BLOOD
RITES

ALSO BY BARBARA EHRENREICH

The Snarling Citizen

Kipper's Game

The Worst Years of Our Lives: Irreverent Notes from a Decade of Greed

Fear of Falling: The Inner Life of the Middle Class

The Hearts of Men: American Dreams and the Flight from Commitment

Re-making Love: The Feminization of Sex (with Elizabeth Hess and Gloria Jacobs)

For Her Own Good: 150 Years of the Experts' Advice to Women (with Deirdre English)

Witches, Midwives, and Nurses: A History of Women Healers (with Deirdre English)

Complaints and Disorders: The Sexual Politics of Sickness (with Deirdre English)

The Mean Season: The Attack on the Welfare State (with Fred Block, Richard A. Cloward, and Frances Fox Piven)

BLOOD RITES

Origins and History of the Passions of War

Barbara Ehrenreich

AN OWL BOOK
Henry Holt and Company • New York

Henry Holt and Company, LLC
Publishers since 1866
115 West 18th Street
New York, New York 10011

Henry Holt® is a registered trademark
of Henry Holt and Company, LLC.

Distributed in Canada by H. B. Fenn and Company Ltd.

Library of Congress Cataloging-in-Publication Data
Ehrenreich, Barbara.
Blood rites: origins and history of the passions of war /
Barbara Ehrenreich.
p. cm.
ISBN 0-8050-5787-0
Includes bibliographical references and index.
1. War—Psychological aspects. 2. War. I. Title.
U22.3.E37 1997 96-50891
355.02—dc21 CIP

First published in hardcover in 1997 by Metropolitan Books

First Owl Books Edition 1998

Designed by Paula R. Szafranski

Printed in the United States of America

11 13 15 17 19 20 18 16 14 12

Contents

Acknowledgments

This project was made possible, in part, by a grant for Research and Writing from the John D. and Catherine T. MacArthur Foundation, for which I am truly grateful. My extremely able research assistants have included, over the years, David Glenn, Linda MacColl, and Maura McDermott. I thank them all for their ingenuity and good-humored attention to detail; with special thanks to Ben Ehrenreich for his delightful memos on nineteenth-century nationalism, Virgil, and other matters.

A number of people—friends, relatives, acquaintances, and assorted scholars—read and commented on drafts: Bill Angelbeck, Julianne Unsell, Christopher Faraone, Vincent Crapanzano, Ben Ehrenreich, Laura Slatkin, John Ehrenreich, Larry Shames, Annie Dillard, John Leslie, Janet Susan McIntosh, Richard Barnet, Marcus Raskin. Even those who were not the least sympathetic to the project contributed valuable remarks. I also thank the many scholars who took time to answer my calls and questions—including, among others, John Dower, Paul Martin, Robert Blumenschine, Jack Bradbury, Paul Stern, Robert Wencke, and Chris Knight.

It has helped, of course, that I have the greatest editor in the world, Sara Bershtel, whose relentless lucidity shines through, I hope, on every page. Sara got invaluable back-up on this project from her colleague Tom Engelhardt, whom I am indebted to for salvaging this book, in many spots, from error and mediocrity.

Finally I thank Rosa Ehrenreich and Ben Ehrenreich, for everything from commenting on drafts to sharing their educations with me. When they were little I dedicated a book to them because they were my children. I do so now because they are the adults I am most proud to know.

Foreword

Some years ago I had occasion to need a theory of war. The occasion, fortunately, was only a literary one: I had been asked to write the preface to the English translation of a book about the twentieth-century German warrior elite, Klaus Theweleit's fascinating *Male Fantasies*. I was flattered to be asked, but felt inadequate to the task. After all, my only qualification was that I had written a book about men and masculinity (*The Hearts of Men*), and nothing in that had touched on the subject of war.

I soon found that there are no theories of war or—depending on what you are willing to accept as a "theory"—far too many of them. Ask a scholar for an explanation of war, and he or she will most likely snicker at your naïveté in expecting that something so large and poorly defined could even be explained. Ask a nonspecialist, however, and you will get any of a dozen explanations, each proffered with utter confidence: It is because of our innate aggressiveness . . . or because of innate male aggressiveness . . . or because of imperialism and greed . . . or overpopulation and a shortage of resources . . . or manipulation by evil, bloody-minded elites . . . or it is simply a manifestation of unknowable evil.

Our understanding of war, it occurred to me, is about as confused and unformed as theories of disease were roughly 200 years ago. At that time there was no consensus among men of science as to whether disease arose from sources within the afflicted individual, such as ill "humours" and bad habits, or whether its source lay in something outside us—in the night air, for example, or dangerous "miasmas." Among the public at large, sin—which played the same role in early theories of disease as "innate aggressiveness" plays in those of war—remained a popular explanation. None of this would be cleared up until the middle of the nineteenth century, when the discovery of a heretofore invisible and unsuspected agent of disease—germs—would open the way to seeing all diseases as biological afflictions, traceable to molecular and cellular events, though of course embedded in the social ecology of cities and classes and migrations and conquests.

In one way, our prospects of understanding war are far bleaker than the prospects of understanding disease were two centuries ago. At least at that time, the period of "Enlightenment" in Western thought, educated people were convinced that a theory was discoverable and well worth the effort of seeking. Today there is no such self-confidence among the people most entitled to possess it. The social scientists to whom one might naturally turn for some understanding of an institution like war have, in all too many cases, given up on big questions and sweeping theories of any sort and are engaged instead in narrow empirical studies or, what is safer yet, critiques of studies already done.

But the silence of the academics can only frustrate the curious layperson. There is something in us, or at least something in some of us, that urgently seeks to make sense out of disconnected data and unassimilated experience, to draw links between people "like us" and people not at all like us, between what happened long ago and what is happening right now or could happen next. The urgency increases when the subject at hand, like war or disease, involves life and death, including the potential death of all people on earth. We need to know, and we need to know something more than piles of unrelated observations.

So the reckless amateur rushes in where the prudent scholar fears to tread. Eleven years ago, prodded by the assignment of a two-thousand-word preface to a book unknown in my own country, I began my study of war. Unrestrained by loyalty to any particular academic discipline, I read widely and at first almost randomly, puzzling over ethnographic and historical detail, savoring the sweeping perspectives of those few who dared to propose them. Being a journalist as well as an amateur scholar, I not only read people's books and articles but also tracked down the authors at their homes or offices and pestered them with my questions. I shamelessly borrowed from my children's higher educations, studying over their shoulders, as it were, anthropology at Oxford and religious studies at Brown. I gave talks which were initially mostly questions, and left with new insights and long lists of suggested readings.

In keeping with my original preoccupations, as well as with Theweleit's theme, my suspicions first centered on the theme of gender. Wars, after all, have been fought, in almost all cases, by men, and sometimes for the stated purpose of "making" them men. But as I pressed back further in time and broadened my inquiry to include other forms of organized and socially sanctioned violence—such as rituals of blood sacrifice—a deeper and far more ancient explanatory theme emerged. This was not something I had ever thought about before; in fact, it lay entirely outside my conceptual framework and analytic approach to the world. What it amounts to is a new evolutionary perspective on war and related forms of violence, but—if I am right about the direction in which the relevant scholarship is tending—one that will not remain new and startling for long.

This is a theory about the feelings people invest in war and often express as their motivations for fighting—where these feelings might have originated and how they have played out in history. I should emphasize at the outset that human feelings do not account for all that we might want to know about war or particular wars—why they start, in each instance, or end in the ways that they do. On the question of what "causes" war or any particular war, Tolstoy still has the last word:

> The deeper we delve in search of these causes the more of them we discover, and each single cause or series of causes appears to us equally valid in itself, and equally false by its insignificance compared to the magnitude of the event.[1]

It was a long time before I was able to make this distinction—that is, to understand that the feelings we bring to war are not, in themselves, a full and complete explanation for the persistence of war. What war is, why it "really" happens, and what we might do to keep it from happening are questions we will return to in the second half of this book, and especially at the very end. Until then, the focus will be on the feelings we bring to war, with the understanding that they are not the sole "cause" of war. They are the way it digs its talons into us; no more than that, and no less.

A note of caution: The standards of proof in an endeavor like this are hardly as firm as those that prevail in the natural sciences which constituted my formal education. Speculation plays a definite role here, though I will try to alert you to where it begins and leaves off. But the occasional foray into speculation does not mean that we can be content with any old "story" which suits our tastes and fits a smattering of the data. I have done my best here to make sense of certain recurrent and disturbing patterns of human behavior. If the result fails the test of careful scrutiny or future findings, others will have to do better.

Part I
PREDATION

> So elemental is the human need to endow the shedding of blood with some great and even sublime significance that it renders the intellect almost entirely helpless.[1]
>
> —Martin van Creveld

1
The Ecstasy of War

Different wars have led to different theories of why men fight them. The Napoleonic Wars, which bore along with them the rationalist spirit of the French Revolution, inspired the Prussian officer Carl von Clausewitz to propose that war itself is an entirely rational undertaking, unsullied by human emotion. War, in his famous aphorism, is merely a "continuation of policy . . . by other means," with policy itself supposedly resulting from the same kind of clearheaded deliberation one might apply to a game of chess. Nation-states were the leading actors on the stage of history, and war was simply one of the many ways they advanced their interests against those of other nation-states. If you could accept the existence of this new super-person, the nation, a battle was no more disturbing and irrational than, say, a difficult trade negotiation—except perhaps to those who lay dying on the battlefield.

World War I, coming a century after Napoleon's sweep through Europe and northern Africa, led to an opposite assessment of the human impulse to war. World War I was hard to construe as in any way "rational," especially to that generation of European intellectuals, including Sigmund Freud, who survived to ponder the unprecedented harvest of dead bodies. History textbooks tell us that the "Great War" grew out of the conflict between "competing imperialist states," but this Clausewitzian interpretation has little to do with the actual series of accidents, blunders, and miscommunications that impelled the nations of Europe to war in the summer of 1914.[2] At first swept up in the excitement of the war, unable for weeks to work or think of anything else, Freud was eventually led to conclude that there is some dark flaw in the human psyche, a perverse desire to destroy, countering Eros and the will to live.[3]

So these are, in crude summary, the theories of war which modern wars have left us with: That war is a means, however risky, by which men seek to advance their collective interests and improve their lives. Or, alternatively, that war stems from subrational drives not unlike those that lead individuals to commit violent crimes. In our own time, most people seem to hold both views at once, avowing that war is a gainful enterprise, intended to meet the material needs of the groups engaged in it, and, at the same time, that it fulfills deep and "irrational" psychological needs. There is no question about the first part of this proposition—that wars are designed, at least ostensibly, to secure necessaries like land or oil or "geopolitical advantage." The mystery lies in the peculiar psychological grip war exerts on us.

In the 1960s and '70s, the debate on the psychology of war centered on the notion of an "aggressive instinct," peculiar to all humans or only to human males. This is not the place to summarize that debate, with its endless examples of animal behavior and clashes over their applicability to human affairs. Here I would simply point out that, whether or not there is an aggressive instinct, there are reasons to reject it as the major wellspring of war.

Although it is true that aggressive impulses, up to and including murderous rage, can easily take over in the heat of actual battle, even this statement must be qualified to take account of different weaponry and modes of fighting. Hand-to-hand combat may indeed call forth and even require the emotions of rage and aggression, if only to mobilize the body for bursts of muscular activity. In the case of action-at-a-distance weapons, however, like guns and bows and arrows, emotionality of any sort can be a distinct disadvantage. Coolness, and the ability to keep aiming and firing steadfastly in the face of enemy fire, prevails. Hence, according to the distinguished American military historian Robert L. O'Connell, the change in the ideal warrior personality wrought by the advent of guns in the fifteenth and sixteenth centuries, from "ferocious aggressiveness" to "passive disdain."[4] So there is no personality type—"hot-tempered," "macho," or whatever—consistently and universally associated with warfare.

Furthermore, fighting itself is only one component of the enterprise we know as war. Wars are not barroom brawls writ large, or domestic violence that has been somehow extended to strangers. In war, fighting takes place within battles—along with much anxious waiting, of course—but wars do not begin with battles and are often not decided by them either. Most of war consists of *preparation* for battle—training, the organization of supplies, marching and other forms of transport—activities which are hard to account for by innate promptings of any kind. There is no plausible instinct, for example, that impels a man to leave his home, cut his hair short, and drill for hours in tight formation. As anthropologists Clifton B. Kroeber and Bernard L. Fontana point out, "It is a large step from what may be biologically innate leanings toward individual aggression to ritualized, socially sanctioned, institutionalized group warfare."[5]

War, in other words, is too complex and collective an activity to be accounted for by a single warlike instinct lurking within the individual psyche. Instinct may, or may not, inspire a man to bayonet the first enemy he encounters in battle. But instinct does not mobilize supply lines, manufacture rifles, issue uniforms, or move an army of thousands from point A on the map to B. These are "complicated, orchestrated, highly organized" activities, as social theorist Robin Fox writes, undertaken not by individuals but by entities on the scale of nations and dynasties.[6] "The hypothesis of a killer instinct," according to a commentator summarizing a recent conference on the anthropology of war, is "not so much wrong as irrelevant."[7]

In fact, throughout history, individual men have gone to near-suicidal lengths to avoid participating in wars—a fact that proponents of a warlike instinct tend to slight. Men have fled their homelands, served lengthy prison terms, hacked off limbs, shot off feet or index fingers, feigned illness or insanity, or, if they could afford to, paid surrogates to fight in their stead. "Some draw their teeth, some blind themselves, and others maim themselves, on their way to us," the governor of Egypt complained of his peasant recruits in the early nineteenth century.[8] So unreliable was the rank and file of the eighteenth-century Prussian army that military manuals forbade camping near a woods or forest: The troops would simply melt away into the trees.[9]

Proponents of a warlike instinct must also reckon with the fact that even when men have been assembled, willingly or unwillingly, for the purpose of war, fighting is not something that seems to come "naturally" to them. In fact, surprisingly, even in the thick of battle, few men can bring themselves to shoot directly at individual enemies.[10] The difference between an ordinary man or boy and a reliable killer, as any drill sergeant could attest, is profound. A transformation is required: The man or boy leaves his former self behind and becomes something entirely different, perhaps even taking a new name. In small-scale, traditional societies, the change was usually accomplished through ritual drumming, dancing, fasting, and sexual abstinence—all of which serve to lift a man out of his mundane existence and into a new, warriorlike mode of being, denoted by special body paint, masks, and headdresses.

As if to emphasize the discontinuity between the warrior and the ordinary human being, many cultures require the would-be fighting man to leave his human-ness behind and assume a new form as an animal.[11] The young Scandinavian had to become a bear before he could become an elite warrior, going "berserk" (the word means "dressed in a bear hide"), biting and chasing people. The Irish hero Cuchulain transformed himself into a monster in preparation for battle: "He became horrible, many-shaped, strange and unrecognizable," with one eye sucked into his skull and the other popping out of the side of the face.[12] Apparently this transformation was a familiar and meaningful one, because similarly distorted faces turn up frequently in Celtic art.

Often the transformation is helped along with drugs or social pressure of various kinds. Tahitian warriors were browbeaten into fighting by functionaries called Rauti, or "exhorters," who ran around the battlefield urging their comrades to mimic "the devouring wild dog."[13] The ancient Greek hoplites drank enough wine, apparently, to be quite tipsy when they went into battle;[14] Aztecs drank pulque; Chinese troops at the time of Sun Tzu got into the mood by drinking wine and watching "gyrating sword dancers" perform.[15] Almost any drug or intoxicant has served, in one setting or another, to facilitate the transformation of man into warrior. Yanomamo Indians of the Amazon ingest a hallucinogen before battle; the ancient Scythians smoked hemp, while a neighboring tribe drank something called "hauma," which is believed to have induced a frenzy of aggression.[16] So if there is a destructive instinct that impels men to war, it is a weak one, and often requires a great deal of help.

In seventeenth-century Europe, the transformation of man into soldier took on a new form, more concerted and disciplined, and far less pleasant, than wine. New recruits and even seasoned veterans were endlessly drilled, hour after hour, until each man began to feel himself part of a single, giant fighting machine. The drill was only partially inspired by the technology of firearms. It's easy enough to teach a man to shoot a gun; the problem is to make him willing to get into situations where guns are being shot and to remain there long enough to do some shooting of his own. So modern military training aims at a transformation parallel to that achieved by "primitives" with war drums and paint: In the fanatical routines of boot camp, a man leaves behind his former identity and is reborn as a creature of the military—an automaton and also, ideally, a willing killer of other men.

This is not to suggest that killing is foreign to human nature or, more narrowly, to the male personality. Men (and women) have again and again proved themselves capable of killing impulsively and with gusto. But there is a huge difference between a war and an ordinary fight. War not only departs from the normal; it inverts all that is moral and right: In war one *should* kill, *should* steal, *should* burn cities and farms, should perhaps even rape matrons and little girls. Whether or not such activities are "natural" or at some level instinctual, most men undertake them only by entering what appears to be an "altered state"—induced by drugs or lengthy drilling, and denoted by face paint or khakis.

The point of such transformative rituals is not only to put men "in the mood." Returning warriors may go through equally challenging rituals before they can celebrate victory or reenter the community—covering their heads in apparent shame, for example; vomiting repeatedly; abstaining from sex.[17] Among the Maori, returning warriors could not participate in the victory celebration until they had gone through a whaka-hoa ritual, designed to make them "common" again: The hearts of slain enemies were roasted, after which offerings were made to the war god Tu, and the rest was eaten by priests, who shouted spells to remove "the blood curse" and enable warriors to reenter their ordinary lives.[18] Among the Taulipang Indians of South America, victorious warriors "sat on ants, flogged one another with whips, and passed a cord covered with poisonous ants, through their mouth and nose."[19] Such painful and shocking postwar rites impress on the warrior that war is much more than a "continuation of policy . . . by other means." In war men enter an alternative realm of human experience, as far removed from daily life as those things which we call "sacred."

The Religion of War

Not only warriors are privileged to undergo the profound psychological transformation that separates peace from war. Whole societies may be swept up into a kind of "altered state" marked by emotional intensity and a fixation on totems representative of the collectivity: sacred images, implements, or, in our own time, yellow ribbons and flags. The onset of World War I, for example, inspired a veritable frenzy of enthusiasm among noncombatants and potential recruits alike, and it was not an enthusiasm for killing or loot or "imperialist expansion" but for something far more uplifting and worthy.

In Britain, the public had been overwhelmingly opposed to involvement until the moment war was declared, at which time screaming crowds poured into the streets and surrounded Buckingham Palace for days. In Berlin, the crowds poured out "as though a human river had burst its banks and flooded the world."[20] In St. Petersburg a mob burned the furnishings of the German embassy while women ripped off their dresses and offered them to soldiers in the middle of a public square.[21] When the United States entered the war, on April 6, 1917, the audience at the New York Metropolitan Opera House stood up and greeted the announcement with "loud and long cheers."[22]

Hardly anyone managed to maintain their composure in the face of the oncoming hostilities. Rainer Maria Rilke was moved to write a series of poems extolling war; Anatole France offered to enlist at age seventy; Isadora Duncan recalled being "all flame and fire" over the war. Socialists rallied to their various nations' flags, abandoning the "international working class" overnight. Many feminists, such as England's Isabella Pankhurst, set the struggle for suffrage aside for an equally militant jingoism, and contented themselves with organizing women to support the war effort. "The war is so horribly exciting but I cannot live on it," one British suffragette wrote. "It is like being drunk all day."[23] Even pacifists like the German novelist Stefan Zweig felt a temptation to put aside their scruples and join the great "awakening of the masses" prompted by war.[24] In India, young Gandhi recruited his countrymen to join the British army; even Freud, as mentioned above, briefly lost perspective, "giving all his libido to Austria-Hungary."[25]

But Freud failed to reflect on his own enthusiasm; otherwise he would never have hypothesized that men are driven to war by some cruel and murderous instinct. The emotions that overwhelmed Europe in 1914 had little to do with rage or hatred or greed. Rather, they were among the "noblest" feelings humans are fortunate enough to experience: feelings of generosity, community, and submergence in a great and worthy cause. There was little difference, in fact, between the fervor that greeted the war and the emotional underpinnings of the socialist movement, which promised land (or bread) and *peace*. As historian Albert O. Hirschman has written:

> [For] important sectors of the middle and upper classes . . . the war came as a release from boredom and emptiness, as a promise of the longed-for community that would transcend social class.[26]

Just after the war, the American psychologist G. E. Partridge observed that the mood of war had been, above all—and despite the war's acknowledged horrors—one of "ecstasy." Drawing on the work of early-twentieth-century German psychologists, he enumerated, in a way that can now only seem quaint, the various "ecstasies" associated with war: that of heroism, of "taking part in great events," or of victory ("Siegestrunkenheit"); the "joy of overcoming the pain of death"; and, summing up all the other ecstasies, the "social intoxication, the feeling on the part of the individual of being a part of a body and the sense of being lost in a greater whole."[27] The thrill of being part of a vast crowd, of abandoning ordinary responsibilities in order to run out into the streets, of witnessing such "great events" as declarations of war: This was "ecstasy" enough for the millions who would never see actual combat.

It was the sense of self-loss, Partridge opined, of merger into some "greater whole," which showed that war was an attempt to meet the same psychological needs otherwise fulfilled by "love, religion, intoxication, art."[28] A historian of our own time, Roland Stromberg, would agree, writing of the men who volunteered to fight in World War I:

> Doubtless they found hell, but they did not go seeking it; rather than an itch to kill, hurt, or torture their fellow men, as Freud claimed, they felt something much more akin to love.[29]

The mass feelings inspired by war, many noted right after World War I, are eerily similar to those normally aroused by religion. Arnold J. Toynbee, the British historian, had been caught up in World War I like most of his peers, and produced several volumes of "atrocity propaganda" as his contribution to the war effort.[30] Later, repenting for that brief burst of militarism, he argued that war had in fact become a religion, moving in to fill the gap left as the traditional forms of worship lost their power over people. "Man," he wrote, requires "spiritual sustenance," and if man was now less inclined to find it in a church, he would find it in the secular state and express it as a militant nationalism in which "the glorification of War [is] a fundamental article of faith."[31]

To say that war may be, in an emotional sense, a close relative of religion is not to pass moral judgment on either of these ancient institutions. We are dealing with a very basic level of human emotional experience, which can be approached just as well at, say, a labor rally as at a nationalist gathering or a huge outdoor mass. Coming together in a large crowd united by some common purpose, people feel a surge of collective strength, and they may project this sense of power onto God, the Nation, or the People. *El pueblo unido*, goes the left-wing chant, *jamas sera vencido* (The people united cannot be defeated). As the nineteenth-century theorist of crowd psychology, Gustave Le Bon, observed, somewhat haughtily:

> In crowds the foolish, ignorant, and envious persons are freed from the sense of their insignificance and powerlessness, and are possessed instead by the notion of brutal and temporary but immense strength.[32]

Individually we are weak, but with God, or through "the fatherland" or "the working class," we become something larger than ourselves—something indomitable and strong. Even those of us who will never experience battle, or for that matter, God, can know the thrill of being swept along with a huge and purposeful crowd.

This is one of humankind's great natural "highs," and is, perhaps paradoxically, as likely to be experienced at an anti-war demonstration as at a pro-war rally. But it is a high that can be most reliably experienced in contemplation of an enemy—the "Viet Cong" or, for that matter, the military-industrial complex—which both excites our adrenaline and serves to unite us. All "minor" differences (as, for example, of class) disappear when compared to the vast differences (construed as moral, cultural, and sometimes racial) that supposedly separate us from the "jerries," the Communists, the Arabs, or the Jews.

Through the mass rally or the spontaneous gathering in the streets, large numbers of people can experience something analogous to the transformation that makes a man into a warrior. Just as the ancient warrior fasted, took drugs, danced all night, and even became a monster, the crowd, too, leaves mundane things behind and transmutes itself into a new kind of being, larger than the sum of its parts, more powerful than any single individual. Consider the British psychologist Roger E. Money-Kyrle's eyewitness description of a Hitler rally:

> The people seemed gradually to lose their individuality and become fused into a not very intelligent but immensely powerful monster, which was not quite sane and therefore capable of anything. Moreover, it was an elemen-

> tary monster . . . with no judgment and few, but very violent, passions. . . . [W]e heard for ten minutes about the growth of the Nazi Party, and how from small beginnings it had now become an overpowering force. The monster became self-conscious of its size and intoxicated by the belief in its own omnipotence.[33]

But there is more to the "religion" of war than the thrill of the mass rally or of the battle itself. In between wars, there are ample reminders of the collective high induced by the threat or actuality of war. The tribal war chieftain had his collection of skulls or similar trophies to contemplate in times of peace; the ancient emperor had his stelae commemorating victories, his temples to Mars or Minerva. In the modern European world, according to historian George Mosse, war cemeteries and monuments serve as the "sacred spaces of a new civil religion"[34]—lovingly tended and solemnly redecorated year after year. The grave of the "unknown soldier" is an especially stirring reminder of the moral transcendency of war: In war the individual may be entirely obliterated for the higher cause, made nameless as well as dead. Yet even in this abject condition, he, or at least some remnant of the "glory" associated with his passing, lives on forever, symbolized by a perpetual flame.

By the twentieth century, war, and the readiness for war which is so much a part of nationalism, had become the force unifying states and offering individuals a sense of transcendent purposefulness. Today, even in peacetime, the religious side of war is everywhere manifest. No important state function can go forward without the accompaniment of drumrolls and soldiers at attention. The inauguration of presidents, the coronation of monarchs, the celebration of national holidays—these events require everywhere the presence of the soldier as a "ceremonial appurtenance."[35] Where there are no true soldiers, exclusively ceremonial ones may be maintained: Even the Vatican—which, one might imagine, needs no further embellishment with quasi-religious pompery—has its Swiss Guard.

The word "sacrifice" summed up the religious passion of war for generations of Europeans and Americans. In the rhetoric of religious militarism, killing the enemy was almost an incidental outcome of war compared to making "the supreme sacrifice" of one's own life. Dying in war was not a mishap inflicted on the unfortunate, but the point, almost, of the whole undertaking. "Happiness," the German poet Theodor Korner declared at the time of the Napoleonic Wars, "lies only in sacrificial death."[36] Mosse has commented on the extensive "cooptation of Christian symbolism and ritual to sanctify the life and death of the soldier" in World War I.[37] The war was compared to the Last Supper, the soldier's death to the martyrdom of Christ—in, for example, postcards showing angels hovering over handsome, contented-looking, and apparently unwounded corpses.[38]

Not all Europeans, at all times, have seen war as an occasion for a beautiful, sacrificial death, of course, but the notion is a widespread one and not only among urban, industrialized cultures. In his groundbreaking study of "primitive" war, the American anthropologist Harry Turney-High offered numerous examples of similar sacrificial fervor among tribal peoples. He reports dryly that on Mangaia, for example, in Polynesia,

> [the] high-born, noble Tiora did not shrink when informed by the war priests that their god demanded his sacrificial death at the enemy's hands. He went against the foe alone and they obligingly killed him, unaware that his immolation was intended to accomplish their own defeat.[39]

Caesar reported that the Aquitanians had an elite society of fighters called *solidurii*, or "bound-by-duty," who were sworn to share one another's deaths in battle or else to kill themselves.[40] There were similar "no retreat" societies among North American Indian tribes. A Crow could "vow his body to the enemy," which meant he was prepared to die in an attack against hopeless odds.[41]

Self-sacrifice is perhaps the least "rational" of all human undertakings. Anthropologists may debate whether it is rational, in a self-serving sense, to fight for land or women or to avenge some wrong. But there is no straightforward biological calculation that could lead a man to kill himself, like one of the *solidurii*, or to die—possibly unwed and childless, like the Crow warrior—because he has sworn a vow.* "At bottom, the reason why fighting can never be a question of interest," the military theorist Martin van Creveld writes, "is—to put it bluntly—that dead men have no interests."[42]

A cynic might dismiss the religiosity of war as a mystification of its mundane, ignoble aims, all the rhetoric of "sacrifice" and "glory" serving only to delude and perhaps intoxicate otherwise unwilling participants. At some level, the cynic would be right: The results of war—the burned villages, bombed cities, sobbing orphans and captives—are the same whether the war was undertaken in the noble spirit of self-sacrifice or was driven by less worthy motives, like vengeance or greed. Thus most scholars have no doubt felt themselves justified in slighting the high-flown rhetoric and rituals of war to concentrate on its technology and impact. Of all the volumes on war listed in the bibliography of this book, only a half-dozen at most concern themselves directly with the passions that have made war, to so many of its participants, a profoundly religious undertaking.[43]

But there are at least two reasons to take seriously the religious dimension of war. First, because it is the religiosity of war, above all, which makes it so impervious to moral rebuke. For millennia, and long before the Enlightenment or even the teachings of Jesus, people have understood that war inverts all normal morality; that it is, by any sane standard, a criminal undertaking. Buddhism, arising in the fifth

*The biologically "rational" explanation for certain kinds of altruism is that it promotes the survival of one's kin, and hence of genes that are similar to one's own. It could be argued that this explanation applies to situations in which men die defending their immediate clan or families (although the practice of exogamy has guaranteed that even clans and families will be of varied genetic makeup). But it is somewhat more of a stretch from a band or tribe of loosely related individuals to the mass, genetically polyglot armies of both ancient and modern states.

century B.C., condemned war, and one of the most bluntly reasoned anti-war arguments ever made comes to us from the Chinese philosopher Mo Ti in the fourth century B.C.:

> When one man kills another man it is considered unrighteous and he is punished by death. Then by the same sign when a man kills ten others, his crime will be ten times greater, and should be punished by death ten times. . . . Similarly if a small crime is considered crime, but a big crime such as attacking another country is applauded as a righteous act, can this be said to be knowing the difference between righteousness and unrighteousness?[44]

But war, as Mo Ti must have realized, enlists passions which feel as "righteous" to those who experience them as any of the arguments against it.

The other reason to study the religiosity of war is for what it has to say about us as a species, about "human nature," if you will, and the clichéd "problem of evil." Other creatures, including our near relatives the chimpanzees, have also been known to kill their own kind with systematic zeal; certain species of ants even do so on a scale and with a tactical ingenuity fully deserving of the label "war." But of course no other species exhibits behavior we recognize as "religious," and none can be said to bring exalted passions to their acts of intraspecies violence.

So, we might well ask of ourselves: What is it about our species that has made us see in war a kind of sacrament? Not all wars, of course, have excited the kind of passion aroused by World War I. But does the fact that humans *can* and often do sacralize the act of killing mean that we are more vicious than any other creature? Or is it the other way around, with our need to sacralize the act of killing proving that we are, deep down, ultimately moral creatures? Which are we: beasts because we make war, or angels because we so often seek to make it into something holy?

A psychologist might offer one sort of answer, based on the anxieties that seem built into the individual life cycle, but here I am interested in another kind of answer, drawn from efforts to reconstruct our collective biography as a species, our history and prehistory. Since the search for prehistoric "origins" has become distinctly unfashionable among contemporary anthropologists, I should explain, first, that the kind of origin I seek is not a hypothetical event, or "just-so" story, like the mythical rebellion, in Freud's *Totem and Taboo*, of the "primal horde" against its patriarchal leader. "Antecedent" may be a better word for what we are after here: Hunting is an antecedent of war, almost certainly predating it and providing it with many valuable techniques; here we seek a similarly long-standing antecedent to the *sacralization* of war.

Second, it should be acknowledged at the outset that to know the origin of something is not, of course, to know why it persists or plays itself out, over and over. But in the case of repetitive, seemingly compulsive patterns of behavior, the first step to freedom may be to know how it all got started. Like a psychologist facing an individual patient, we need to uncover the original trauma.

We begin, in the next chapter, with the most clear-cut case of sacralized violence that human cultures have to offer: religious rituals of blood sacrifice. Even in times of peace, the religions of many traditional cultures were hardly aloof from the business of violence. In fact, their rituals have very often centered on the act of killing, either mimed or literally enacted, of humans or animals. As René Girard emphasized in his classic *Violence and the Sacred*, violence was, well into the historical era, at the very core of what humans define as sacred, and the first question we will address is *why*.

In the conventional account of human origins, everything about human violence is explained as a result of our species' long prehistoric sojourn as hunters of animals. It is the taste for meat and the willingness to kill for it that supposedly distinguish us from other primates, making us both smart and cruel, sociable and domineering, eager for the kill and capable of sharing it. We are, in other words, a species of predators—"natural born killers" who carried the habit of fighting over into the era of herding and farming. With the Neolithic revolution, wild ungulates were replaced as prey by the animals in other people's herds or the grain stored in other villages' fortresses; and the name for this new form of "hunting" was war. In this account, the sacralization of war arises only because the old form of hunting, and probably also the sharing of meat, had somehow been construed as sacred for eons before.

No doubt much of "human nature" was indeed laid down during the 2½ million years or so when *Homo* lived in small bands and depended on wild animals and plants for food. But it is my contention that our peculiar and ambivalent relationship to violence is rooted in a primordial experience that we have managed, as a species, to almost entirely repress. And this is the experience, not of hunting, but of being preyed on by animals that were initially far more skillful hunters than ourselves. In particular, the sacralization of war is not the project of a self-confident predator, I will argue, but that of a creature which has learned only "recently," in the last thousand or so generations, not to cower at every sound in the night.

Rituals of blood sacrifice both celebrate and terrifyingly reenact the human transition from prey to predator, and so, I will argue, does war. Nowhere is this more obvious than in the case of wars that are undertaken for the stated purpose of initiating young men into the male warrior-predator role—a not uncommon occurrence in traditional cultures. But more important, the anxiety and ultimate thrill of the prey-to-predator transition color the feelings we bring to *all* wars, and infuse them, at least for some of the participants, some of the time, with feelings powerful and uplifting enough to be experienced as "religious."

Having made that case—convincingly, I hope—in the first half of this book, Part II will consider the sacralization of war in historical times, and its evolution from an elite religion observed by a privileged warrior caste to the mass religion we know today primarily as nationalism. It is in our own thoroughly "modern" time, we will see, that the rituals and passions of war most clearly recall the primitive theme of resistance to a nonhuman threat.

> All religions are cruel, all founded on blood; for all rest principally on the idea of sacrifice—that is, on the perpetual immolation of humanity to the insatiable vengeance of divinity.[1]
>
> —Bakunin

2

Sacred Meat

In war, men "offer their lives" and sometimes make "the supreme sacrifice." This rhetorical convention links war and religion in a far more literal way than one might suspect. To the modern ear, "sacrifice" has a passive, almost bloodless sound; we confuse it with self-denial and renunciation, and associate it with images of pale maidens and marble statuary. But sacrifice first appears in the historical record as a well-defined religious ritual, varying in detail from culture to culture, but almost always featuring, at its climactic moment, an act of public bloodshed: the killing, torture, or mutilation of an animal or a human, followed by the ritual disposal of the blood and, in most cases, the consumption of the dead.

Ritual sacrifice is the most clear-cut instance of violence made sacred. When the victim is nonhuman, the central act of violence is essentially a familiar and understandable one: the slaughter of animals for food. The fact that the simple act of butchery has so often been sacralized hints at a sinister side to the deities so honored and is suggestive, as we shall see, of an anxiety far older than either religion or war, and possibly central to both.

Few religions today openly practice blood sacrifice.* The idea is repulsive to most modern, Western people, who prefer the slaughter of animals to go on unceremoniously and out of sight, in thoroughly secular "meat-packing plants." But contemporary historians of religion remind us of what religious practitioners often prefer to ignore or forget: that blood sacrifice is not just "a" religious ritual; it is the central ritual of the religions of all ancient and traditional civilizations. For thousands of years, the core religious ritual from the highlands of the Andes to the valley of the Ganges was the act of sacrificial killing. The temple that housed the altar, or the raised platform or stone circle that constituted a holy place, was also an abattoir.

The Judeo-Christian religions, for example, no longer demand—or for that matter, permit—blood sacrifice. But sacrifice, including human sacrifice, remains a central theme of the Jewish and Christian texts. In the Old Testament, the decisive event, and the one that defines the relationship between the Jews and Jehovah, is the aborted sacrifice of Isaac by his father, Abraham. In the New Testament, it is the sacrifice of Jesus by his "father," the deity himself. And throughout the first five books of the Old Testament, with obsessive regularity, huge numbers of animals are sacrificed as "offerings" to God.

This fixation on sacrifice is not peculiar to the Judeo-Christian tradition, but can be found in almost all cultures that have possessed animals to sacrifice. "Sacrificial killing," the eminent Swiss classicist Walter Burkert tells us, "is the basic experience of the sacred."[2] Before war became a widespread and massive enterprise, it was proba-

---

*Hinduism and Santeria are among the exceptions. In Hinduism, however, animal sacrifice is practiced within popular, and often lower-caste, goddess cults. The mainstream male deities have long since been weaned from blood to candies, butter, and fruit.

bly through ritual killing that humans approached the experience of the transcendent—that something "larger than ourselves" which uplifts the patriot at a pro-war rally. Hence, for example, the linguistic link between the words that touch on holiness—"sacred," "sacrament," "sacerdotal," "sacrilege"—and "sacrifice," which denotes ritual violence. All are cognate with *saklais* or *shaklaish*, the ancient Hittite word meaning "rite."

Not all cultures have possessed animals they deemed suitable for sacrifice, and some anthropologists reserve the term "sacrifice" for herding peoples, like the ancient Hebrews and Greeks. But those cultures which lack appropriate animal victims often feature acts of self-mutilation which, while not properly "sacrifices" in the classic Hebrew and Indo-European sense, are equally focused on bloodletting as a public spectacle. In Mayan culture, for example, "human sacrifice and blood-letting were continuous and pervasive throughout the Classic period," and the aim "seems to have been less the life of the victim and more his blood, perhaps as the 'sustenance' demanded by the gods."[3]

Even without accompanying rituals or acts of violence, the flow of blood is an arresting spectacle. The color alone demands attention and calls to mind violent acts of piercing or cutting and the shocking sameness of all living creatures beneath the skin. Sacrificial rituals often seem, in fact, aimed at the production of blood as much as at any other by-product of death, including edible meat. Among the varieties of sacrificial killing, strangling and hanging are not unknown, but are far less common than methods productive of the flow of blood. Ancient Greek, Hebrew, and Hindu rituals feature elaborate attention to the handling of the victim's blood, which may be collected in a trough or chalice, daubed on the foreheads of those seeking the benefits of sacrifice, or even poured over the body of a person in need of purification.

Mayan royalty threaded cords through their penises (or, in the case of queens, their tongues) as their assembled subjects watched in awe. In an annual sun dance, Blackfoot and Arapahoe males of the

American plains tore their flesh open as they danced backward from a pole to which they were attached by thongs hooked into their chests.[4] Men of traditional Hawaiian and Australian aboriginal cultures ritualistically cut their penises in order to induce bleeding. Almost any body part—limbs, face, genitals, trunk—has been exploited, in some culture, as a source of ritual blood.[5] Among the Gahuka-Gana and Gururumba tribes of Papua New Guinea, the nose was the favored organ:

> The boys [undergoing initiation] are brought to a river amid the shouts, chants, and flute music of warriors. There they are confronted by a group of masturbating men who wade into the river and stick sharp leaves up their own noses until they hemorrage profusely. The initiates also induce nasal hemorrage. . . . They then spend a year in the men's hut, have little contact with women, and practice nose bleeding, vomiting, and flute playing.[6]

In the ancient world, according to Burkert, the ritual of animal sacrifice was a profoundly gripping, even terrifying, spectacle. First there were complex preparations, often involving bathing and sexual abstinence on the part of the human participants. In ancient Greece, the rite itself began with a procession in which the sacrificial animal was led to the holy place, where the altar had been set up, usually with a fire blazing on top of it. Water was then sprinkled on the animal, followed by a shower of barley grains:

> Hidden beneath the grains in the basket was the knife, which now lies uncovered. The leader in this incipient drama . . . steps toward the sacrificial animal, carrying the knife still covered so that the animal cannot see it. A swift cut, and a few hairs from the brow are shorn and thrown into the fire. . . . Now comes the death blow. The women raise a piercing scream: whether in fear or triumph or both

> at once, the "Greek custom of the sacrificial scream" marks the emotional climax of the event, drowning out the death-rattle.[7]

The blood is collected in a bowl and sprinkled on the altar stone. The animal is carved up and disemboweled. After a seer has studied them for omens, the entrails are cooked over the altar fire and eaten at once by the participants. The rest of the meat may be eaten later, with a portion going to the priest, priestesses, or other functionaries associated with the holy place.

Among the ancient Greeks, nothing of any importance could occur, no decisions could be made, without the accompanying flow of sacrificial blood. Funerals required sacrifices, as did celebrations and homecomings, vows and agreements. Risky ventures, such as journeys and wars, could not be undertaken without sacrifices both to reveal the likely outcome and to win the support of the gods. During campaigns, the military leader served also in the priestly role of sacrificer. As historian John Keegan reports of Alexander the Great:

> Bizarre though it seems to us . . . his day began with his plunging of a blade into the living body of an animal and his uttering of prayer as the blood flowed.[8]

Calamities and misfortunes could, of course, be overcome only through the appropriate sacrifices. In fact, one of the major functions of the famed Delphic oracle was to regulate the economy of sacrifice: to dictate which creatures had to be sacrificed, in what quantities, and to which gods, in order to achieve the desired result. Large animals, such as bulls, counted more than small ones, and quantity was another important measure of devotion. The historian Xenophon relates that before a battle with the Persians, the Athenians

> had vowed to Artemis to sacrifice as many goats as they should kill Persians; but they could not find enough, so

> they resolved to sacrifice every year five hundred, and they do so still.[9]

The ancient Hebrews were equally obsessed with sacrifice. In his book *In the Shadow of Moloch*, Martin Bergmann points out that the Hebrews, who went to such lengths to distinguish themselves from their neighbors in other religious matters, had sacrificial rituals very similar to those of the Canaanites and other despised "idolators." Whole pages of the Old Testament are devoted to the enumeration and description of animal sacrifices in minute anatomical detail. In Leviticus (9: 3–4), for example, Moses prescribes

> a kid of the goats for a sin offering; and a calf and a lamb, both of the first year, without blemish, for a burnt offering. Also a bullock and a ram for peace offerings . . . and a meat offering mingled with oil. . . .

The fate of each resulting animal by-product is described, down to the fat, the caul, the kidneys, the liver, and the rump.

"Animal sacrifice," Burkert tells us, "was an all-pervasive reality in the ancient world."[10] Hebrew sacrificial ritual resembled that of the Greeks, which in turn resembled that of the Egyptians and Phoenicians, the Babylonians and Persians, the Etruscans and the Romans. The names of the gods who were the recipients of the sacrifices varied from culture to culture, but the main elements of the ritual were everywhere recognizable and familiar to the ancients: the procession, the climactic throat-slitting or beheading, the butchering, the examination of entrails, the ritual uses of the fresh blood, the burning or cooking of the remains.

All these bloody rituals belong in the same broad category of socially sanctioned violence where we might locate war, and appear to be speaking to some of the same concerns as war. Death is clearly among these concerns, as is the power to bring about death, to kill or at least draw blood. If nothing else, both war and ritual bloodlettings are spectacular demonstrations of the human power to injure and kill. But there is another connection suggested by René Girard in his wonderfully imaginative *Violence and the Sacred*. He speculates that war and sacrifice may originally have served the same end: to damp down the aggressive energy which could tear a community apart and redirect that energy toward an "external" focus—the sacrificial victim or the foreign enemy, in the case of war.

Girard seems to assume the existence of an aggressive tendency, or at least syndrome, which, left to itself, would lead to endless feuds and squabbling. The entire function of religion, he argues, is to redirect this violence "outward":

> *Religion* in its broadest sense . . . must be another term for that obscurity that surrounds man's efforts to defend himself by curative or preventative means from his own violence.[11]

But one does not have to accept the idea of innate aggressiveness to apply Girard's line of reasoning. The violent tendencies he postulates could just as well be the product of circumstance—the rebellious tendencies of a people oppressed by their chief or king, for example. In either case, the "function" of sacrifice would be to redirect the violence toward more socially acceptable targets: Instead of killing one another or the king, the sacrificers, or their priestly representatives, ceremoniously kill the victim.

The god to whom the sacrifice is offered is irrelevant in Girard's view, a mere mythological gloss on the proceedings. What matters is the selection of a victim and his or her violent and public death. The sacrificial victim must be seen primarily as a scapegoat, Girard argues, citing the ancient Greek ritual in which a pauper who had been maintained at public expense, the designated *pharmakos*, or "cure," was driven out of the city and possibly killed in order to ward off a calamity, such as plague, foreign invasion, or internal dissension. Even an animal could serve as the designated victim; the term "scapegoat" comes from the Yom Kippur ritual of heaping the sins of the people on the head of a goat, and then slaughtering the animal along with the memory of the sins. In the process, according to Girard, the "old pattern of each against another gives way to the unified antagonism of all against one."[12] Social cohesion is preserved at the expense of the unfortunate scapegoat.

Thus, Girard speculates, war is "merely another form of sacrificial violence"[13] arising from the need to deflect internal strife outward:

> We see here the principle behind all "foreign" wars: aggressive tendencies that are potentially fatal to the cohesion of the group are redirected from within the community to outside it.[14]

Whether Girard is right or not about the historical functions of sacrifice, few would quibble with his insight that war has served, again and again, to promote acquiescence to the political status quo. In our own time, Americans credited the Gulf War with "bringing us together." Serbian and Croatian leaders solved their people's postcommunist economic discontents with an orgy of nationalist violence. World War I at least temporarily abolished the threat of internal class warfare within most of the belligerent nations; socialism was tamed, and henceforth contained within the familiar structure of the militaristic nation-state, in the form of that war's most notable product, the Soviet Union.

Food for the Gods

But Girard passes too quickly over the issue of the nature of the deity who is the recipient of the sacrifice, for herein lies an important clue to the human habit of sacralizing violence. Practitioners of sacrifice have interpreted the rite in a highly specific and concrete way: Sacrifice is the means by which humans *feed* the god or gods; the victim is in fact a meal. Thus the Olympian gods savored the smell of roasting meat arising from the sacrificial altars and, at least in the work of the ancient Greek comic poets, complained about the size of their share of the meat;[15] the Aztecs' sun god would be extinguished without its steady diet of sacrificial human blood; the Mayan gods seem to have required blood for sustenance; Inca gods "ate" sacrificial llamas; Hawaiian gods "smack[ed] their lips" at the sight of their intended victims.[16] The Hebrew god was too ethereal to be imagined actually eating, but in the Bible, the divine fire sometimes spurts forth excitedly and literally consumes the flesh lying upon the altar.[17] The Hebrew king David acknowledges Jehovah's carnal interest in the sacrificial ritual when he resolves at one point to set things right between himself and the deity by "let[ting] him smell an offering."[18]

Thus the ritual of sacrifice reveals an almost universal attribute of the archaic deity to whom the sacrifices are offered: He or she is a carnivore. This deity may have many other attributes—as a parental figure, a judge, a leader in war—but the animals sacrificed are, in all cases, *edible* animals, at least in the view of the sacrificers. They are domestic animals like goats and sheep or occasionally wild animals such as deer, but seldom anything deemed unappetizing, such as insects or lizards. In his *Theory of Religion*, Georges Bataille offers a rather high-flown explanation of why the victim should be edible. "One sacrifices *what is useful*," he writes, precisely to lift that thing out of the realm of utility and into the realm of "immanence."[19] But the far more direct explanation is that *the gods prefer a meal of meat*. What, after all, turned Cain against Abel and thus, according to the Bible, initiated the whole tragic cycle of intrahuman violence? Cain, recall, was a farmer, and gave offerings of the "fruit of the soil." Abel was a shepherd, and gave "the firstlings of his flock." God much preferred the meat offerings and unabashedly favored Abel, hence Cain's murderous envy. The philosophically respectable explanation is that Cain, like Job later on, was being taught a lesson in God's arbitrariness and the necessity of accepting his will no matter what that will demands.[20] But a couple of thousand years ago, when this story was being recorded, God's behavior probably did not seem so arbitrary: He simply wanted meat.

Humans, too, are carnivores; and it is humans, for the most part, who actually consume the sacrificial meat. The countless animals sacrificed in the Old Testament do not, from an unbeliever's perspective, go to waste; they become the Hebrews' dinner. Some portion of the dead animal goes to the priests who perform the sacrifice, another portion to the lay participants who contributed the animal, yet another portion—usually something rather insubstantial like the smoke from the sacrificial fire—to the deity. Even so, tensions sometimes arose over the relative size of the portions allotted to humans and gods; in the Book of Samuel we find that wicked priests are taking too much and even demanding the whole, raw animal instead of their proper share of the cooked remains.

In some ways, the institution of blood sacrifice is little more than the prelude to a meal. Anthropologist Bruce Lincoln observes that in ancient Indo-European cultures, "every offering is followed by a meal,"[21] and ritual sacrifice continued to serve a culinary function well into the modern era—sometimes shading over into unceremonious butchery. The temple of Kali in nineteenth-century Calcutta could handle eight hundred goats in three days, far more than Xenophon's Athenians could muster:

> The temple serves simply as a slaughterhouse, for those performing the sacrifice retain their animals, leaving only the head in the temple as a symbolic gift, while the blood flows to the Goddess.[22]

The great temple at Jerusalem played a similar role in the lives of the ancient Hebrews, and the rituals of kosher slaughter remain as reminders of the thriving biblical tradition of animal sacrifice. No animal could be eaten without having suffered a ritual death, just as the laws of ancient Greek cities stipulated that all meat offered for sale had to have been produced by ritual slaughter.[23] Similarly, among the contemporary reindeer-herding Chukchi people of northeast Asia, there are no "secular kills." Every animal sacrificed is eaten, and every animal that is eaten represents a ritual offering to the gods. If the gods demand more sacrifices than the herds can reasonably provide, the Chukchi give them fake reindeer fashioned out of tallow, pounded meat, crushed leaves, or even snow.[24]

But even though sacrifice is in some sense no more than an elaborate preliminary to a meal—analogous, perhaps, to saying grace—it contains an element of anxiety which has usually been interpreted as *guilt*. The meat may be deemed necessary as food, the ritual killing may be deemed necessary if the meat is to be eaten at all, yet still there is uneasiness over the slaughter. Hubert and Mauss, the renowned nineteenth-century historians of sacrifice, report that some rituals required apologies to the victim. Excuses might be made for the act; the animal might be mourned as if it were a relative; the rest of the species the victim belongs to might be entreated not to seek revenge; the sacrificer himself might be punished.

> At Athens the priest at the sacrifice of the *Bouphonia* [where an ox was sacrificed] fled, casting his axe away. . . . The purification which the sacrificer had to undergo resembled . . . the expiation of a criminal.[25]

In an ancient Babylonian rite, the priest apologized to the severed head of the sacrificial bull, saying, "This deed was done by all the gods; I did not do it."[26]

Sacrifice was the core religious rite, but at the same time, according to Girard, it was understood to be a moral transgression, akin to murder. He opens *Violence and the Sacred* with the observation:

> In many rituals the sacrificial act assumes two opposing aspects, appearing at times as a sacred obligation to be neglected at grave peril, at other times as a sort of criminal activity entailing perils of equal gravity.[27]

The ritual of sacrifice legitimates the act of killing for meat, yet somehow the ritual is never quite enough. The killing has still occurred; it is always right there, at the center of the ritual. Hence the need for the charade of denials and apologies to the victim. Conversely, Girard implies, the ritual would be nowhere near so awe-inspiring if it did not include the element of transgression, so thrillingly registered by the "sacrificial scream" of the Greek rite.

But guilt toward the animal victim is only one possible explanation for the angst that seems to surround the sacrificial rite. There is an alternative explanation, which hinges on the possibility, implicit in so many cultures' rituals of animal sacrifice, that the victim was once or might someday be not animal but human. In the Hebrew and Greek traditions, myths preserve the notion that the original, and perhaps most desirable, victim from the divine point of view was in fact human, and that the animal victim is only a substitute. A ram replaces Isaac on the altar at the last minute; a deer may or may not have replaced Agamemnon's daughter Iphigenia. In some cases of animal sacrifice, the victim is first feted as if it were human, dressed in human clothes, perhaps treated like a human child—even nursed by human females in the case of infant bears designated as sacrificial victims by the Aino of Japan.[28] The people of Tenedos in ancient Greece would treat a pregnant cow as if it were a woman, and the calf, when it was born, would be dressed as a human child and sacrificed to Dionysus.[29]

Or, as we shall see in a later chapter, the victim may in fact be human. When the victim is human or is an animal construed as a substitute for a human, the act of sacrifice takes on new meanings. The drama is heightened; a new frisson is introduced—not that of transgression, but of menace. "It is the intriguing equivalence of animals and man," Burkert suggests,

> as expressed in mythology in the metaphors of tragedy, but also in rituals of substitution, that casts the shadow of human sacrifice over all those holy altars in front of the temples.[30]

If this creature can be killed, and if this creature is somehow a stand-in for a human victim, then the spectator must wonder, Why not me? Herodotus captures this anxiety in his story of Heracles in Egypt. The Greek hero arrives to great celebration. He is crowned and led in a procession to the altar, where he suddenly realizes "that he is not the hero of the feast but the victim designated for the sacrifice."[31] Fortunately, being a hero, he is able to massacre the entire assemblage and escape unharmed.

In the sacrificial ritual, the spectator is invited to identify not only with the sacrificer wielding the knife, but with the helpless creature who is about to be served up to the gods. Thus the ritual has a terrible lesson to teach: that, from the point of view of a carnivorous deity, humans are also meat.

> First, men lived apart from each other and no city existed. Because of this they were destroyed by animals that were always and everywhere stronger than they, and their industry that sufficed to feed them was yet inadequate to fight against the wild animals.[1]
>
> —Plato

3
The True Mark of the Beast

Ask about the origins of any aspect of human behavior and science was, until very recently, likely to give a one-word answer: hunting. Hunting, especially of large animals, is the activity that distinguishes prehistoric humans from other primates; hence, according to the theory of human evolution that prevailed in the 1970s, hunting must be the reason for the distinction. Imaginative depictions of our prehistoric ancestors, as in museum displays, still invariably feature "man the hunter," scanning the horizon with sharpened stick in hand. In this account of our origins, there is nothing mysterious about the human propensity for violence. "Man," or anything worthy of the name, has always been a predator—a killer of animals and eater of meat.

According to the "hunting hypothesis," as it is known, prehumans emerged from the African forests into the savannah 2 to 3 million years ago, developed a taste for meat, and began to organize their lives around its acquisition. Supposedly, everything "human" followed from this carnivorous predilection. Gender roles were laid down by the impossibility of taking infants and children along on the hunt. The use of tools—or, more narrowly, weapons—tightened hand-eye coordination and sharpened the hominid brain. The cooperation required for the hunt called forth speech and some of the earliest forms of social organization. Humans' distinctly avid sexuality evolved to keep the male hunter-providers loyal to the child-bound females who waited at home for their share of the meat. And so on. Hunger was the original challenge, meat was the answer, and all else followed from that.

If violence was, almost from the beginning, the means of human survival, then, according to some advocates of the hunting hypothesis, it must be bred into our genes—an evolutionary version of "original sin." This was the view of paleontologist Raymond A. Dart, who offered the following, somewhat overwrought, summary of the connection between Paleolithic hunting, sacrificial killing, and war:

> The blood-bespattered, slaughter-gutted archives of human history from the earliest Egyptian and Sumerian records to the most recent atrocities of the Second World War accord with early universal cannibalism, with animal and human sacrificial practices or their substitutes in formalized religions and with the world-wide scalping, head-hunting, body-mutilating and necrophiliac practices of mankind in proclaiming this common bloodlust differentiator, this predaceous habit, this mark of Cain that separates man dietetically from his anthropoidal relatives and allies him rather with the deadliest of Carnivora.[2]

But theories of man-the-bloodthirsty-carnivore do not account for the peculiar human tendency to sacralize the act of killing, to surround it with ritual and awe. There is a gap here, which scholars have sought to fill with specifically "human" feelings of altruism or guilt. In Walter Burkert's account, sacrificial ritual is rooted in the feelings of guilt human hunters must have felt toward their animal victims—the beginnings, one might imagine, of an admirable ecological consciousness. Humans needed to kill, this line of reasoning goes, but killing filled them with a deep unease. As historian of religion Karl Luckert put it:

> For their sins of killing, primitive hunters developed and performed religious retreat rituals—primarily to alleviate feelings of guilt. They atoned for their trespasses.[3]

The evidence usually cited for such guilt among early humans is the elaborate arrangements of animal bones left in some sites by hunters of the Upper Paleolithic. These remains testify, Karl Meuli argued in the 1940s, to the ritual aspects of animal-killing even in very distant times. The hunters, it has been inferred, must have worried that what they were doing was wrong—although, as Burkert observes with a rueful "alas," some surviving hunting peoples "are said to laugh at the convulsions of the dying animal."[4]

So the hunting hypothesis—plus some allowance for paternal responsibility and the supposed delicacy of human feelings—was made to account for everything. Hunting was believed to be the great triumph that lay at the threshold of human existence, and simultaneously the original trauma. Humans are killers, according to this hypothesis, but somehow not "natural" killers like lions or wolves. Only through the consolations of religion and ritual could our species sustain its bloody career.

But in just the past ten or fifteen years, the hunting hypothesis has declined rather precipitously to the status of "myth."[5] Certainly big-game hunting was, or at least became at some point, an important part of how prehistoric humans earned their livelihood, but the hypothesized status of hunting as the nearly exclusive factor driving human evolution is now thought to be grossly overstated. It had always seemed a bit suspicious that the sexual division of labor postulated by the hunting hypothesis—with the males striding out to hunt while the females remain home with the young—bears such an uncanny resemblance to that of American suburbanites in the mid-twentieth century, when the framers of the hunting hypothesis were coming of age. It is at least unlikely, as Donna Haraway argues, that an exclusively male activity (if hunting was indeed that) could have been the sole "motor" of human evolution.[6]

In fact, studies of existing hunting-gathering societies suggest that it may have been the presumably male activity of hunting, rather than the female work of gathering, which should be regarded as a supplemental activity.[7] Proud "hunters" like the !Kung people of the Kalahari Desert derive only a fraction of their calories from hunting; the rest come from the gathering activities undertaken mainly by women. Similar proportions hold for other hunting-gathering cultures, except those in the plant-poor Arctic region.[8] Furthermore, careful reexamination of the archeological evidence in a number of sites has led to the conclusion that hominids and even early *Homo sapiens* were more likely to obtain the meat they did eat by scavenging the kills left by more effective predators, such as the big cats, than by hunting for themselves.[9] Big-game hunting, as opposed to scavenging, may be a fairly recent innovation, going back, in anthropologist Lewis Binford's estimation, to no more than 70,000 to 90,000 years ago.[10] So if we want our theories of human culture to be based firmly on material need, it might be better to start with "woman the gatherer" or "man (and woman) the scavengers of carrion" than with "man the hunter."

But, for our purposes, the real problem with the hunting hypothesis is that it completely obscures an aspect of the human-animal relationship which may have been far more important in shaping human evolution. Humans, and before them, hominids, could not always have been the self-confident predators depicted in the standard museum diorama. The savannah that our hominid ancestors strode (or, more likely, crept warily) into was populated not only by edible ungulates, but by a host of deadly predators, including a variety of big sabertooth cats as well as the ancestors of lions, leopards, and cheetahs. Before, and well into, the age of man-the-hunter, there would have been man-the-hunted.

Advocates of the hunting hypothesis—and there certainly remain some—have tended to pooh-pooh the threat of predation to early humans. "Man," the archeologist and popular writer Louis Leakey proclaimed, "is not cat-food."[11] Until recently, big-cat predation on primates of any kind was thought to be the work of rare pathological individuals who were too disabled or demented to catch their normal prey. Besides, whether or not primate meat is distasteful to carnivores, the thought of being eaten is definitely distasteful to *us*.

But the evidence of predation both on hominids and on modern primates has become overwhelming. The turning point came in the early eighties, with the reexamination of certain hominid bone deposits found in southern Africa. For years, these assemblages of hominid and animal bones had been interpreted in the light of the hunting hypothesis: The reason why the hominid bones were commonly found intermixed with those of other animals, according to Raymond Dart, was that *Australopithecus*, who lived three-quarters of a million years ago, had hunted and killed the other animals. Dart's follower Robert Ardrey went further: *Australopithecus* was a murderer as well as a hunter. The wounds found in one of the hominid skulls were evidence, he argued, of "purposeful," armed assault.[12]

And so it went until the South African paleontologist C. K. Brain did a little further detective work. He measured the puncture marks in the skull of the supposedly murdered *Australopithecus* and found that the distance between them precisely fit the gap between the lower canines, or stabbing teeth, of the leopard. The reason, he argued, that hominid and animal remains so often ended up together was that *both* had been eaten by leopards.[13]

Hominids and prehistoric humans were almost certainly never numerous enough to constitute the sole foodstuff of any predator species. But even if no other species specialized in predation on early humans, our biology is alone enough to suggest an alarming level of vulnerability to the exceptionally hungry or casual prowler. Humans and primates generally (with the exception of the muscular gorillas and certain baboons) are individually, and in the natural, unarmed state, rather dainty creatures. Compared to the big cats, our teeth are blunt, our muscles weak, our nails good for little more than scratching away at lice. Nor do we have the natural defenses possessed by other large land animals: the elephant's thick skin, the buffalo's horns, the antelope's speed. Until recently though, predation on primates was downplayed because primatologists seldom witnessed it. There was, as it turns out, a good reason for this: Primatologists do their work in the daytime, while predators tend to do theirs at night. More careful observations—including the analysis of carnivore feces for primate remains—have established that predation is indeed a serious threat to modern primates and was most likely to ancient ones as well. A 1991 study found that leopard predation was the number-one cause of death among a forest chimpanzee population, accounting for 39 percent of deaths over a five-year period.[14] Two years later, evidence was reported for significant *lion* predation on chimpanzees.[15] Field observations suggest that troops of savannah-based baboons, which are sharp-toothed, formidable fighters, lose 25 percent of their members to predation annually.[16]

If primatologists have not always appreciated the threat of predation, primates certainly have. Savannah-dwelling chimpanzees, which share their habitat with lions, cluster in large groups, presumably for defense, and use alarm calls to warn of approaching predators.[17] Similarly baboons enter the savannah warily, falling into a defensive marching order, with the young males on the periphery. A sick baboon will try so hard to keep up with the group that it will neglect to find food, and thus weaken all the more quickly. For an individual to fall behind the troop is to be eaten "within hours after the troop has gone and probably before its heart stops beating."[18] Reviewing the evidence for carnivore predation on nonhuman primates, the Dutch biologist Adriaan Kortlandt concludes that "for the early hominids, breaking a leg while walking alone would often have been fatal, due to carnivore predation."[19]

Modern *Homo sapiens*, too, can be tasty prey. Despite the conventional wisdom that wild predators do not like the flesh of primates, or will not attack unless "bothered,"* wild carnivores have been a threat to human communities right into historical times. One of the few systematic studies of carnivore predation on humans—conducted near the Gir Forest of western India between 1978 and 1991—found up to forty lion attacks on humans per year, forcing the unhappy villagers to remain indoors after sunset or go out only in groups of four or five.[20] Lions significantly impeded the construction of the Ugandan Railway in 1895–1901, killing twenty-eight Indian laborers and about a hundred African villagers living near the construction sites. Surviving laborers were forced to set up camp on top of water towers, dig pits beneath their tents, or sleep in beds lashed to trees.[21]

Tigers, far more than lions, have restricted human opportunities in the Indian subcontinent. According to Franklin Russell's *The Hunting Animal*, when the British East India Company received its charter from Elizabeth I in 1600,

---

*In our own time, most of the large predators have become endangered species, and this has led to an understandable tendency to see them as victims rather than as victimizers, and of no great danger to respectful humans. Hikers are routinely reassured that the ambient wildlife will not bother them if they refrain from bothering it. But there have been a number of cases, in recent years alone, of attacks on humans by apparently undisturbed predators—mountain lions attacking joggers, for example, or bears attacking sleeping campers. Some of these attacks can perhaps be rationalized as unnatural behavior resulting from too much contact with humans or with the waste left at human campsites. But clearly *some* predators, in *some* settings, do in fact stalk humans as food. The tigers of the Sundarbans are an undeniable example, and have even been known to modify their behavior in response to the evasive tactics of humans. In 1986, realizing that tigers almost never attack a human from the front, someone designed plastic face masks to be worn on the back of the head. The masks fooled the tigers for five or six months, after which the tigers figured out that the masks were not faces at all, and resumed their attacks (Montgomery, p. 39—see n. 24 this chapter).

> many thousands of square miles—some said half a million—of India were depopulated by tigers. Farmers, after establishing crops, grazing animals, residences, and roads, were driven from their lands by tigers, the stock destroyed, their workers taken in the fields, and their families plucked from out of their residences. Travel on roads . . . was impossible without either firearms or great numbers of travelers banded together.[22]

The British started recording the numbers of humans lost to tigers in 1800, and found that by the end of the century, approximately three hundred thousand people had been killed, along with 6 to 10 million farm animals.[23] In the Sundarbans region of India, where the tigers routinely stalk humans as food, even today,

> so many are killed by tigers here that some villages are known as *vidhaba pallis*—tiger widow villages. Arampus, near Gosaba, is one such village; in each of its 125 families is a woman whose husband or brother or son was killed by a tiger.[24]

Today most large land carnivores are either extinct or too wary of firearms to attack a group of humans—or so, at least, the conventional wisdom goes—but individuals still fall prey to alligators, bears, mountain lions, and packs of hyenas or wild dogs. Among the more lurid twentieth-century cases of predation on humans catalogued by C. K. Brain is a leopard in Rudraprayag, India, that killed 125 people between 1918 and 1926, even in one instance forcing open a door to get to a boy sleeping inside. A Zambian leopard killed sixty-seven people in 1936–7,[25] and, according to Brain, some African villages practiced a grisly form of euthanasia by leaving old, sick, or feeble individuals outside the village at night so that animals would dispose of them.[26] "People living in the perfect safety of their homes in a Western country have no conception of the insecurity felt by blacks in their kraals in the interior of Africa," a white hunter, James Sutherland, wrote in 1912:

> The cause of this feeling of insecurity is chiefly the man-eating lion, and no other animal of the forest inspires such terror. . . . In villages far in the heart of the pori, where the white man is never seen, not hundreds but thousands of Africans are killed annually by these monsters.[27]

Wolves, it is often claimed, never attack humans.[28] But in the summer of 1996, the Indian state of Uttar Pradesh experienced thirty-three fatal wolf attacks on children and twenty maulings. As the *New York Times* reported:

> When the man-eating wolf came into this tranquil village [Banbirpur] toward dusk on an evening in mid-August, it was every child's worst nightmare come true. The wolf pounced while Urmila Devi and three of her eight children were in a grassy clearing at the edge of the village. . . . The animal, about 100 pounds of coiled sinew and muscle, seized the smallest child, a 4-year-old boy named Anand Kumar, and carried him by the neck into the luxuriant stands of corn and elephant grass that stretch to a nearby riverbank. When a police search party found the boy three days later, half a mile away, all that remained was his head.[29]

In the Paleolithic setting, humans (or hominids) would not have had to be any animal's favorite meal in order to be thrust into constant conflict with predators. For one thing, as we will see in chapter 7, the population of predators—and, indeed, of all large land animals—was much larger in the Paleolithic period than it has been ever since. Furthermore, if early humans obtained their meat primarily by scavenging, they would have been drawn, again and again, to the kill sites left by more successful hunting animals, where there was always the possibility of the predator's return. Leopards and lions will fight any poachers they discover at their kill sites—wild dogs or hyenas, for example—and unarmed hominids would have been easily driven off or even added to the predator's meal. Though scavenging may be a sinecure compared to hunting for oneself, it is hardly a low-risk occupation.

Yet somehow it offends human vanity to think of ourselves or our predecessors as vulnerable prey, potential meat for other species. Darwin himself glided right over the problem of human vulnerability. On one page in *The Descent of Man* he calls "man" "the most dominant animal that has ever appeared on earth." Twenty pages later he acknowledges that if hominids had been any stronger, they

> would probably . . . have failed to become social; and this would most effectually have checked the acquirement by man of his higher mental qualities. . . . Hence it might have been an immense advantage to man to have sprung from some comparatively weak creature.[30]

But a "comparatively weak creature" could not have become "the most dominant animal" overnight. Here is what we might call the missing link within the theory of human evolution itself: how a poor, shivering creature grew to unquestioned dominance. Before and well into the age of hunting, there must have been a long, dark era of fear when the careless and the stragglers were routinely picked off, when disease or any temporary weakness could turn a man into meat.

It is not only vanity which has kept us from acknowledging the tragic vulnerability of our predecessors. There is a special conceit that we tend to bring to any contemplation of "primitives," contemporary or prehistoric: We have a bias against believing that "primitives" also experience history and change. We imagine that whatever we find them doing at the moment of contact—or excavation—is what they must have been doing for "untold thousands of years," as if there could be no migrations, no catastrophes, no innovations, until we moderns arrive on the scene. But prehistory was not one blank, smooth screen on which the same actions—hunting, dragging the carcass back to camp or cave, sharing the meat, and so forth—were enacted over and over. The very notion of "prehistory" is simply an admission of our ignorance of what had to have been an immensely complex and varied *history*. Glaciers came and went, forcing early humans to migrate or invent new ways of living. The outlines of continents changed; land bridges appeared, as between Asia and North America or Australia and Tasmania, only to vanish again under impassable seas. Human technologies were also changing. The first evidence of artificial fire-making—an iron pyrites ball with deep grooves from repeated striking—comes from a Belgian site only 15,000 years old.[31] And it was only about 15,000 years ago that our ancestors developed effective action-at-a-distance weapons, like the bow and arrow,[32] that did so much to make our species "the most dominant animal" on earth.

So we could say, without disrespect to the known facts, that there were at least two broad and overlapping epochs in prehistory: one in which our ancestors confronted the world, for the most part, as potential prey, and another in which they took their place among the predators which had for so long oppressed them—an epoch of cowering and perpetual vigilance, and an epoch in which other species learned to cower and flee from us. The transition from one status to the other would have been halting and gradual, as the means of defense—both weapons and forms of social organization—evolved into the means of attack and offense. And well into the epoch of man-the-hunter, humans still had good reason to fear the tall grass, the forests, and the night.

But there *was* a transition, and even if Darwin could not bring himself to think of it, it had to be the single greatest advance in human evolution, this progress our distant ancestors made from the status of anxious prey to that of unrivaled predator. We were not given dominion over the earth; our forebears earned it in their long, nightmarish struggle against creatures far stronger, swifter, and better armed than themselves, when the terror of being ripped apart and devoured was never farther away than the darkness beyond the campfire's warmth. If we seek an "original trauma" that shaped the human response to violence, we have no need to postulate some primal guilt over hunting and killing. The original trauma—meaning, of course, not a single event but a long-standing condition—was the trauma of *being* hunted by animals, and eaten. Here, most likely, lies the source of our human habit of sacralizing violence: in the terror inspired by the devouring beast and in the powerful emotions, associated with courage and altruism, that were required for group defense.

Animals and Human Evolution

We are unaccustomed to thinking of animals as anything other than instruments of human ambition, or at best as pets. They occur in history buried within adjectives modifying forms of human culture: There have been "herding peoples," "hunting peoples," "horse peoples," with the adjectival status of the animal emphasizing its total subordination to human needs. Or, what is worse, urban people in the industrialized north have almost ceased to think of animals even as useful servants, and find them merely cute. Bears have been trivialized as teddy bears; the mighty dinosaurs have been given witty television personae; in children's books, the animals speak and play human roles, to evoke a whole world of cuteness. It is almost beyond us to think of animals as actors in their own right, following their own agendas—much less as actors which might have shaped the course of human destiny.

But animals played a much more vivid and active role in the "primitive" or ancient human mind. The modern reader is often baffled by the predominance of animals in the art and myths of our progenitors. Paleolithic cave art features masterfully drawn animals—bison, rhinoceroses, bears, deer, aurochs, lions—interacting with humans who are often no more than stick figures and sometimes dressed with bird or stag heads themselves. The earliest civilizations worshipped hybrid human-animal gods, like Sekmet, the lion-headed Egyptian goddess of war. The intricate geometric ornamentations in ancient Chinese art turn out to be animals—mostly, in fact, sacrificial animals—in abstract form.[33] In the Hindu pantheon, Ganesh still takes the form of an elephant, Hanuman a monkey. Even the highly anthropomorphic Greek gods have their animal familiars—like Demeter and her pigs—and it may be that the animal was the form the deity originally took.

In myth and folklore, there is no sharp, clear boundary dividing animals from humans. Animals can become humans or humanlike gods and vice versa. Just as frogs turn into princes in European fairy tales, Zeus becomes a swan in order to rape Leda; Actaeon is transformed by Artemis into a stag; men, as we have seen, can becomes wolves or bears on their way to being warriors. Quite aside from all this shape-changing, the human and animal protagonists of myth interact promiscuously and with no regard for genetic compatibility. Pasiphaë, the mythical Cretan queen, has sex with a bull and gives birth to the monstrous Minotaur. The Deer Woman of Plains Indian mythology sneaks off at night from her human brothers to mate with bucks and give birth to fawns.[34] In the Hindu epic the Mahabharata, Rama calls on the gods to mate with "the wives of the foremost of monkeys and bears" in order to produce a generation of superhuman warriors who have "the strength of the elephant and the speed of the wind."[35]

All of this comes to us from a world that is almost impossible to imagine today—a world in which humans were everywhere decisively outnumbered by large land animals and lived in intimate connection with them. Even in Homer's age, when humans had already domesticated the large edible animals and subdued many of the wild predators:

> Domesticated animals provided food, clothing, and various by-products; teams of sweating oxen reduced the farmer's labor in the fields, and the dog kept off human and animal robbers. Many shared, like Eumaios, a bed in common with their domesticated animals. Beyond the cultivated

> areas wild animals—rabbit, deer, and the boar—provided sport for the huntsman and his hounds and trained adolescents for war. On the peripheries lived the cattle-robbers and scavengers, the lion and the jackal . . . who preyed on men's cattle and ease of mind.[36]

But of all the animals that populate myth, none have more forceful and active roles than the fighting animals which represent a danger to humans: the large, horned ungulates and especially the predator beasts. The Hindu goddess Durga saves the entire pantheon of gods by defeating the buffalo-demon. The Greek hero Heracles battles the Nemean lion; Theseus subdues giant boars as well as the bull-headed Minotaur. And what are we to make of the fantastic zoology of ancient myth—the dragons and sea monsters and beastly amalgams of familiar animals? Probably the single most universal theme of mythology is that of the hero's encounter with the monster that is ravaging the land or threatening the very foundations of the universe: Marduk battles the monster Tiamat; Perseus slays the sea monster before it can devour Andromeda; Beowulf takes on the loathsome, night-feeding Grendel. A psychiatrist might say that these beasts are projections of the human psyche, inadmissible hostilities deflected to mythical targets. But it might be simpler, and humbler, on our part to take these monsters more literally: as exaggerated forms of a very real Other, the predator beast which would at times eat human flesh.

Myth may represent the oldest and crudest form of "history," shot through, of course, with fantasy. The next refinement, which brings us closer to the actual historical record, is the epic tale, and here too the beasts abound. Enkidu, comrade of Gilgamesh in the Sumerian epic, has the job of protecting human settlements from animal marauders:

> He took his weapon
> To chase the lions,
> That shepherds might rest at night.
> He captured wolves,

He captured lions,
The chief cattleman could lie down;
Enkidu is their watchman,
The bold man,
The unique hero![37]

In Homer's world, humans have far more to fear from one another than from predator animals, but still it is the beast that defines ferocity. Similes compare warriors to hounds, wild dogs, lions, or men confronting lions.[38] In the *Iliad*, we even get a glimpse of a time when men went to war, not against one another, but against the wild beasts: Achilles attacks Aeneas, we are told, like a lion "whom men, when a whole community has gathered itself, are furious to kill."[39]

Perhaps the saddest theme of the whole blood-drenched epic is Achilles' transformation from a beautiful young hero into a kind of cannibal beast himself. At the close of the climactic battle, he refers to his dying enemy Hektor as "meat," rather than "flesh," and wishes that his own appetite were stronger:

I wish only that my spirit and fury would drive me
to hack your meat away and eat it raw . . .[40]

Moving closer to what might be called the historical record, we can still find evidence of humankind's war against the predator beasts. A stele erected by the Assyrian king Assurbanipal in the seventh century B.C. recounts the ferocity of the lions and tigers after torrential rains had flooded the land; the inscription boasts of his efficiency in stamping out these beasts in their lairs.[41] In the Old Testament, which certainly reflects some historical events, lions are a common menace. Samson killed a lion, and God sent lions among the Assyrians when they occupied Samaria, killing many of the invaders.[42] As late as the fifth century B.C., Herodotus reports lions attacking Xerxes' pack camels during a march through Thrace.[43] And it may be that the walls built around early human settlements—such as those supposedly erected by Gilgamesh—were meant not only to foil human foes, but to keep out predators and stampeding wild herds as well. Defense against animals might also explain the peculiar design of the Anatolian Neolithic community Çatal Hüyük: There are no walls around the town, but the entrances of dwellings all lead out through the roof—easy enough for a human enemy to penetrate, but probably baffling to lions and wild bulls.

There are other reasons to think that wild animals were still perceived as menaces by the ancients in their cities and towns. Classicist Christopher A. Faraone points out that frightening images of dogs, lions, and monsters were commonly posted at the entrances of temples or cities to ward away evil, and one of the evils they were meant to repel was beasts like themselves. He cites a Hebrew manuscript from the third or fourth century A.D. (and reflecting, he says, far earlier traditions), advising:

> If you wish to expel from the city every dangerous wild animal, whether lion, or wolf, or bear, or leopard . . . make a bronze image in the likeness of the one [which you desire to expel] and . . . bury it at the entrance of the city and let its face be facing north.

This concern made sense, he argues, in "very early agricultural communities in the eastern Mediterranean, where the sudden and devastating attack of actual predators (wolves, wild dogs, bears, lions) on men and livestock" was a real and vivid possibility.[44]

But we do not have to look so far back in time to find traces of the marauding beast, faint paw prints left deep in the human psyche. Children's first nightmares are often of devouring beasts; their most thrilling games are of capture and pursuit; their bedtime stories feature cannibal witches and wolves intent on human flesh. A 1933 study of urban children's fears found high frequencies of fear of animals and hybrid animal-human monsters, and this before television had brought monsters into every living room. A later study of American schoolchildren, in 1965, found them not much concerned about practical threats like nuclear war, traffic, and germs. "The strange truth," concluded the author of the study, "is that they fear an unrealistic source of danger in our urban civilization: wild animals." In response to the question "What are the things to be afraid of?" 80 percent of children ages five and six mentioned wild animals, predominantly snakes, lions, tigers, and bears.[45]

Similarly, studies of dreams reported by urban adults show a surprising prevalence of menacing animals, given their virtual absence in real life. Japanese and American college students, for example, reported high frequencies of dreams involving "creatures, part human, part animal," "wild, violent beasts," snakes, and "being frozen with fright"—subconscious preoccupations which, biologist Balaji Mundkur speculates, may reflect "basic sensitivities imprinted during the psychological evolution of primates."[46]

The Defense Hypothesis

Once we acknowledge that our distant ancestors were prey as well as predators, we can imagine human evolution being driven, not only by appetite, but by the imperatives of defense. The evolution of human intelligence, for example, has often been credited almost entirely to cooperative big-game hunting, with its requirements of communication and weapon use. But obviously defense would also have required insight, cooperation, and new technologies. In fact, Johns Hopkins paleobiologist Steven M. Stanley has recently proposed that the turning point in hominid evolution came when climatic changes pushed our ancestors out of the trees and into the predator-infested savannah. It was, he argues, "the need for self-defense while living freely on the ground [that] was the primary driving force behind the natural selection that created the large brain of *Homo*."[47] Similarly, the first use of fire may not have been for warmth or cooking so much as to ward off predators in the night;[48] the first sharpened stones may have been defensive weapons as well as tools of the hunt. Even that supremely human accomplishment, language, may have roots in simple alarm calls, such as those used by animals to warn their fellows of a predator's approach.

Then there is the fact that hominids evolved as social animals, which, as Darwin surmised, might not have happened if they had been strong enough to withstand predators one-on-one. The hunting hypothesis traced human sociality entirely to the demands of cooperative hunting, but science increasingly emphasizes the threat of being hunted.[49] It is known, just to give one particularly vivid example, that the presence of predators has a dramatic effect on the living arrangements of modern hunter-gatherers: Australian Aborigines in the predator-free Western Desert space their campsites a generous forty meters apart on average, while the !Kung people in the predator-rich Kalahari Desert arrange theirs in close-knit circles.[50] There is safety in numbers, especially when the individuals are bound together, as humans often are, by loyalties that help motivate collective evasion and defense.[51] Self-confident creatures like the tiger and the bear can afford to live alone; the group—or herd or flock or school—is the natural shelter of the weak.

And paradoxically, a certain amount of weakness may have been the evolutionary price we paid for our triumph over the beasts. Group living, and with it the possibility of collective defense, was one reason for the human triumph; the other was the dramatic increase in individual intelligence suggested by the expansion of hominid cranial capacity in the last 2 to 3 million years. Because the size of the human skull at birth is limited by the width of the female pelvis, humans are born soft and small and must do most of their growing after birth, in the dangerous world *ex utero*. Human young, then, are ideal prey from a predator's point of view: helpless, tender, inexperienced. No matter how wily and strong "man" may have been, his children would have depended on the shelter of the group. Again, the impact of predation is illustrated by modern hunter-gatherers: Among the lion-endangered !Kung, "young children tend to remain in close proximity to the campsite and contribute little to the economic life of the community" until well into their teens, while the Australian children, who have no predators to fear, hunt and forage on their own from the age of eight or ten, often ranging one hundred kilometers from home entirely on their own.

Predation may, incidentally, help explain the separation anxiety which babies begin to express at the age of about nine months.[52] "Anxiety" is too mild a word for this. Left alone in a room for a moment, the baby may start bawling, red-faced, at the top of its lungs. To a parent this response seems bafflingly intense and out of all proportion to the cause. But in the archaic situation, even momentary abandonment could mean exposure to predators and the chance of being snatched or eaten. Natural selection would probably have favored those babies who responded with the loudest fuss and could not accidentally, even for a moment, be left behind.

The imperative of protecting the vulnerable young in a predator-rich environment no doubt played a major role in shaping human sex differences and sexuality. *La différence*—the sexual dimorphism characteristic of humans and many other animals—is now believed to reflect, in large part, the greater role of males in actual combat with predators.[53] Hunting, too, if it were a male-only activity, would have favored bigger, stronger males. But long before the male hunting band, males were probably deployed as baboon males are: to guard the periphery of the group. The male, so used, is the primordial sacrifice—an offering to the beast, but an offering which may, with skill and luck, survive. Among baboons, males have been known literally to sacrifice themselves in defense of the group, and it has been estimated that, among primates generally, 80 percent of young males do not survive to maturity.[54]

Of course, this kind of specialization is helpful only if the males remain loyal to their band and to the females and children within it. Usually they do, in part because humans are so strongly motivated by sex. Compared to the many primate females whose interest in sex is confined to brief periods of fertility, human females are sexually receptive virtually all the time. Furthermore, we often prefer to copulate face-to-face, making sex a more personal and sometimes emotional affair than it can be in the typical mammalian dorsal position. Finally, humans are capable of dragging the pleasure of intercourse out for many minutes or even longer, in contrast to the hasty, in-and-out encounters of other primates.

With an emphasis on predation, though, we no longer need to see females as homebound "wives," dependent on their males. The hunting hypothesis has natural selection acting primarily on males, and selecting them almost exclusively for hunting-related traits. Females, in a hunting-centered scheme, need only be attractive enough to keep their males faithfully bringing the meat home to the campsite at night. But if we acknowledge the relentless danger of predation, the entire picture of homebound females and roving male hunters falls apart. It would be at least unwise for the males to leave the females and children alone and unguarded during the hunt. And it would be foolish indeed to drag bleeding carcasses home to the campsite, where they would be a magnet for lions and canid scavengers.

More likely, both sexes were involved in scavenging meat and defending the young, meaning that females, too, were selected for strength and courage and cunning. Human females are not *that* much smaller than human males, relative, for example, to the gap between male and female gorillas or baboons, and probably had a significant defensive role themselves. As animal behaviorist John Alcock writes, the vulnerability of human babies

> exerts selection on mothers to be especially solicitous to their offspring, to provide the kind of care that will help ensure their survival during early development and throughout the period of dependency.[55]

In a predator-infested environment, successful mothering might involve not only tender care, but the ability to evade or repel carnivorous intruders and the wisdom to transmit this ability to the young.

Here we cannot explore all the explanatory possibilities that have opened up since the hunting hypothesis gave way, in the 1980s, to what we might call the defense hypothesis. Clearly, the problem of predation by wild carnivores throws a new light on every aspect of human evolution, from group living to the relation between the sexes. No doubt many other aspects of human behavior and psychology will find, in time, at least speculative explanations in our prehistory as prey. The pathologies of paranoia—for example, chronic anxiety and the fear of abandonment—may all have evolutionary roots in the perpetual vigilance of potential prey. For our purposes, though, the important point is that none of this new thinking in paleoanthropology has so far made its mark on theories of intrahuman violence and war. Without exception, these remain loyal to the hunting hypothesis, according to which "man" was always a killer.

Robert L. O'Connell, for example, finds only two primordial analogs for intrahuman violence: hunting and the often violent, but usually nonlethal, sexual competition between male animals such as stags. Even in his most recent book, the sweeping *Ride of the Second Horseman*, the human story begins with hunting and gathering; there is no acknowledgment of the problem of defense.[56] John Keegan, who is perhaps the world's most preeminent military historian, focuses his discussion of "war and human nature" on the debate over an "aggressive instinct"—without any mention of human vulnerability.[57] Similarly, Dudley Young, in his *Origins of the Sacred: The Ecstasies of Love and War*, emphasizes the dense populations of predators hominids would have encountered in Africa—including the now extinct *Dinofelis*, a big cat which may have specialized in killing large primates—but only as a "pressing incentive for the improvement of our hunting skills."[58] Defense itself, apparently, was never a problem, our carnivorous enemies serving only as rivals and role models.

But the defense hypothesis challenges all past thinking on human violence and our peculiarly human ambivalence toward it. To man-the-hunter, the sight of bloodshed need have no more profound and ominous implications than the sound of a dinner bell. But to man-the-hunted, even human acts of violence carry disquieting reminders of human vulnerability. Man-the-hunter no doubt invented war; at least he invented the weapons of war. But for the tendency to sacralize violence—to ritualize the slaughter of animals and bring "religious" feelings to war—we must go back further, to a time when "man" was an object of prey.

> Can one be sure of making a distinction between the sacrificer holding a knife and the wolf with gaping jaws reddened with blood?[1]
>
> —Marcel Detienne and Jesper Svenbro

4
The First Blood Sacrifice

There is no question that the sacrifice of animals reenacts human predation on animal life. Certain forms of sacrifice, however, have a very different dramatic function: that of reenacting the predation of animals on humans. Through the sacrifice of animals as stand-ins for human victims—or the sacrifice of humans themselves—human beings not only celebrated their own status as predators, possessed of the power to kill. They also acknowledged, and thrillingly replayed, their own long, long prehistory as prey.

If predation played as significant a role in human prehistory as I have suggested, and if it remained a concern well into historical times, we might expect to find some trace of that horrifying experience in cultural rituals. One obvious place to look is at the category of ritual which is termed apotropaic, referring to actions aimed at warding off evil in the form of enemies, disease, or malevolent spirits.

Powerful evil forces must be frightened or appeased, and in some cases these forces are, or once were, literal beasts. In European folk tradition, for example, children run through the town at some point in spring or winter, cracking whips—a custom probably left over from a time when whips were used to drive marauding wolves away.[2]

Many forms of sacrifice could also be regarded as apotropaic rituals insofar as the failure to perform them is, in the view of the sacrificers, an invitation to disaster. Here, too, the original danger may have been predation by carnivorous animals. Walter Burkert, who in *Homo Necans* explained sacrifice as a way of dealing with the guilt occasioned by the hunting and killing of animals, took a very different approach in a later essay. Attempting to imagine the "unritualized, real situation" from which sacrificial ritual might have evolved, he proposes

> a group surrounded by predators: men chased by wolves, or apes in the presence of leopards. The utmost danger is met with excitement and anxiety. Usually there will be but one way of salvation: one member of the group must fall prey to the hungry carnivores, then the rest will be safe for the time being. An outsider, an invalid, or a young animal will be most liable to become the victim. This situation of pursuit by predators must have played a momentous role in the evolution of civilization, while man, as a hunter, became a predator himself.[3]

In general, he suggests, the demons who must be pacified in various apotropaic rituals "cannot but assume the features of predators."[4]*

---

*Intuitively, Burkert's conjecture has a definite appeal. Situations in which one individual must be sacrificed so that others may live both haunt and intrigue us. In the familiar grade-school "values clarification" exercise, students must decide which occupant of a hypothetical lifeboat—the homemaker, the banker, the nun, and so forth—should be tossed overboard to lighten the load. In this case, it is the sea which will consume the sacrificial victim, but often we imagine a literal predator. A recent *New York Times* story was headlined "An Offering to the Wolves: A Shuffling of His Staff Buys Time for Clinton," and began:

If sacrificial ritual was shaped in part by animal predation on humans, we would expect to find evidence of a tradition of *human* sacrifice in the archaic world. What better way to evoke the horror of predation and the emotions inspired by it than through the ritual killing of actual humans? Unfortunately, though, the archeological record is often ambiguous, and great care must be taken to distinguish between the remains of a ritual sacrifice and those of, say, an execution (as of a criminal) or the burial of a murder victim. Furthermore, we have no reliable eyewitness accounts to turn to. When the Greek geographer Pausanias visited Mount Lykaion in the second century A.D., he heard rumors of the yearly murder, dismemberment, and devouring of a child at the mountaintop sanctuary of Zeus. But he did not investigate. "I could see no pleasure in delving into this sacrifice," he wrote, adding cryptically: "Let it be as it is and as it was from the beginning."[5]

Until a few years ago, scholarly opinion tended to see human sacrifice as an anthropological oddity, if not a figment of overheated imaginations. Modern people's distaste for the practice has often impeded objective investigation. On the one hand, there was no doubt a tendency for Europeans to attribute human sacrifice to subjugated peoples in order to discredit their cultures; one of the nineteenth-century arguments in support of the slave trade was that it at least saved the captured Africans from a worse fate at the hands of their own people.[6] On the other hand, scholars themselves have often been too prone to overcorrect for past imperialist distortions by denying or ignoring the evidence for human sacrifice, in both the ancient as well as the modern world. They have tended to file human sacrifice, along

---

> It is one of the oldest rites of government: when things are not going well, when the leader is in trouble, a member of his retinue must be sacrificed. At least the wolves will be silenced for a while.

As Hubert and Mauss, the nineteenth-century historians of sacrifice, pointed out, the meat left by ancient Greek sacrificial rituals was sometimes literally carried off by wolves.

with cannibalism, under the category of sensationalism and intercultural slander.

Today, however, the evidence has accumulated to a point where it can no longer be ignored. A consensus is emerging that human sacrifice, far from being an oddity, has been a widespread practice among diverse cultures, from small-scale tribes to mighty urban civilizations such as that of the fifteenth-century Aztecs,[7] and that it has played a role in almost every conceivable form of religious observance. The most clear-cut cases are provided by the large number of skeletons found interred, along with a king or other important personage, in royal tombs—presumably slaves and wives who were intended to accompany their master into the netherworld. Such remains have been found in China, Sudan, and Mesopotamia, dating to the second and third millennia B.C.[8] But human sacrifice has also very likely been employed in one setting or another to ensure the fertility of the earth, to consecrate buildings, to guarantee success in war, and, in all cases, to "feed" or appease the gods. If we have collectively forgotten the practice, this may be because it is so difficult for us to acknowledge that what is morally repulsive to us could once have been deemed morally necessary by people no less human than ourselves.

Still, much of the history of human sacrifice remains frustratingly obscure, including the obvious question of its temporal relationship to the far less controversial practice of animal sacrifice. Did animals replace human victims, as many myths imply, or, in some cases, did humans replace animals? In myth, the striking thing is how interchangeable the two types of victim seem to be. Artemis may have been willing to accept a deer instead of Agamemnon's daughter Iphigenia; Jehovah asks for Isaac but will take a ram. What ultimately concerns the ancient gods is *meat* or, more commonly in the case of human victims, blood. Where we do find an exclusive concentration on human sacrifice, as among the Aztecs, whose obsession with this ritual is documented by their own records as well as by the Spanish conquerors' accounts, we also find a marked shortage of animals that might have substituted for humans. If the Aztecs had possessed large animals, such as cattle and sheep, these creatures might have nourished the Aztec gods just as well.

What does seem clear is that human sacrifice played a role in the ancient religions—Greek, Hebrew, and Hindu—that were also so preoccupied with animal sacrifice. Turning first to the ancient Greeks, we know at least that they believed human sacrifice was an important part of their religious and historical legacy. Mythological references to human sacrifice, in one form or another, are rampant. The cannibalistic Titan Cronus required human victims. The maenads—frenzied female worshippers of Dionysus—were said to tear living victims apart with their hands and eat them on the spot. In the *Iliad*, twelve captured Trojan youths were sacrificed along with numerous animal victims at the funeral of Patroklus, and according to legend, the funeral of Achilles required the sacrifice of the Trojan princess Polyxena. Finally, in a remarkable feat of archeological sleuthing, the American scholar Joan B. Connelly has recently made the controversial proposal that the giant frieze set high on the Parthenon in fact depicts the preparations of three Athenian princesses, daughters of King Erectheus, for sacrifice:

> The youngest girl's funerary dress is being unfolded; she will go first. The oldest daughter . . . is in the process of handing down a stool to her mother. The daughter at the far left faces to the front, with a garment [presumably her funerary dress] still folded and carried upon the stool on her head.[9]

The Hebrews, too, saw human sacrifice as a relic of the not-so-distant past. Psalms 106: 37–38 says clearly of the early Israelites:

> Yea, they sacrificed their sons and their daughters unto devils and shed innocent blood, even the blood of their sons and of their daughters, whom they sacrificed unto the idols of Canaan.

According to Bergmann, the prophets "waged a relentless war against the ritual murder of children," and associated it with the worship of pagan gods such as Chmosh and Moloch. Micah 6: 7, for example, inveighs against both human and animal sacrifice, barely bothering to distinguish between them:

> Will the Lord be pleased with thousands of rams, or with ten thousands of rivers of oil? Shall I give my firstborn for my transgression, the fruit of my body for the sin of my soul?

Circumcision may well be a remnant of a tradition of human sacrifice, with the foreskin serving as a substitute for a whole human victim. Some historians speculate that an archaic version of the deity, quite possibly a goddess, demanded human sacrifices and later came to accept the destruction of the male genitals as a sufficient substitute for the whole man; castration may, in fact, have been a prerequisite for the priesthood in the archaic age, when the chief deity was herself female and accustomed to being represented by priestesses. Later even this requirement was softened, and the foreskin allowed to substitute for the genitals as well as the man.[10]

At least one ancient city, Carthage, left what has been interpreted as direct archeological evidence of human sacrifice. Thousands of burial urns containing the charred remains of infants and young children have been unearthed in the Tophet, or sacred precinct, of that North African city, which had been founded about 3,000 years ago by settlers from Asia Minor. Two facts suggest this was no ordinary cemetery: Inscriptions on the commemorative markers sometimes mention vows made to the deities—the goddess Tanit (Astarte in Asia Minor) and her consort Baal Hammon—implying that the children were offerings made in exchange for some divinely granted boon; and many of the urns contain the cremated remains of more common, animal offerings. These findings would seem to bear out the accusation, made by the prophet Jeremiah, that the worshippers of Baal "consigned their sons and daughters to the fire."[11]

For the Indian subcontinent, we have not only references to human sacrifice in ancient religious texts, but descriptions of practices encountered by the British in modern times. The Vedas refer to human sacrifice and offer special incantations and instructions for it.[12] Texts from around 900 B.C. mention human sacrifices to Rudra, a wild version of the mainstream Vedic god Shiva, who in the Rig-Veda "kills those who walk on two feet as well as those who walk on four feet."[13] The British claimed to have found and attempted to outlaw a variety of forms of human sacrifice still being practiced in India in the eighteenth and nineteenth centuries: widows burned to death on their husbands' funeral pyres in the practice of suttee; random victims being offered to Kali by members of the cult from whose name we derive the word "thug"; children and sometimes adult victims being sacrificed by the tribal mountain peoples known generically as Kondhs.[14]

Thus the records of literate ancient peoples are at least strongly suggestive of archaic traditions of human sacrifice. As for nonliterate peoples, we have again only the word of the conquerors. The Romans reported human sacrifice among the Carthaginians, the Scythians, and the tribes of Britain, who were, according to Tacitus, accustomed "to drench their altars in the blood of prisoners and consult their god by means of human sacrifice."[15] Some of these allegations may be slanderous, but the Romans attributed human sacrifice to the Celtic peoples of northern Europe and, indeed, as Patrick Tierny, author of *The Highest Altar: Unveiling the Mystery of Human Sacrifice*, reports, archeologists have found the remains of sacrificial victims under Celtic holy sites:

> A man shot to death by arrows lies buried at the main entrance of Stonehenge; the Greek geographer Strabo wrote that Druids performed human sacrifice by arrow shooting. And within two miles of Stonehenge there is another circle, built of wooden posts, called Woodhenge. In the center of Woodhenge excavators found a three-and-a-half-year-old girl whose skull had been split "before burial"

> with an ax. . . . Forensic analysis of [cremated] bones at fifty Scottish stone circles revealed that there were too few individuals for family burials, and that a disproportionate number were children.[16]

The most dramatic and large-scale cases of alleged human sacrifice come not from the ancient world but from quite recent times: fifteenth-century Mexico and nineteenth-century western Africa. At the opening of the great temple of Tenochtitlán, the Aztecs are said to have sacrificed well over ten thousand people, prisoners of recent wars.[17] Each killing must have been a gripping, if not terrifying, sight, conducted at the top of a pyramid within easy view of the assembled populace below. First the victim mounted the steps of the pyramid upon which the sacrifice was to take place:

> He was awaited at the top by the satraps or priests who were to kill him, and these now grabbed him and threw him onto the stone block, and, holding him by feet, hands and head, thrown on his back, the priest who had the stone knife buried it with a mighty thrust in the victim's breast and, after drawing it out, thrust one hand into the opening and tore out the heart, which he at once offered to the sun.[18]

To the modern reader, as to the Spanish conquerors who encountered and destroyed Aztec culture in the sixteenth century, the practice of human sacrifice is profoundly disturbing. But to the Aztecs themselves, ritual murder was the ultimate act of piety, serving to keep the universe functioning in an orderly and predictable manner. Without its meals of human blood, the sun would die and the world would be plunged into darkness. Hence the need for perpetual war to provide the captives whose blood would feed the sun:

> Convinced that in order to avoid the final cataclysm it was necessary to fortify the sun, they undertook for themselves

> the mission of furnishing it with the vital energy found only in the precious liquid which keeps man alive. Sacrifice and ceremonial warfare, which was the principal manner of obtaining victims for all sacrificial rites, were their central activities and the very core of their personal, social, military, religious, and national life.[19]

It was war that allowed human sacrifice to achieve a truly spectacular scale. Certainly, the sacrifice of a single well-loved child within a tribal group would be a compelling spectacle in itself, but with war the process could be magnified to hundreds or thousands of deaths at a time. Like the Aztecs, the nineteenth-century African kingdom of Dahomey waged war for the stated purpose of collecting victims for sacrificial rites. In these rites,

> the king sat on a platform among his dignitaries while the people stood below in a dense throng. At a sign from the king the executioners set to work. The heads of the murdered prisoners were thrown onto a heap; several such heaps were to be seen. There were processions through streets lined with the naked corpses of executed enemies hanging from gallows; to spare the modesty of the king's innumerable wives these had been mutilated. . . . People fought for the corpses; it was said that in their frenzy they ate them. Everyone wanted to get a piece of the enemy dead; it might be called a communion of triumph. Human beings were followed by animals, but the chief thing was the enemy.[20]

Clearly there were simpler ways to dispose of excess prisoners, but spectacles of slaughter served a function of their own. Whatever the spectators may have felt—horror or religious awe—human sacrifice compelled them to witness the power of their own leaders, their priests and kings, over individual life and death. At some point in prehistory, historian Lewis Mumford writes, "the exhibition of armed might became one of the most important attributes of kingship." Egyptian and Mesopotamian monarchs boasted on their monuments and tablets of "their personal feats in mutilating, torturing, and killing with their own hands their chief captives."[21] Apparently the mass human sacrifices of precolonial Mesoamerica and western Africa were also intended, in part, to intimidate. According to the Spanish chronicler Diego Durán, Aztec sacrifices had the desired effect on their witnesses, who often included, as invited guests, the leaders of areas subjugated by the Aztecs:

> The lords and principals who were called to the feast and sacrifice were horrified, beside themselves, on seeing the killing and sacrificing of so many men, so terrified that they dared not speak.[22]

Studies of Mayan glyphs and iconography suggest a similar role for human sacrifice in the Classic Maya period:

> The true Maya lord expressed his political dominance through the taking of captives but achieved the sacralization of that dominance only by the sacrificing of those captives.[23]

And an Ashanti king stated in the mid-nineteenth century that "if I were to abolish human sacrifice, I should deprive myself of one of the most effectual means of keeping the people in subjection."[24]

The Attack of the Gods

For whatever reasons it was performed, with animal or human victims, the sacrificial ritual in many ways mimics the crisis of a predator's attack. An animal or perhaps a human member of the group is singled out for slaughter, often in a spectacularly bloody manner: The

Aztecs ripped the victim's heart out; in the Greek rite of *spiragmos*, which is referred to in myth, the victim was torn to pieces. The audience screams; the victim's blood is sprinkled about or even poured over objects and people requiring purification. Describing his responses to an animal sacrifice performed in our own time, Tierny reports emotions which would be appropriate to someone witnessing a successful predator attack on a fellow human: There is high excitement, "frenzied screaming," a sense of "ultimate risk," followed by "infinite relief," and finally guilt that "he died instead of me."[25]

In fact, Greek mythology offers numerous cases in which humans are offered directly to a predator beast in order to save the larger community. Laomedon must expose his daughter Hesione to a sea monster sent by Poseidon; Andromeda is tied to a rock to be eaten by another one of Poseidon's monstrous envoys; in Thespiae, a young man was selected by lot each year to be offered to a dragon that was ravaging the land. These myths are not, of course, evidence that any such events actually occurred, but they do at least show that the *possibility* of having to appease a predator beast with a human sacrifice had powerful dramatic resonance for the Greeks.

In one particularly gruesome story, which recaptures the terror of an actual predator's attack, a familiar deity takes the form of a predator and demands a human victim. The god Dionysus, angry at three sisters who refuse to join in his revels, appears to them successively in the form of a lion, a bull, and a panther. Driven insane by these visitations, one of the women offers her own son as a sacrifice. The three sisters, whose madness has by this time merged them with the god as surely as if they had participated in his orgiastic revels, then tear the child to pieces and devour him on the spot.[26]

One of the few rituals of human sacrifice to survive into modern times was, in part, an explicit attempt to appease very real predator beasts. Until Christian missionaries succeeded in dissuading them from the practice, certain of the Kondh tribes of India sacrificed a human victim, the *meriah*, who might have been captured or even raised locally for this purpose. Before the killing, the priest offered prayers to the "earth goddess" for "full granaries, increase of children, cattle, pigs and poultry and for *the decrease or disappearance of tigers and snakes*"[27] (italics added). The priest then stabbed the victim while the villagers joined him in singing:

Here we sacrifice the enemy
Here we sacrifice the "*meriah*"
The gods eat-up this sacrifice
The enemy is thus worshipped
Let there be no collective loss
Let no tigers prowl
The gods need so many bribes
So many offerings.[28]

Later in the song, the deity being sacrificed to is identified as Durga, the goddess who is stereotypically portrayed riding on a tiger:

Durga eats
Durga eats everything.

Once sated on the *meriah*, Durga would presumably leave the rest of the villagers alone.

But for all the intuitive appeal of the apotropaic scenario, in which the sacrifice is designed to ward off the predator beast, there is also an intuitive problem: The beast may be temporarily appeased by the victim that is tossed to it, but it will return. In fact, the sacrificial strategy seems guaranteed to habituate the predator to seek out human encampments as a source of food. If you want to attract a stray cat or dog, you leave it "offerings" of milk or meat. Bear attacks in contemporary American national parks have been attributed to the human habit of leaving garbage out near dwellings and campsites. Thus it seems likely that in the prehistoric situation, the wolves that were satisfied one night with an infant or a hunk of animal meat would be back the next night for more.

One possibility is that "sacrifice," in its most archaic form, was not a ritual at all, but a face-saving euphemism for death by predation. Perhaps no victims were ever thrown to the wolves or lions, but it somehow pleased our hominid ancestors to think of those who died in the jaws of predators as victims voluntarily offered by the group. Before the practice of burying the dead, all those who died of any cause would have ended up as some predator's—or scavenger's—meal anyway. If it is difficult for modern humans to think of themselves or others like them as prey, the idea may have been equally upsetting to our ancestors. Thus religion, or some dim and gory predecessor thereof, may have helped soften the harsh reality of predation; the loss of a child to wild beasts becomes more bearable when it is understood as a "sacrifice" that will ward off further evils. As "sacrifice," the horror of random victimization is in part redeemed.

There is another possibility, however, suggested by the proposal that hominids and early humans may have obtained their meat by scavenging dead animals, including the kills of other creatures. Scavenging would have thrown our hominid ancestors into a highly ambivalent relationship with the predator beasts. On the one hand, the predators are of course destroyers, winnowing out the weak and the unwary from the hominid band. On the other hand, the beasts who kill become, in their own way, providers: Partly eaten kills left by big cats, for example, attract hyenas, wild dogs, and at one time, probably inept carnivores like our hominid ancestors, who initially had no means of felling a large game animal on their own. Even the more peaceable ungulates, such as deer, it should be noted, can be dangerous and challenging prey for humans hunting on foot.

Thus a certain dependency would have entered into the hominid relationship with the predator beast, terrifying as that beast may have been. Anthropologist Curtis Marean has argued, for example, that the extinction of sabertooth cats approximately 1.7 million years ago was a major turning point in hominid evolution: Without these forest-based cats to scavenge from, hominids were forced to venture out into the savannah, where they scavenged from lions and other big cats. The increased danger of predation in the savannah, Marean suggests, exerted a selective pressure for a larger hominid body size, more like that of modern humans.[29]

So the presence of carnivores encouraged by "sacrificial" offerings may even have been desirable in certain situations, despite the obvious dangers: It would not have helped early humans to be surrounded by luscious and abundant game animals if there were no predator animals to do their hunting for them. At least one form of predator beast—the wolf or wild dog—was apparently seduced by human offerings of meat into servitude as a hunting aide.

To some scholars, the idea of hominids scavenging is almost as distasteful as the idea of their being prey.[30] But scavenging from more skillful predators takes courage and ingenuity, especially in the case of what anthropologists call "active" or "confrontational" scavenging, in which the scavenger must drive away the beast that made the kill. Hyenas scavenge from lions but are fierce predators themselves, capable of matching lions tooth for claw. Imagine, then, the audacity of our toothless, clawless, unarmed ancestors, creeping out from the underbrush to steal the leavings of the mighty leopard or lion. Imagine, too, the role the predator would come to play in the prehuman and early human mind: both giver of sustenance and taker of life.

If the beast that kills also nourishes, then the idea of archaic sacrifice as a literal offering to the beast begins to make more sense. In addition to whatever apotropaic function the offering serves—calming the beast for the moment—it is a profound acknowledgment of human dependency. Should the predator animals leave the area in search of more plentiful game animals, the hominid band might suffer also. Thus hard times, in which game animals are scarce, might seem to demand extraordinary "sacrifices," just as they did in the ancient civilizations that institutionalized sacrifice as a religious ritual. Perhaps, too, there is a psychological need to see the hominid-predator relationship as more reciprocal than it actually is: Before humans are equipped to capture their own game, they can convince themselves, through offerings to the beasts, that they have somehow earned their meat.

The myths and practices of a surviving hunting-gathering people, the Koyukon of northwestern Alaska, are suggestive of the kind of reciprocal relationship that could have arisen between early humans and more skillful predators. The Koyukons are hunters, but they are also scavengers and believe that wolves deliberately leave fresh kills for them to find:

> In the Distant Time, a wolf-person lived among people and hunted with them. When they parted ways, they agreed that wolves would sometimes make kills for people or drive game to them, as a repayment for favors given when wolves were still human. . . . Koyukon hunters still find wolf kills, left clean and unspoiled for them, and it is their right to take what is found.[31]

In return, the Koyukons sometimes leave out treats for the wolves:

> When hunters leave cache behind they might place some fat apart from the rest of the meat, and if wolves happen along they are expected to take this rather than disturb what people want for themselves.[32]

Presumably this method is effective, and the wolves are content with their share.

A similar relationship existed between the Indians of southern California and the mountain lion, which was venerated as a provider of meat:

> When they saw buzzards gathering, they sought out and feasted upon the lion's kill. The lion's success as a hunter meant their own survival. Cheyenne mythology went even further: their women suckled panther cubs like children, and in turn the panthers killed deer for them. . . . Maybe it was the use of mountain lion food by people that generated a body of lore, prominent in parts of Central and South America, of the lion as a friend and even loving helper of humankind.[33]

Here we must confront the unsettling equivalence, implicit in the discussion so far, between the predator beast and the deities of ancient and traditional religions. As we saw in chapter 2, these deities have carnivorous tastes. The sacrificial offering is the "food" of the gods, and the food must, in almost all cases, be meat. This may mean simply that the gods are anthropomorphic and share the human preference for meat. Or it may mean that the sacrifice-devouring gods represent the killer beasts that were the original meat eaters. Anthropologist Karl Luckert would seem to favor the latter explanation, asserting that the gods of hunting peoples "were mostly greater-than-humanoid hunters who, accordingly, appeared mostly in the form of predators."[34]

If the idea of the deity as a predator beast seems preposterous, recall Jehovah's furious appetite for animal offerings and his obsessive demands for foreskins, which may have been a substitute for human sacrificial victims. Zeus, too, often seems to take a more predatory than parental interest in his human subjects. He is sometimes known as Zeus Lykaios, the wolf, a rapist and insatiable consumer of blood offerings. But here we can let an acknowledged expert do our generalizing for us. In his study of initiation rites among tribal societies, Mircea Eliade found that

> the Divine Beings who play a part in initiation ceremonies are usually imagined as beasts of prey—lions and leopards (initiatory animals par excellence) in Africa, jaguars in South America, crocodiles and marine monsters in Oceania.[35]

And while we have no idea what, if any, deities Paleolithic humans worshipped, it may be significant that caverns recently discovered near the town of Vallon-Pont-d'Arc in southern France contain "the skull of a bear, placed on a large rock set in the middle of a gallery against a backdrop of bear paintings." To Jean Clottes, France's leading specialist in Paleolithic art, this configuration is suggestive of "some kind of altar," presumably dedicated to bears or a bearlike deity.[36]

Within human memory, there are numerous examples of the worship of predator animals, and while these tell nothing about Paleolithic practices, they at least show that such worship is within the repertory of human possibilities. Lions were worshipped at the mouths of desert wadis in ancient Egypt, where hunters and caravans entered the lions' desert habitat;[37] jaguars were worshipped in Central and South America;[38] the Toltec deity Tezcatlipoca was closely associated with, and sometimes represented as, a jaguar.[39] Indians of the tiger-ridden Sundarbans region still worship the pre-Vedic tiger god Daksin Ray, who, according to myth, once demanded human sacrifices.[40] Until he converted to vegetarianism recently, Daksin Ray required animal sacrifices offered up in orgiastic rites:

> The yard of worship overflows with the blood of the sacrificed birds and beasts. Marking their foreheads with the blood of bleeding beasts, the drunken devotees, with torches in hand, dance and make obscene gestures and utterances. Stunning shouts and pealing music are raised.[41]

Sometimes the recipient of sacrificial offerings is an actual, living predator animal. The ancient Hawaiians, for example, worshipped sharks as deities and made sacrifices to them.[42] A particularly fervent case of shark worship was reported by the Portuguese missionary and adventurer Sebastian Manrique, who observed sacrificial rites at the mouth of the Hugli River in seventeenth-century India. According to this observer—and I have no way of judging his reliability—both men and women went into a state of ecstasy and offered themselves to the sharks:

> They enter the sea up to their breasts and are very soon seized and devoured . . . and since they [the sharks] are accustomed and thus encouraged constantly by tasting human flesh, they become so bloodthirsty that they rush up fiercely at a mere shadow.[43]

Or a god may be represented by predators that eat the sacrificial victims for him. According to one interpretation, the episode in the Norse saga of the Volsungs in which the evil king Siggeir "takes the sons of Volsung as prisoners of war and exposes them in fetters to be devoured by a wolf, represents a ritual of human sacrifice to Odin."[44]

There are hints, too, that human sacrifice in the Classic period of Mayan culture may have—literally as well as symbolically—fed a jaguar god. The highest order of Mayan priests was the "Jaguar priests," who officiated at rites in which the heart was torn out of a living victim's chest;[45] and one of the more terrifying tools left by the Mayan clergy was the "claw-knife," which was "designed to inflict lacerations similar to those caused by claws, probably those of the jaguar."[46] (Interestingly, the obsidian blades used for Aztec sacrificial killings also seem to have been symbolic "analogues of jaguar fangs and claws."[47]) Archeologists speculate that Classic Maya human sacrifice simulated, in part, a jaguar's kill—the victim being lacerated with claw-knives either before or after the removal of the heart. In fact, according to Maya scholars Francis Robicsek and Donald Hales,

> it is conceivable that the final act of Classic heart sacrifice was to offer the body of the victim (*sans son coeur*) to be mangled by jaguars, who were regarded as high-ranking deities of the Classic period Mayan pantheon.[48]

Mayan art depicts what indeed appears to be human offerings to jaguars. One polychrome vase shows a priest holding out the limp body of an infant or child to a jaguar whose paw reaches out toward the child's head.[49] In a scene from another polychrome artwork, the archeologists' caption tells us, "the body of an infant, whose lower chest or midriff is cut open, is being offered (?) to a jaguar by a knife-wielding priestly personage."[50]

There is another reason to suspect that religion may be rooted in the primordial encounter with the predator beast. Writing in the 1960s, Konrad Lorenz noted the physiological parallels between what humans experience as religious awe and the arousal experienced by animals in the face of a threat. What is known in German as the *heiliger Schauer*, or "holy shiver" of awe, may be a "vestige," he suggested, of the widespread and entirely unconscious defensive response which causes an animal's fur to stand on end, thus increasing its apparent size.[51] Deities are usually imagined as potential helpers, but they are also objects of fear. "The fear of God is the beginning of wisdom," or, as the Roman poet Statius wrote, "Fear, first of all, produced gods in the world."[52]

Why, the modern reader cannot help but wonder, would human beings want to reenact, through religious ritual, the terror of predation? Probably for the same reason that "civilized" people today pay to see movies in which their fellow humans are stalked and devoured by flesh-eating ghouls, vampires, and extraterrestrial monsters. Nothing gets our attention like the prospect of being ripped apart, sucked dry, and transformed into another creature's meal. As Elias Canetti has written:

> The narrow gorge through which everything has to pass is, for the few who live so long, the ultimate terror. Man's imagination has been continually occupied by the several stages of incorporation. The gaping jaws of the large beasts which threatened him have pursued him even into his dreams and myths.[53]

We are drawn back compulsively, in both nightmares and moments of fun, to that primordial encounter with the devouring beast. The "fun," of course, is that in the fictional encounter, we can look into the very jaws of the beast—and live to do it again. Rituals and other sorts of spectacles that replay the possibility of being eaten are one way of celebrating what must have been, for our entire species, a terrifyingly narrow escape.

> To the humble seeker of biological truth there cannot be the slightest doubt that human militant enthusiasm evolved out of a communal defense response of our prehuman ancestors.[1]
>
> —KONRAD LORENZ

5
The Rebellion Against the Beast

The great advance in human evolution, the transition from the status of prey to that of predator, must have been, at some level, an act of transgression—a rebellion against the predator beast. It took enormous courage and defiance for our clawless, blunt-toothed, hominid ancestors to in any way challenge the beast's dominion. And insofar as the predator may also have been a provider and perhaps a kind of deity, the human rebellion against it surely ranks with Lucifer's uprising against heaven—the difference being that humans won.

The myths of many cultures seem to recall this rebellion as a discrete and singular event, often the slaying of a fantastic beast by a male hero/god. Perseus defeats the sea-dwelling, man-eating Gorgon. Indra defeats the monster Vrtra. Saint George battles the dragon Dajjal. In early Japanese myth, it is the storm god Susanoo no Mikoto who destroys the dragon.[2] The defeated serpent or dragon has been interpreted as representing the chaos "of matter still unformed and undifferentiated," or of human societies before the imposition of the hierarchies of gender and class.[3] In the Sumerian origin myth, the hero is the god Marduk and the monster of chaos is Tiamat, his own mother, described by Joseph Campbell as "terrifying, dragon-like, attended by swarms of demons—a female personification of the original abyss itself."[4]

In reality, of course, there could have been no single, decisive victory, and certainly not one achieved by a single, miraculously gifted individual. If these heroic myths tell us anything, it is that, on the eve of remembered history, enormous prestige attached to the man who could defend his community against the incursions of predatory animals. But the human ascent to the summit of the food chain took hundreds of thousands, if not millions, of years and, especially in the earlier stages, no doubt utilized forms of defense, widespread in the animal world, that involve females as well as males, young as well as old. In this chapter we look at the forms which the rebellion might have taken and consider their possible relevance to the practices, in far more recent times, of ritual sacrifice and war.

One familiar practice which could be counted as a form of "rebellion" is the burial of the human dead. At some point about 150,000 years ago, early humans were no longer content to leave their dead exposed and began to bury them with some apparent ceremony. All kinds of meanings can be read into this practice, including belief in a soul and an afterlife. But one obvious consequence was to deprive the wild carnivores of an easy meal. Even lions are not above devouring animal remains, and less formidable scavengers—dogs, vultures, crows, rats, and so on—often have little choice but to eat the already dead. Hence, in historical times, the widespread concern that the dead have a "proper burial." The heroes of the *Iliad* fear death not only because it means being reduced to thinghood, as Simone Weil wrote,[5] but because it could mean being reduced to meat. Hektor threatens to lop off Patroklus's head and feed his body to the "Trojan bitches," and Achilles' vengeance, as we have seen, includes the promise that the birds and dogs will dine on Hektor himself.

To die unburied is to be doubly defeated—first by the enemy and then by the scavenging creatures who clean up the battlefield when the fight is over. In Sumerian myth, after the warrior-goddess Anath defeats the god Mot:

> Birds eat his remnants,
> Consuming his portions,
> Flitting from remnant to remnant.[6]

Conversely, to bury the human dead is to cheat the beasts: to refuse, even in death, to accept the status of prey.

But at the core of the hominid rebellion was the decision, no doubt predating by millennia the practice of burying the dead, to confront the beast itself. The natural impulse, in the face of danger, is to flee. The predator is sighted—perhaps as it snatches a child or an injured adult from the group. The alarm call sounds, and the band scatters into bush and trees. At some point, though, our hominid ancestors, or some brave souls among them, decided not to flee but to stand and face the threat. Those who stepped forward to confront the predator risked their own lives, of course, but evolutionary biologists tell us that the act of resistance can be, in a genetic sense, self-serving. By protecting others who are genetically related to them—children, for example, and siblings—the defenders help ensure that their genes, or at least genes closely resembling theirs, have some chance of living on. Heroism has its own (genetic) rewards.

This does not mean, of course, that the threatened hominid must pause to calculate the genetic payoffs of various courses of action. In the moment of confrontation, emotions take over, serving as a primitive kind of decision-making algorithm overriding the more cumbersome processes of calculation and rational thought. As evolutionary psychologists Leda Cosmides and John Tooby put it:

> When a tiger bounds toward you, what should your response be? Should you file your toenails? Do a cartwheel? Sing a song? Is this a moment to run an uncountable num-

> ber of randomly generated response possibilities through the decision rule? And again, how could you compute which possibility would result in more grandchildren? The alternative: Darwinian algorithms specialized for predator-avoidance, that . . . upon detecting a potential predator, constrain your responses to flight, fight, or hiding.[7]

The emotional "algorithm" that shapes our response to danger is the well-known "fight or flight" response, which we share with other mammals. At the sight of danger, the heart and respiratory rate increase, and blood is withdrawn from the surface of the body and the viscera in favor of the voluntary muscles (hence the "gut-wrenching" feelings and blanching of the skin)—all in preparation for the sudden exertion of fighting or fleeing. Subtler changes take place, too: The pupils dilate, the bronchi distend, glucose is released by the liver for use by the muscles, and blood clotting is sped up in anticipation of wounds. All these changes are automatic, taking place within seconds or minutes of the perception of a threat, without any conscious intervention.

Subjectively, the fight-or-flight response may feel like panic, rage, or even a mad surge of superhuman strength. In Greek myth, Queen Ino of Boeotia is attacked by a lynx while hunting. A torn and blood-stained fragment of her tunic convinces her husband that she has been killed by wild beasts. In reality, a "sudden Bacchic frenzy had seized her" at the moment of the attack. "She had strangled [the lynx], flayed it with her teeth and nails, and gone off, dressed only in the pelt, for a prolonged revel on Mount Parnassus."[8]

The practice of scavenging would have greatly increased the likelihood of hostile encounters with predator beasts. Drawn to the kill site by the sound of crows or the sight of vultures circling in the air, early humans would have found, in many cases, the predator still busy at its meal. The Gond tribespeople of north-central India still, or at least until very recent times, obtained meat by scavenging from tiger kills. "If the tiger is still there, they stand at a safe distance and shout and toss stones and wave sticks" to drive the tiger away and then move in to "devour every scrap of meat."[9]

In myth, confrontations between humans and beasts often occur at a potential kill site and leave the predator deprived of its meal. Hesione and Andromeda were not devoured by the monsters they were intended for but, rather, were rescued by the heroes—Heracles and Perseus, respectively—they would end up marrying. In Thespiae, the practice of choosing a young man by lot every year to be fed to the dragon ended when the male lover of one chosen victim volunteered to be sacrificed in his stead, then killed the beast. In all these cases love triumphs over fear, the sacrifice is subverted, and a potential meal becomes a mate.

How exactly did our hominid ancestors confront and, with luck, repel predator animals? Most likely hominid resistance predated any effective weapons technology and, as in the case of other social animals, invoked the strength of numbers. Birds and nonhuman primates will often drive away dangerous intruders by "mobbing" them: All members of the group—male and female, mature and immature—close ranks and advance on the intruder, making the most threatening noises and gestures at their command. Modern humans, such as unarmed campers confronting a bear, tend almost instinctively to do the same—banding together, shouting, and banging on pots and pans. Summarizing the ways nonhuman primates respond to predators, anthropologists Lisa Rose and Fiona Marshall write:

> Once potential predators have been detected, the reactions of extant primates are often coordinated and aggressive. . . . Individuals typically respond rapidly to the alarm calls of others; in chimpanzees and capuchins, dispersed groups will quickly coalesce and join in aggressive displays. . . . Baboons mob and chase cheetahs or jackals and will attack and fight even lions or leopards. . . . Whenever Tai Forest chimpanzees notice the presence of a leopard, they "search for it and chase it away cooperatively."

Rose and Marshall suggest that these cases of collective defense among nonhuman primates may well be a model for the defensive behavior of hominids, who "would have responded similarly to the risk of carnivore predation by intensifying cooperative behaviors, perhaps using branches or stones as simple defensive weapons."[10]

The behaviors required for collective resistance may have helped establish the rudiments of hominid "culture." In his most recent book, historian William H. McNeill addresses the human propensity for "keeping together in time," as through group dancing and military drilling, and suggests that it can be traced to the primordial sociality of the hominid band confronting a wild animal.[11] Possibly the invention of music, as well as the nearly universal practice of dancing, owes much to the exigencies of anti-predator defense.

In creatures that have some chance of succeeding at group resistance, the perception of danger may trigger powerful feelings of group solidarity. Not in everyone, of course; there are always those who choose to hide or climb a tree. But chimpanzees, for example, "may become highly aroused at the mere sight of a killing, screaming loudly as they watch the action and running about and throwing their arms around one another."[12] Male colobus monkeys, sweetly enough, prepare for group resistance to a predator by "run[ning] to one another and embrac[ing] for reassurance."[13] And we know from quite recent human experience that nothing pulls a group, or a nation, together like the appearance of an enemy or external threat. It is a shame, perhaps, that hatred and mortal fear seem to draw us together so much more reliably than love and camaraderie, but as any demagogue knows, a crowd is most likely to bond into a purposeful entity when it has an enemy to face. Millennia of terror seem to have left us with another "Darwinian algorithm": that in the face of danger, we need to cleave together, becoming a new, many-headed creature larger than our individual selves.

The final stage of the rebellion occurs when humans learn to hunt and kill for themselves—game animals and even, at times, the predator beasts themselves. Hunting in the early stages may have been, like early forms of defense, an activity involving the entire group, females and children included. The stratagem of "mobbing" would have lent itself to such hunting techniques as driving animals over cliffs to their death, beating the underbrush to force the game out from cover, or simply overwhelming a cornered animal. Our prime tutors in the subject of hunting were probably not the big cats, which usually hunt alone, but the wolves and wild dogs, which know how to work in a pack.

But it is through hunting that humans come to imitate individual beasts, as well as the behavior of packs. Stones which have been pounded until they acquire an edge, as well as sticks which have been brought to a point with sharpened stones, become the human equivalent of the teeth and the claws of the beast. Thousands of years later, with the subjugation of the horse and the emergence of the mounted archer, humans finally achieved both the speed and the deadliness of a leopard or lion. Perhaps the "fearful symmetry" Blake saw in the face of the tiger was his own human face, reflected back.

Reenacting the Rebellion

The transformation from prey to predator, in which the weak rise up against the strong, is the central "story" in the early human narrative. Some residual anxiety seems to draw us back to it again and again. We recount it as myth and reenact it in ritual, as if we could never be sufficiently assured that it has, indeed, occurred. In folktales, lions are defeated by foxes, wolves outwitted by clever monkeys, and in general,

> small, tiny, and physically weak animals or birds are shown as wiser than the big animals or birds and essentially victorious in their tasks and struggles against them.[14]

In religious narratives and rituals, few themes are as ubiquitous as that of the potential victim who is resurrected or otherwise upgraded to the status of victor. The British anthropologist Maurice Bloch concludes, remarkably enough, that this is, in fact, what religion is *about*: "The dramatic transformation of prey into hunter . . . underlies in different forms the practices which can easily be subsumed under the English word 'religion.'"[15]

Origin myths are one way in which the transformation story is retold. Mircea Eliade found that an origin myth commonly

> tells of a primordial Animal who killed human beings in order to resuscitate them; in the end, the Animal was itself killed, and this event, which took place in the beginning, is ritually reiterated.[16]

The animal might have been a python or a monster; it may have eaten humans and regurgitated them; it might have been killed because it *stopped* regurgitating its victims, or did not regurgitate enough of them. In any case:

> a Supernatural Being had attempted to renew men by killing them in order to bring them to life again "changed"; for one reason or another, men slew this Supreme Being, but they later celebrated secret rites inspired by this drama; more precisely, the violent death of the Supreme Being became the central mystery.[17]

Just as the entire species had to undergo the prey-to-predator transformation long ago in the Paleolithic past, so does each child undergo a version of it in the course of growing up. We start as helpless infants, weighing less than one-tenth as much as adults and unable to support even that tiny weight on our infant limbs. We start, in other words, as potential prey, and remain at the mercy of giants for many years before we find our way, through learning and growth, to a more commanding status. Most cultures have marked the transition from potential prey to potential predator with initiation rites, and these often seem to be quite vivid and literal reenactments of the primal encounter with a man-eating predator beast.

Consider the initiation rites practiced by the Orokaiva people of New Guinea. The children to be initiated, both boys and girls, are first menaced by masked adults leaping out from the bush. The intruders, who are supposed to be "spirits," chase the children, shouting "bite, bite, bite" at them, and herd them onto a platform of the kind usually used for the slaughter of pigs. The terrified children are then covered in a "blinding cape" and taken to an isolated hut in the bush, where they undergo various ordeals and are inducted into tribal secrets. "Not infrequently," the anthropologists tell us, some of the children die during the course of these ordeals. Finally the surviving initiates return to the village, dressed in masks and feathers like the "spirits" who first menaced them, and participate in a pig hunt. They return, Bloch reports, "not as prey but as hunters of pigs, shouting the same formula which had been addressed to them, Bite, bite, bite."[18]

Australia and New Guinea lack large terrestrial carnivores, and in these places it is spirits, monsters, deities, or medicine men who frighten the initiates in the first phase of the ritual. But these also usually turn out to be man-eating creatures, hungry for human flesh. In the Indo-Tibetan rite of *tchoed*, for example, a sword-wielding goddess attacks the novice, "decapitates him and cuts his body to pieces; then he sees demons and wild beasts fling themselves on the fragments of his flesh and devour them."[19]

In places where dangerous animals are common, they or their surrogates play a central role in rites of initiation. Among the Nootka, Kwakiutl, and Quillayute peoples of the Pacific Northwest, it is "wolves"—men in wolf masks—who menace the initiates, abduct them into the forest, subject them to ordeals (including ritual scarring, which may imitate the effect of claws), and finally introduce them to the secrets of the wolf cult.[20] Among the Luiseño and Diegueño Indians of California, the boys being initiated are threatened with death from attacks by pumas, bears, ravens, tarantulas, and rattlesnakes.[21] In some African ceremonies, the central ordeal of male initiation is circumcision, which is performed by men dressed in lion and leopard skins. As Eliade writes: "They incarnate the divinities in animal form who in mythical times first performed initiatory murder. . . . But soon afterward the novices are themselves dressed in leopard or lion skins."[22]

In at least some instances, females too undergo violent initiatory encounters with beasts. In the rites of initiation into the African female secret society of the Pangwe, one of the leaders symbolizes a leopard, who attacks, "kills," and "eats" the novices. Finally the other leader "kills" the leopard and frees the novices from the belly of the first one. ("This ritual motif is bound up with hunting and, consequently, properly belongs to men," Eliade comments huffily.)[23]

Northern European myths emphasize the need to become a beast in order to become a warrior.[24] The initiate "became a dreaded warrior in the measure in which he behaved like a beast of prey."[25] He wore a wolfskin and behaved wolfishly, or he donned a bear skin in order to run around "berserk," biting people as if he were a bear. As Eliade summarizes:

> To behave like a beast of prey—wolf, bear, leopard—betokens that one has ceased to be a man . . . that one has in some sort become a god. . . . On the level of elemental religious experience, the beast of prey represents a higher mode of existence.[26]

In some ancient settings, conflicts between humans and predator beasts were staged as almost purely secular events—a form of entertainment. Roman gladiators fought not only other men but wild animals, and—except when pitted against unarmed victims, such as the early Christians—the animals were usually the losers. The emperor Augustus boasted of the killing of 3,500 animals during his regime, while the later emperor Titus supplied 5,000 to be killed in a single day.[27] According to a contemporary observer, "should the arena become too sodden with blood, it is raked over and fresh sand is scattered."[28] One result of this form of entertainment was that the most skillful animal combatants, such as lions, were largely exterminated in many parts of the Roman world.[29]

DNA and Bedtime Stories

Obviously, the human fascination with the drama of predation has survived much longer than the kinds of situations which originally inspired it. If we were to guess, somewhat arbitrarily, that the human prey-to-predator transformation was more or less complete only as recently as 25,000 years ago—a time of big-game hunting and, at least in the European archeological record, self-confident artistic production—then we must still account for the continuing human preoccupation with this transformation for another thousand generations. Even if we take as our starting point the far more recent rise of settled agricultural communities, which would have seen wild carnivores as a threat primarily to livestock, many generations intervene between the terrifying actuality and its encryption in familiar myths. How are we to explain the compulsive repetition, as noted by Maurice Bloch, of rituals and entertainments recapitulating the terror of predation and the triumph of the prey-to-predator transformation?

The easiest, and perhaps the laziest, hypothesis would be that we simply *inherit* this preoccupation—that much of the emotional response to predation is somehow hardwired into the circuitry of the human brain. We know, from very recent research, that other species retain responses and abilities apparently derived from encounters with long extinct predators. California ground squirrels, for example, are still capable of "stereotypic anti-rattlesnake behavior"—throwing dirt and fluffing up their tails—although they have been rattlesnake-free for 70,000 to 300,000 years. North American pronghorn antelopes can achieve speeds of about sixty miles per hour, although any local predators capable of outrunning them have been extinct for at least 10,000 years.[30] Could it be that humans are similarly haunted by the "ghosts of predators past"? Darwin pondered the question when his two-year-old son developed a fear of large caged animals at the zoo: "Might we not suspect," the great amateur biologist wondered, "that the . . . fears of children, which are quite independent of experience, are the inherited effects of real dangers . . . during savage times?"[31]

I hesitate to even raise this possibility, knowing that genetic explanations of human behavior are controversial for reasons quite apart from their potential scientific validity. At the present time, scholarly opinion is sharply divided on the role of heredity—and even of biology generally—in framing human behavior and personality. The more biologically inclined seek genetic explanations for almost every aspect of human personality, and make a case for specific genes for such seemingly complex traits as intelligence, risk-taking, and homosexuality. The more culturally inclined, on the other hand, tend to see each new generation as a tabula rasa, waiting to be filled in with notions "socially constructed" by its particular culture. Loosely put, *nurture* has been the rallying cry of the scholarly left, because it seems to maximize human options, while *nature* has tended to be the province of the scholarly right, because it has so often been deployed to ratify the social status quo. What better way to argue that things cannot change than to claim that they are the way they are because this is what nature has decreed?

As sensible people have repeatedly pointed out, this is hardly an either/or proposition. Whatever we may inherit by way of behavioral propensities are just that—propensities, which may or may not be expressed as actual behavior, depending on whether the environment calls them forth. A gene for alcoholism, for example, will do little damage in a culture innocent of the technology of fermentation or in an individual—a nun, for example—committed to abstinence. We inherit only certain potential responses, and it is up to our environment to evoke or suppress them.

But those who value human freedom have little to fear from genetic types of explanations anyway. Even in an environment favorable to their expression, the existence of inherited predispositions does not condemn us to enact them. If it could be shown, for example, that humans have an innate taste for male domination, or for bloodshed, or any other form of nastiness, we could seek to order our social arrangements so as to counter this tendency. The biologist Richard Dawkins, who has been much maligned in certain circles for his alleged overemphasis on the role of genetics, assures us that

> it is perfectly possible to hold that genes exert a statistical influence on human behaviour while at the same time believing that this influence can be modified, overridden or reversed by other influences.[32]

To offer a medical analogy: Just because a disease is genetic, like Tay-Sachs or Huntington's disease, we are not absolved from the obligation to cure it. In fact, it is the *failure* to acknowledge an inborn tendency, like the failure to reckon with a subconscious urge, that inexorably condemns us to live it out.

Furthermore, the fact that some response or pattern of behavior may be entirely *culturally* determined hardly means that each generation is free to alter it at will. Just as biology is not a dictatorship—at least when it comes to human behavior—neither is culture a realm of freedom. If we decide that something like war, for example, is an artifact of culture rather than the imperative of, say, a genetically determined "killer instinct," then we are acknowledging that culture is at least as full of hideous snares as the human genome may be.

The question, though, is not whether a genetic hypothesis is politically congenial, but whether it is true. How would we determine the ways in which the experience of predation may have, through millennia of natural selection, left its mark on our neuronal circuitry? What responses, to what images or situations, would we look for? Could these responses be humanely sought in experiments with infants? Could we find variations in these responses from one individual to another, and evidence of familial transmission among individuals? If so, could we rule out nongenetic mechanisms for such transmission? (Chronic anxiety, for example, could easily be transmitted from one generation to the next by other than genetic means.)

The data we have now, however, are enough to establish that the human brain contains, at least, some innate residue of the experience of predation. The fight-or-flight response is the most obvious example, but more lasting states of mind have also been traced, at least speculatively, to the evolutionary experience of predation. In neurobiological terms, anxiety is a close relative of panic,[33] and akin to the constant vigilance displayed in the wild by animals which are at risk of predation. Just as panic is a response to an imminent attack, generalized anxiety may well be a response to an environment in which attacks can be expected to occur.[34] Psychiatrists Isaac Marks and Randolph Nesse argue that panic disorders, phobias, and chronic anxiety all represent evolutionary adaptations to a dangerous environment, replete with predators and nonliving threats such as lightning and heights.[35] Interestingly, some of the same drugs—fluoxetine, or Prozac, for example—which are used to treat anxiety in humans have the effect of rendering mice dangerously nonchalant in the face of a traditional predator, the rat.[36]

The likelihood that states of chronic anxiety reflect the evolutionary experience of predation does not, by itself, explain the continuing prominence of predation in rituals practiced long after wild animals had ceased to be a common threat. Why should the anxiety continue to focus on the specific fear of being devoured? The available studies suggest that humans and other primates are not born with a fear of their natural predators, or even of the most ancient antagonists known to mammals—snakes and other reptiles—so it is hard to imagine a purely genetic explanation for the prominence of animal predation in cultural rituals and myth. There is, however, experimental evidence that human subjects can much more readily *develop* phobic reactions to so-called archaic threats, such as snakes, than to modern ones, such as cars and guns.[37] Unfortunately, the only archaic threats that seem to have been studied are snakes and spiders, rather than, say, lions and leopards. These creatures, though, elicited phobic reactions more readily than did other environmental cues, and the reactions they elicited were more lasting and slower to fade.

What we seem to inherit, then, is not a fear of specific predators, but a capacity to acquire that fear—for example, by observing the reaction of adults to various potential threats—with efficiency and tenacity. Hence, perhaps, the surprising frequency of predator animals in dreams, as mentioned earlier.

So we can say, without, I hope, offending the social-constructionists, that human beings inherit certain patterned responses to threats and that the threat which originally selected for these responses was probably that of predation. It seems likely, then, that the primordial experience of predation at least *colors* our emotional responses to situations other than predation itself—the sight of violence or bloodshed occasioned by our fellow humans, for example. This does not mean that we "remember," in any Jungian or mystical sense, the alarm felt by our distant ancestors when a leopard pounced on one of their comrades and began to rip him apart; only that there was an evolutionary advantage to the ability to feel this alarm, and that this ability has been passed along to us. We who live now are the descendants of those early humans who reacted strongly and quickly to the sight of violence, whether by fleeing or banding together defensively; those who failed to react would have left far fewer descendants. Thus, even in our relatively predator-free modern environment, the sight of bloodshed can trigger the fight-or-flight response, or at least a mild version of it: Our hearts beat faster, we breathe more rapidly, our skin may blanch and viscera contract. We pay attention.

But if biology left us with a capacity for powerful physiological responses to predation, it is culture which continued to activate this capacity long after the actual threat had vanished or declined. One can easily imagine how highly specific predator-related fears might be transmitted, by entirely cultural mechanisms, from one generation to the next. Initiation rites such as those of the Orokaiva and so many other cultures, in which children are terrorized by mimed threats of predation, can be seen as sources as well as reflections of predator-related anxieties. In addition, children in many cultures are warned that monsters, bogeymen, or wild carnivores will "get them" if they fail to obey their elders. At least in the northern European tradition, children's stories routinely feature devouring beasts and cannibals. Babies even *look* like prey to grown-ups: We tell them, lovingly, they are so cute that we could "eat them up." An urban myth which, as a nervous first-time mother, I encountered in widely different ethnic settings has the parents returning home to find that the baby-sitter has roasted their infant in the oven "like a turkey."

The fact that most cultures entrust the care of small children almost entirely to women might also favor the cultural transmission of predator-related anxieties. To the extent that women have been barred from the use of effective weapons, even in predator-infested locales, and to the extent that male domination takes on the symbolic coloration of predator-prey interactions, women might be expected to be especially fearful of the possibility of predation and likely to communicate their fears to children. Among the Inuit for example,

> women were taught from an early age to fear the bear. Many stories told how women were attacked, mutilated, and devoured by hungry bears that unexpectedly appeared in camp when the men were away hunting, or which intercepted solitary and defenceless women along the paths.[38]

The anthropologist does not comment on whether this fear was rational in terms of the likelihood of an actual bear attack or whether it simply reflected women's subordinate status in a culture where, as he relates, the bear is an important symbol of masculine power and sexual potency. Either way, women's relative defenselessness would probably be communicated to children as a predator-related fear. And from a mother's point of view, it is far safer for the children to fear too much, or to fear unlikely threats, than to fear too little.

Could the practice of scaring children with threats and stories of predator beasts account for the continuing human anxiety about predation, even in locales, like New Guinea and Australia, where there have been no terrestrial predators to worry about for thousands of years? The literature I have found has little to say on this point.[39] We do know, however, that fears implanted in early childhood are far more intense and "irrational" than those acquired later on, and hence could conceivably be transmitted through many generations in a fairly specific form. Such fears, Dawkins suggests, are "*self-perpetuating*," because of their "deep psychological impact" on each generation in turn.[40] If a woman feared lions and communicated this fear urgently enough to her daughters, the fear might persist in her grandchildren long after all the lions had been driven away.*

But the cultural transmission of predator-related anxiety from parent to child would not work without another biological "given": the prolonged helplessness of human young. Children are susceptible to fears implanted by their elders not only because of their ignorance and inexperience, but because of their actual vulnerability. Even a friendly terrier looks very different from a height of two feet than from an adult's five feet or more. And adults are tempted to instill such fears not only because they may be insensitive, or irrationally driven to replicate the traumas they themselves experienced as children, but because fear helps children to survive.

However this anxiety is transmitted from generation to generation—through cultural practices, biological inheritance, or, more likely, a mixture of both—cultures address it in many ingenious ways. There are blood rites, as we have seen, that mime predation, and blood sports, such as the Roman games, that act it out. In our own time, the spectacle of anti-human violence is replayed endlessly by a commercial entertainment industry which thrives on people's willingness to pay for the frisson inspired by images of their fellow humans being stalked by killers, sucked dry by vampires, or devoured by multi-mouthed beasts from outer space. There is even a vogue of what could be called "predation porn": depictions (on the Discovery channel, for example) of actual predators in acts of actual predation. An hourlong show on the Fox channel, "When Animals Attack," offers tapes and reenactments of recent incidents in which humans were

*The widespread human disgust for feces may be similarly transmitted. Humans are not born with this sensitivity—in fact, babies have been known to play with or even eat their feces—but it seems to be communicated to them readily enough. The fact that a trait so essential for disease avoidance can be entrusted to nurture rather than nature suggests that cultural forms of transmission can be highly reliable indeed, and over many generations.

attacked by bears, mountain lions, or other wild predators. All such spectacles and rites offer a "safe" version of the trauma of predation, one in which we approach the nightmare—and survive. Though, fortunately for the purveyors of such entertainments, the very spectacles that safely scare us probably help perpetuate the anxiety that drives us to them.

In addition to such safe reenactments, humans have another way of addressing their predation-related anxieties, and this is through the thrill of defensive solidarity. The crowd that gathers to stone the scapegoat chosen as a sacrifice, or that cheers the gladiators in the arena, experiences a burst of fear-dissolving strength. It is through collective effort that our distant ancestors defeated the beast that was the ancestor of our fears, and we still seek the kind of élan our ancestors found in that archaic confrontation. Give us an "enemy" and a team or tribe with which to face that enemy down, and all anxiety dissolves, temporarily, in a surge of collective aggression against the threat.

The capacity for defensive solidarity is, I would suggest, another legacy of the prehistoric war against animal predators. This does not mean we are "programmed" to band together and fight, any more than we are programmed to turn tail and flee. But obviously we possess both the capacity for collective action and the capacity to be rewarded for such action with pleasurable feelings of potency. The most likely source of these capacities was the experience of predation, which may have given a selective advantage to those individuals who rallied to the group's defense and, in so doing, saved the lives of their children or grandchildren. We are wired, in a sense, for solidarity, although clearly this is a neurobiological possibility that many of us, in a highly individualistic and competitive culture, manage to repress or ignore for months or years at a time.

Thus there are two likely psychological legacies of predation which would appear to be relevant to the institution of war. One is the automatic response of alarm in the face of a threat—or of anxiety in a continuously threatening environment—which we inherit from a time when our ancestors faced the world largely as prey. "Designed" to ready us physiologically to fight or flee a dangerous animal, this response is what makes war, or any other spectacle of carnage, so gripping to us. In historical times, people stayed up late, night after night, to hear the epics and *chansons* of war retold. In our own time, the threat of war can keep us glued to the television set, as Americans were during the buildup to the Gulf War in 1990 and '91.

The other, apparently weaker, response readies us emotionally for collective action and possible self-sacrifice for the sake of the group. Many culturally contrived events, from sacred rituals to televised team sports, allow us to recapture the elemental potency of the group united against the beast; but few do so more reliably than war, if only because in war—as opposed to, say, soccer—the threat of death is real.

Neither of these responses is the "cause" of war. They are simply part of the repertory of emotional responses we *bring to* war, no matter what happens to have "caused" it. But it is these responses, I am suggesting, that color war with the profound feelings—dread, awe, and the willingness to sacrifice—that make it "sacred" to us. The alarm response infuses war and stories of war with urgency and excitement, while the solidarity response, if we may call it that, mobilizes our most altruistic and exalted impulses. And these are the very feelings which give us some purchase on our notions of a mystic entity—a nation, or an all-encompassing deity—of which we individuals are only the parts.

To put it another way: We will not find the roots of the human attraction to war by searching the human psyche for some innate flaw that condemns us to harass and kill our fellows. In war we act as if the only enemies we have are human ones, but I am proposing that the emotions we bring to war are derived, in an evolutionary sense, from a primal battle that the entire human species might easily have lost. We are not alone on this planet, and we were once decisively outnumbered by creatures far stronger and more vicious than ourselves.

Medicine offers a useful analogy. In an autoimmune disease, the body's immunological defenses turn against the body itself. Cellular responses which evolved to combat invading microorganisms start combatting, instead, the tissues of heart or muscle. We do not understand exactly why, in all cases, the immune mechanism becomes so confused that it can no longer distinguish "self" from "other." But we could not even begin to comprehend these perverse ills if we had no inkling of humankind's long struggle against an external enemy—the viruses, bacteria, and parasites that cause so many diseases—because it was out of that struggle that the immune system evolved in the first place.

Similarly with war: The weapons have changed beyond recognition over the millennia, but the basic emotional responses represent defensive mechanisms which evolved in combat with a deadly, nonhuman "other."

> The Great Goddess everywhere demands sacrifices, because the decisive moments in the life of the female—menstruation, deflowering, conception, and childbearing—are intimately bound up with a sacrifice of blood.[1]
>
> —Erich Neumann

6

When the Predator Had a Woman's Face

Some of the earliest deities worshipped by humans were female,[2] but they were hardly the nurturing "earth mothers" imagined by so many later scholars, both male and female. The archaic goddess unearthed from Mediterranean and Mesopotamian ruins or recalled in Mesoamerican mythology is far more likely to hold a snake in her clenched fist than a child in her arms. Only rarely a mother and seldom a wife,[3] she reigned in the company of her lion, serpent, or leopard familiars. She was a huntress, a consumer of sacrificial offerings, and, most strikingly, an anthropomorphized version of the predator beast.

In Anatolia the predator goddess is Cybele, the commander of lions. In Egypt she is Sekmet, portrayed as a lioness whose "mane smoked with fire, her back had the colour of blood, her countenance glowed like the sun, her eyes shone with fire."[4] In India she is Durga, also known as Kali, who rides on a tiger and is associated, in Brahmanic texts, with an actual forest region infested with lions and tigers.[5] In Sumer she is Inanna, one of whose names was Labbatu, or lioness, and who is often shown standing with her feet planted on the backs of two imperious lions.[6] In Canaan she is Astarte, who is depicted similarly, on a lion's back.[7] In Mycenae she is flanked by lions; at Çatal Hüyük she sits between leopards. In Crete she is shown playing with lions or standing on a lion-flanked mountain before a worshipping youth. In the Homeric epic, she is Artemis, of whom the poet says:

> Zeus has made you a lion
> among women, and given you leave to kill any at your pleasure.[8]

We do not know what, if anything, these fierce goddesses have to tell us about the status of actual women in the cultures that worshipped them. But our concern here is with human attitudes toward violence, and it is striking that images associated with bloodshed and predation could once have been "gendered" in a way opposite to what we are used to: that there was a time, apparently in many disparate cultures, when imagination gave the beast a human female form. In this chapter, we consider the "feminine" imagery of the predator beast, as suggested by archaic predator goddesses, and speculate on what it meant and why it eventually faded. The data are scant, and the literature is either frustratingly speculative or tainted with romantic notions of femininity from historical times. But it does seem likely that the ascension of "mankind" to the status of predator was followed, near to historical times, by the descent of woman in the opposite direction: from someone who could be imagined as possessing lethal force to a creature more commonly conceived as prey.

To the Jungian scholar Erich Neumann, who put together an exhaustive survey of the mythology of "the Great Mother" in the early 1960s, the beasts that accompany the archaic goddess are not her "guardians"; they are aspects of herself, if not her very essence:

> The terrible nature of the Feminine may take either of two forms: either the Goddess herself may become the terrifying animal or her terrible aspect may become the animal that accompanies and dominates her. Thus she may be a lioness . . . or else she may be enthroned on a lion or ride on a lion; in India she may be a tigress, or else she may ride on a tigress or a lioness; as Artemis she may be a she-bear or the bear may be her companion animal.[9]

Her predatory nature is revealed, in part, by her dominion over the hunt. At least since Sir James George Frazer's *The Golden Bough*, scholars have tended to associate goddess worship with agriculture, and the goddess with the "life-giving" earth. But in the religions of the Aztecs, the ancient Greeks, Egyptians, and Sumerians, a female deity presides over the hunt and wild animals in general (the Aztec goddess of the hunt later evolved into an agricultural deity).[10] Nor is her femaleness incidental to her divine identity as the "mistress of animals" and the hunt: Artemis, like her Sumerian counterpart, Ninhursaga, is goddess not only of the hunt but of that quintessentially female achievement, childbirth.

Artemis presents a particularly baffling persona to those who believe that the moral order was always divided into principles of male violence and female gentleness. Probably far older than the Olympian pantheon of gods and goddesses, and according to Burkert, even Paleolithic in provenance,[11] Artemis was originally a bear or, in more southerly localities, a lioness. Her association with the moon and wild animals links her to the archaic Cretan "Lady of the Wild Things." Dudley Young observes that:

> Her necklace of bull scrotums is usually registered by polite scholars as extra dugs, and the Olympians tried to make her somewhat decent and respectable by casting her as Apollo's sister (her moon to his sun), but with only moderate success; she remains formidably frightening.[12]

When a human hunter, Actaeon, happened to see her naked, bathing, Artemis transformed him into a stag and had him torn to bits by his own hounds. As Burkert tells us, she was exacting in her demands for "cruel and bloody sacrifices."[13]

It is not only as a huntress that early goddesses revealed a predatory, even bestial, side. They were carnivorous and often displayed a special appetite for the bodies and blood of living creatures. An Egyptian document from about 2000 B.C. tells of Sekmet's efforts to slaughter the entire human race—a project from which she was distracted by being given seven thousand jars of beer dyed the color of blood.[14] The Erinyes, or Furies, chthonic goddesses of ancient Greece, were also huntresses, but nonhuman ones, often described as serpents or bitches. Aeschylus has Apollo tell them, disgustedly, "You should make your dwelling the cave of some blood-gorged lion."[15] Tanit, also known as Astarte, who has been described by contemporary goddess enthusiasts as "a goddess of fertility . . . [and] of everything that governed the generation of life,"[16] was, along with her male consort, the recipient of child sacrifices at Carthage.[17]

But for bloodthirstiness, no known or remembered goddess surpasses Kali, who, according to historian D. D. Kosambi, descends from preagricultural religious traditions predating the Aryan invasion of the Indian subcontinent.[18] In the *Devi-Mahatyma* (ca. A.D. 550), Kali is depicted wearing a necklace of skulls and a tiger skin. "Hungry-looking, emaciated, wide-mouthed, with lolling tongue and sunken, reddish eyes," she was capable of devouring whole armies, elephants and chariots included.[19]

No doubt the dark side of the goddess was exaggerated by later adherents of patriarchal religions, just as the "wise woman" of pre-Christian European tradition was discredited by the late-medieval church as a witch. But there is reason to think that the "real" goddess, as known to her original worshippers, deserved at least some of her later reputation for bloodthirstiness. The symbol of the Cretan goddess (also associated with the supreme Sumerian goddess, Inanna) was the labrys, or sacred double ax, probably representing the ax with which sacrificial animals were killed.[20] In historical times, Kali has been particularly demanding of blood sacrifices, including the human blood offered by frenzied, self-mutilating cult worshippers.

Or consider the bloody Great Mother cult that spread to Greece from Anatolia beginning in about 700 B.C., probably basing itself on far more ancient Mycenaean and Cretan traditions of goddess worship. Burkert reports that the Great Mother's priests, or *galloi*, were forbidden to eat anything but meat, as befits admirers of a carnivorous deity, and that

> the main spectacle of the Meter cult, as also of some related Anatolian cults, was the "day of blood," when the *galloi* would flagellate themselves in public and cut their arms with knives and axes, till they streamed with blood, without showing any sign of pain.[21]

If there has been consistent misrepresentation of the archaic goddess, it has been in the direction of downplaying her more savage predilections. By classical times, and certainly in our own time, the associations between masculinity and violence, femininity and nonviolence, had hardened into dogma. The primordial goddess—huntress of beasts and consumer of blood—had to be prettified as a seductress, like Aphrodite, or a motherly figure with a passion for gardening, like Demeter or Ceres. In the Tantric philosophical tradition, Kali underwent a cosmetic makeover into a benign, if still somewhat bloody-minded, lady:

> Her face is sometimes described as beautiful and smiling, her breasts high and youthful, her gauntness gone. Two of her hands still hold the severed head and bloody cleaver but her other two form the gestures of blessing, removing fear and conferring boons.[22]

Ironically, contemporary feminist scholars have been particularly energetic in their efforts to rehabilitate the archaic goddess as a thoroughly gentle and "feminine" figure. The archeologist Marija Gimbutas consistently slighted the goddess's violent side, even conjecturing wistfully that the Minoan and Sumerian goddess's double ax symbolized a butterfly![23] Similarly, in her provocative work on the rise of male dominance, Riane Eisler asserts that in archaic, goddess-centered cultures, "the generative, nurturing, and creative powers of nature—not the powers to destroy—were . . . given highest value."[24] How, then, to explain the goddess's preference for the company of leopards and bulls? These, Eisler says, "represented our forebears' attempt to deal with the darker aspects of reality" and to show, with admirable evenhandedness, that "the destructive processes of nature were also recognized and respected."[25]

Gender biases are revealed, too, in the scholarly bafflement over the goddess's enthusiasm for the hunt and her apparently preagricultural origins. The earliest alleged representations of a female deity are the Paleolithic "Venus" figurines found on the Eurasian land mass from western Europe to Siberia and dating back to almost 30,000 years ago, or roughly 20,000 years before the coming of agriculture.* But compared to agriculture, hunting is a violent and hence, according to modern notions of gender, presumably masculine enterprise. Thus to Gimbutas, the great antiquity of the goddess or her probable forebears seemed to defy logic:

> It would seem logical to look for the origin of the Earth Fertility Goddess at the dawn of agriculture. . . . However, the pregnant-type figurine first appears not in the Early

*Another example of gender bias is the widespread assumption, repeated by Gimbutas, that the Paleolithic Venuses, which presumably prefigure the archaic goddess, were fertility figures. It's true that many of the Venus figurines have exaggerated breasts, bellies, and buttocks, but they are not all visibly pregnant, and some of those that appear to be so may simply be fat. Furthermore, Paleolithic images of males—including cave drawings of stick figures sporting exaggerated erections—are never interpreted as fertility figures. Nor is there any reason to believe that Paleolithic hunter-gatherers were particularly anxious about fertility. Among hunter-gatherers, especially nomadic ones, high fertility can be a distinct disadvantage, and extended lactation is employed to space births.

> Neolithic, but earlier still—in the Paleolithic. The symbol of the fruitful womb is as old as figurine art.[26]

Even as careful a historian as Gerda Lerner states erroneously that "it is from the Neolithic that we derive surviving evidence of cave paintings and sculptures suggesting the pervasive veneration of the Mother-Goddess"[27] when it is, in fact, from the Paleolithic. In the "logic" of our own time, violence is an exclusively male attribute, so that the notion of a predator goddess can only be a cultural oxymoron.

Predation and the Semiotics of Menstruation

One possible explanation for the seeming anomaly of a predator goddess is that she represents a vestige of what was once an actual female economic role. Among surviving hunting-gathering cultures, as well as those encountered by Europeans in the past few centuries, hunting is an almost exclusively male enterprise. But contemporary hunter-gatherers inhabit a world sadly depleted of the large ungulates on which our prehistoric ancestors dined.[28] Hunting today is largely a matter of searching, tracking, and waiting and is generally undertaken by small groups of men at considerable distances from their homes. In the context of far denser animal populations, when vast herds darkened the plains and threatened human bands with being trampled underfoot, "hunting" may more nearly have resembled *herding*[29] and very likely involved all the members of a band. Possibly Paleolithic women participated in "drives" of big-game animals, just as Amerindian women did before the horse transformed bison hunting into a strictly male enterprise.[30] Anthropologist Marvin Harris writes that

> since the paleolithic hunter-gatherers appear to have hunted big-game herd animals mainly by driving them into pitfalls, over cliffs, and into bogs, women would be important at least as drivers and beaters and would render valuable service as butchers and bearers once the wounded

> animals had been dispatched. Nor is there any reason to suppose that women did not carry spears and participate in the actual killing of the trapped animals.[31]

But it is also possible that the link between the predator beast and the human female reflects something even more basic, in a biological sense, than the killing of animals for food. The connection may lie in a phenomenon which is not unique to humans but is uniquely dramatic in its human form: Human females bleed, regularly and in amounts that are profligate compared with other primate species. They bleed at the reproductive turning points of their lives—menarche, defloration, childbirth—and at more or less regular intervals in between. To a person of our own era, female vaginal bleeding is an event of almost zero public import. We see it as a sickness, at best an inconvenience, and usually, thanks to sanitary napkins and tampons, we do not see it at all.

But there are reasons, admittedly of a purely *a priori* variety, to think that menstruation may have figured far more prominently in the lives of Paleolithic people than it does in our own. Humans menstruate more copiously than any other mammals, and before the invention of paper and cloth, it would have been difficult to conceal the flow, especially among groups whose nomadic lifestyle prevented menstruating women from secluding themselves and squatting for days over the absorbent ground. Heightening the potential drama of menstruation is the tendency for human females spontaneously to synchronize their periods. This tendency is known to occur among women living together today, such as female students in dormitories, and has been well documented in the medical literature.[32] Whether it occurs among existing hunter-gatherers has apparently not been investigated, though the British anthropologist Chris Knight points out that the !Kung people of the Kalahari desert "believe . . . that if a woman sees traces of menstrual blood on another woman's leg or even is told that another woman has started her period, she will begin menstruating as well."[33]

Then there is the fact that the periodicity of human menstruation so closely matches the cycle of the moon. For people whose powers of illumination were limited to campfires, the lunar cycle would have been of commanding importance. The sun comes and goes on a reliable twenty-four-hour schedule. The moon, however, vanishes completely for three nights out of the month, nights that would have been terrifyingly, impenetrably dark. For another three or four nights of the month, the full or gibbous moon lights up the nighttime world, making it safer, more friendly to humans, and perhaps allowing daytime activities like hunting and gathering to continue after-hours. Given the likely centrality of the moon in the lives of prehistoric people, it is not surprising that the archaic goddess, from Mesoamerica to the Mediterranean, was a goddess of the moon.

Add to this the fact that, as far as we know, prehistoric people were fairly obsessed with the business of tracking and predicting astronomical events. The linear markings found etched by Paleolithic humans on so many animal tusks and bones have been interpreted as records of the lunar cycle.[34] They might equally well be records of women's menstrual cycles. It is hard to distinguish the astronomical from the menstrual in the human case: Of all the primates, humans have a menstrual cycle that comes closest to matching the 29.5-day cycle of the moon.[35]

Even today this coincidence between the menstrual and the astral goes begging for a theory to explain it. We know enough now to describe the hormonal cycle that underlies menstrual bleeding; we can plot the orbit of the moon. But we have no explanation for the connection between the two cycles. To people who lacked even the concept of a "scientific explanation," it may have seemed that women's cycles control the moon, or else that the divine presence that is the moon expresses itself through the bodies of human females. How prehistoric people construed this remarkable conjuncture we do not and probably cannot know. It does seem likely, though, that the synchronization of menstruation among women, and its further synchronization with the lunar cycle, could have sufficed to make menstruation an event of some public significance, if not an occasion for ritual observance.

But menstruation is not just any cyclical occurrence. It involves the shedding of blood, which is itself a dire event, with or without group synchrony and astral coincidences, and at least intuitively associated with acts of deliberate bloodshed. Aristotle observed in the *Historia Animalium* that menstrual blood runs "like that of an animal that has just been stabbed" in sacrifice,[36] and Hippocratic medical texts utilized the same analogy.[37] Or the blood may be interpreted as symbolizing violence committed by the woman herself, as British anthropologist Camilla Power reports of contemporary African hunter-gatherer societies:

> Of the !Kung girl [upon her first menstruation], people say, "She has shot an eland." . . . A similar metaphor is used by the Hadza for menarche: "she has shot her first zebra!" . . . Among the !Xo, this is ritually enacted. On the final day of seclusion, a gemsbok brow-skin shield is hung at the back of the menstrual hut, and the maiden is helped by the mistress of ceremonies . . . to shoot arrows against it.[38]

Some cultures make a conscious and explicit connection between women's natural vaginal bleeding—both menstrual and postpartum—and acts of ritual bloodletting usually reserved for males. In Papua New Guinea, the self-induced ritual nosebleeds mentioned earlier are seen as parallel to menstruation; the Australian Aborigines who subincise their penises reopen the wounds regularly in order, they say, to simulate menstruation. In ancient Hawaii blood sacrifice was understood to be a "man's childbearing," just as childbearing was a "woman's sacrifice,"[39] and the Aztecs similarly equated men's death in war to women's death in childbirth.[40] War as a kind of ritual bloodletting is linked to menstruation in the myths of the Ndembu people of Africa, and Ndembu male initiates "are implicitly treated like brides at their first menstruation."[41] In the Plains Indian mythology studied by Claude Lévi-Strauss, "there is a link between the menstruating woman, i.e., stained with blood below, and the scalped man, i.e., stained with blood above."[42] "This equivalence is no mere postulation," he reports; "it is clearly stated in the myths themselves . . . [which] bring together in the same story the origin of scalping and that of menstruation or . . . make menstruation responsible for the first trophy head."[43]

But the spectacle of menstruation also hints, disquietingly, at the danger of predation by creatures other than human.* The vagina, in myth sometimes a *vagina dentata*, represents a mouth as well as a "wound," and the mouth of the predator animal is often its most powerful weapon. Long before the male phallus gained its symbolic status as a weapon, the blood-smeared mouth may have been the organ most associated with violence and potency. Traditional and folk imagery sometimes connects blood to the human female's literal mouth: Kali is represented with blood flowing from her mouth (sometimes in highly stylized form, as a red triangle with its apex just under her lower lip); Maori and some Amerindian women tattooed themselves with parallel lines proceeding down along the chin from the mouth, suggesting the flow of blood, and sometimes called "dribble lines";[44] moderns wear lipstick.

The mythologies of some traditional cultures hint at a mysterious

---

*An interesting question is whether menstruation renders women more vulnerable to predator attacks. Bears seem to be attracted to menstrual blood, though it is not clear whether they are more attracted to it than to ordinary blood. But surely, as any contemporary hiker knows, it would be unwise to leave a trail of blood (menstrual or otherwise) behind one in the wilderness, if only because it would seem to signal the presence of someone who is injured and hence vulnerable to attack. Margie Profet, the biologist who has proposed that the evolutionary function of menstruation was to flush out pathogens from the vagina, had not thought about this biological downside of menstruation when I interviewed her by phone in 1995. However, Judy Grahn speculates that the most widespread menstrual ritual observed by ethnographers—the isolation of menstruating women in a special hut—arose as a means of protecting menstruating women and other members of the band from predators which might be drawn by the smell of menstrual blood (though it would take a particularly sturdy hut to deter a determined predator).

affinity between menstruating women and the predatory beasts. In the origin myth of the people of northeast Arnhem Land in Australia, two sisters are swallowed by a monstrous snake which has been aroused by their vaginal blood. One of the sisters gives birth, and her blood flows into the sacred pool inhabited by the Rainbow Serpent, who "emerges in anger":

> "Go away! Go away!" the sisters cried as they saw the immense Snake in the sky. Seized with fear, they sang "menstrual blood"—the most potent and taboo of the songs known to them—and danced to make the Snake go away. But dancing only brought on the second sister's menstrual flow, attracting the Serpent still more.[45]

The sisters flee into the menstrual hut they have built, but the Serpent follows and swallows them alive. From within the Serpent, the sisters proceed to assign names to all the objects on earth, using as their own the "thunder-like 'voice' of the Snake itself," which is male in some versions of the myth, female in others.

Peculiar as this story may sound, it is hardly unique. According to Lévi-Strauss, versions of this myth "appear to belong to all peoples, irrespective of time and race."[46] Among tribal people of southern Venezuela, the Rainbow Serpent is the water-dwelling anaconda, or *mawadi*, which is driven "crazy with desire" by the smell of menstrual blood. The anaconda rise up from the river "in droves," kill all the men, capture the women, and take them down into the snakes' watery home.[47] In other mythologies, the devouring beast associated with menstruation is a wild dog, a jaguar, or a female leopard.[48]

It is tempting to discern, in myths connecting the goddess to the hunt and the menstruating woman to the hunting animal, a time when real women played a central role in the realms of both economies and religion: in the economy, as participants in the hunt; in religion, as beings whose bodies had the seemingly divine gift of bleeding without dying, and doing so regularly, in tune with the most salient cycle of the night skies. Writer Judy Grahn notes the linguistic links between menstruation and words for ritual in the Indo-European languages and suggests that menstruation may have been the forerunner and basis for *all* ritual.[49] Similarly, anthropologist Chris Knight makes an elaborate and, on the face of it, quite plausible argument for menstrual synchrony as a basis of female solidarity and power in Paleolithic times.[50]

But on the intriguing political issue of Paleolithic gender relations, the archeological record is frustratingly noncommittal. All we know for sure is that by the beginning of the historical era, the capacity for violence and bloodletting would be almost universally conceived as a male trait. Hunting would be an exclusively male activity (though still an occasional sport for aristocratic women); the fierce goddesses of an older time would be tamed enough to take their place within pantheons dominated by male gods; menstruation would cease to be a public event. In the new, male-centered scheme of things, it is the boys who enter adulthood through dramatic blood rites of initiation while girls at menarche are shut up in menstrual huts, stitched into hammocks, or simply instructed to hide all evidence of their flow, as if it were a kind of excrement.

The Defeat of the Goddess

In the Sumerian epic of Gilgamesh, which dates from around 2000 B.C., the killing of the predator beast is linked directly to the hero's defiance of the goddess. After Gilgamesh and his companion Enkidu slay the forest monster Humbaba, the goddess Inanna/Ishtar attempts to seduce Gilgamesh: "Come to me Gilgamesh, and be my bridegroom; grant me seed of your body."[51] He rejects her rudely, pointing out that her past lovers, which included a lion and a stallion, have all met terrible ends. Enraged, Inanna sets the Bull of Heaven loose on the two heroes. They make short work of the bull, but the goddess herself is still powerful enough to strike Enkidu with a fatal illness. "My friend," he tells Gilgamesh, "the Great Goddess cursed me and I must die in shame."[52]

Could there have been some real event or trend that brought an end to the predator goddess's reign and ushered in the era of the male warrior-hero? If so, it must have occurred long before the Neolithic revolution brought forth settled agricultural communities, because whatever happened, happened almost worldwide, and it happened also among peoples who continued to make their living exclusively as hunter-gatherers—such as, for example, the indigenous Australians who even now recall in myth the male "theft" of women's magic.[53]

One possible candidate for this crucial "event" is a change in hunting strategies which seems to have occurred sometime near the end of the Paleolithic or the beginning of the Mesolithic period which followed it. This was a time when the supply of large game animals was dwindling in many parts of the world, leaving people scrambling to exploit less efficient food sources, such as birds, fish, and mollusks. Hunting, too, had to change. As large migratory animals became scarce or even extinct, the strategy of the "drive" or the surround, in which a band of humans drove a herd of animals over a cliff or into a cul-de-sac, obviously became less productive. Instead, human hunters turned to tracking individual animals and killing them one by one.[54] With continuing declines in big-game populations in most parts of the globe, hunting everywhere became a matter of quiet and patient *stalking*, better suited to small groups of men than to noisy assemblages that included women and children.[55]

This change in hunting strategy was probably accompanied by the beginnings of what military historian Arthur Ferrill has called the first "arms revolution." Between 12,000 and 8,000 years ago, he writes, humans enriched their armamentarium of spears and clubs with new inventions like the bow and arrow, the dagger, and the sling.[56] The new, more powerful projectile weapons helped make hunting-by-stalking possible: For one thing, it was easier now for small groups of humans to wander far from their home base without fear of becoming prey themselves. The bow and arrow seems particularly well suited to a stalking strategy, while the spear and club may have been most useful in "drive" styles of hunting, when a line of people moved in on the cornered animals for the kill.

Anthropologist Lila Leibowitz argued that this change in hunting strategy may have been responsible for a new sexual division of labor and, with it, a general demotion of the female sex.[57] Instead of the communal hunt undertaken by the whole band, there was now the male hunters' sub-band, with women relegated to the less glamorous job of processing the meat (as well as the skin, bones, and other useful animal products) brought back by men. If so, this might help explain the general decline in depictions of human females in the art of the Upper (or more recent) Paleolithic.[58] On the eve of the Neolithic, the human male was probably a good, goddess-fearing soul. But he held the spear, the sling, and the bow, all firmly in his hand.

In surviving hunting-gathering cultures, not only are women expected to remain behind while men hunt; they are often barred from contact with men's weapons or other "magic" items.[59] Possibly, with the historic change to a male-only hunting strategy, violence in general began to be seen as the exclusive prerogative of males. Even women's involuntary bloodshed must, in most traditional societies, be thoroughly kept from sight. In the patriarchal era, as anthropologist Nancy Jay has written, the blood shed by men in sacrifice or war is powerful and redeeming, while the blood shed by women becomes a dangerous pollutant.[60]

In Greek mythology, a special horror attaches to the image of the violent woman—or, worse, the violent, blood-soaked group of women. In Euripides' play *The Bacchae*, which was based on a far older myth, the god Dionysus has led the women of Thebes, including the king's mother and sisters, off to join his maenads, or *bacchae*, who roam in the wild, dancing, singing, and tearing living animals apart. A herdsman describes these wild women in terms that might have suited the archaic goddess in her role as Mistress of the Animals. Their hair flows loose, their garments are made of fawnskin,

> and they girdled the dappled fur with snakes which licked their cheeks. And some would have in their arms a young gazelle, or wild wolf-cubs, and give them their own white milk.[61]

Angered by some herdsmen, though, the maenads begin to act, quite literally, like beasts. Here the playwright could be describing the anarchy of the old-style communal hunt, where women as well as men rush in among the cornered animals for the kill:

> tearing our cows limb from limb, and you could see perhaps some ribs or a left hoof being tossed high and low; and pieces of bloody flesh hung dripping on the pine-branches.[62]

When King Pentheus goes after the maenads, his own mother, Agauë—"foaming at the mouth, her eyes . . . rolling wildly"—leads the attack on him:

> she set her foot against his ribs, and she tore his arm off by the shoulder. . . . There was a single continuous yell—Pentheus shrieking as long as life was left in him, the women howling in triumph. One of them was carrying an arm, another had a foot with the shoe still on it; the ribs were stripped—clawed clean. Every hand was thick red with blood; and they were tossing and catching, to and fro, like a ball, the flesh of Pentheus.[63]

Still under the spell of the god, and believing that she has killed a lion, Agauë carries what is left of her son back to her father, stating proudly: "I have left weaving at the loom for greater things—for hunting wild beasts with my bare hands."[64]

The moral, of course, is, Stick to your weaving. For women, wilderness is an incitement to wildness; "darkness is treacherous and impure";[65] and the violence of the hunt quickly degenerates into a manic savagery that swallows up humans and animals alike. In Aeschylus's play *The Furies*, another murderous band of females, "blood-dirty" from their predations,[66] must be persuaded to accept a new and gentler role, as household guardians. The violent, bestial female resurfaces briefly centuries later in Virgil's *Aeneid*, where, as the Fury Alecto, she attempts to goad Turnus into waging war against Aeneas. At first he brushes her off ("Let men run war and peace"), but "even as he spoke" a sudden trembling seized him:

> his eyes stared: the Fury hisses with so many serpents, so monstrous is the face she shows. She turned her flaming eyes and thrust him, faltering, back . . . she lifted up two vipers from her hair, her lash was loud, with maddened lips she added this: "Then look at me . . . I come here from the home of the dread Sisters, and in my hand I carry death and wars."[67]

But such monstrous females had no place in the patriarchal order, which attempted to efface every vestige of the archaic association between the human female and the predator beast. Henceforth, for the most part, males alone would be privileged to reenact the transformation from prey to predator. Deprived, in most cases, of a blood rite of initiation, females would have no ritual escape from the child's status as prey. This aspect of the female condition is brought out forcefully in the kind of marriage rites described by early anthropologists as "marriage by capture," in which the groom and his friends abduct the bride from her home while the bride and her family resist (or pretend to resist) the abduction. Such practices are so widespread that "there appear to be no geographical or religious boundaries" to them.[68] Anthropologist Maurice Bloch tells us, for example, that in ancient Rome, "the marriage ritual re-enacted and celebrated the story of the rape of the Sabine women," while in Shinto Japan "marriage is often seen as part of a triumphal consumption of the female by the male."[69]

If females have any ritual transformation to undergo, it is in the opposite direction, from predator to prey. Ancient Greek art features the young, unmarried woman as a "wild animal"—both powerful and virginal, like Artemis, the predator goddess, herself. For example, a fifth-century B.C. terra-cotta relief from Melos shows the mortal Peleus grabbing the goddess Thetis (who is at least a foot taller than him in this depiction) around the waist, while a lion, "represent[ing] one form she assumed in an effort to thwart her suitor," menaces him from her other side. According to art historian Angela M. H. Schuster, the *parthenos*, or unmarried woman, "had to be tamed like a wild animal," and this was to be accomplished through marriage and motherhood. "The taming process was echoed in courtship rituals, which appear in many artistic representations as pursuit scenes with the suitor as hunter, the parthenos as prey."[70] Appropriately, according to British classicist Helen King, the wedding was designed in part to "evoke the preparation of an animal for sacrifice; for example, cutting [the bride's] hair, washing, giving a sign of consent and wearing a garland."[71] The married woman, or *gyne*, King tells us, was at "the opposite pole to the parthenos; she *should* bleed, in menstruation, defloration and childbirth, as part of her role in reproducing society . . . but she should not shed blood. Only a man may shed blood in war and sacrifice"[72] (emphasis added).

By assigning the triumphant-predator status to males alone, humans have helped themselves to "forget" that nightmarish prehistory in which they were all, male and female, prey to larger, stronger animals. Insofar as males have been the human "norm" and females the deviation, weakness and vulnerability could be seen as something aberrant and incidental to the story of humankind. Gender, in other words, is an idea that conveniently obliterates our common past as prey, and states that the predator status is innate and "natural"—at least to men.

Part II
WAR

> It makes no difference what men think of war. . . . War endures. As well ask men what they think of stone. War was always here. Before man was, war waited for him. The ultimate trade awaiting the ultimate practitioner.[1]
>
> —Cormac McCarthy

7

"A Rough Male Sport"

The first evidence of what looks, to modern eyes, like war comes from the Mesolithic, roughly 12,000 years ago.[2] A rock drawing from the Spanish Levant shows bands of stick figures wielding bows and arrows against one another;[3] massed skeletons of the same vintage have been unearthed in southern Egypt and in East Asia, with piercings by spear and arrow points suggestive of deliberate massacres.[4] What these people fought over, no one knows. Agriculture, with its movable treasures of grain and animal herds, was still presumably only a gleam in some hungry woman's eye. Territorial hunting rights are a possibility, or women or injured pride, or even the need, as perceived by the pious, to capture victims for human sacrifice.

On two points there is little controversy, though, if only because they seem so obvious. One is that war has roots in, and in some sense grows out of, prior conflicts with animals. The earliest weapons of war were almost certainly developed for use against animal life,[5] as were the tactics of the wedge and frontal attack. Well into the modern era, in fact, light regiments, which advanced in a line much as Paleolithic hunters may have done in their drives against animals, were called "hunters"—*jaegers, chasseurs*—and were dressed in green.[6]

The second point may be uncontroversial in part because it is seldom, if ever, made; and that is that the rise of war corresponds, roughly, with a global decline in the number of large animals, both "game" and predators, for humans to fight against. Many scholars have attempted to explain war as a function of rising human population density and the attendant competition for resources. But the key factor may be *animal* populations, and these were declining in the Mesolithic on what was, in many settings, a catastrophic scale.

Fast-forward through the last few millennia of prehistory, with some camera capable of taking in whole plains and forests and meadows, and the unmistakable trend will be toward a planet seriously depleted of all large-scale hooved and furry life. Ten or twelve thousand years ago, at the end of the Ice Age, the Northern Hemisphere was still thickly populated by large land mammals: bison, wild cattle, giant ground sloths, mammoths, peccaries, wild goats and camels, rhinoceroses, and so forth. Within a few thousand years, whole species—in fact, whole classes of "megafauna"—were gone forever, extinct. Paleontologists still debate the exact mix of factors that led to these mass extinctions—climatic changes, the retreat of the glaciers, the spread of forests on formerly grassy plains—but one factor which few any longer deny was the advent of the human hunter.

In many parts of the world, the extinction of megafauna coincides neatly with the arrival of human hunting-gathering bands.[7] The German paleontologist W. Schüle writes that

> in Africa, the beginning of the impoverishment [of megafauna] approximately coincides with the evolutions [sic] of the early hominids, in the rest of the world with the first appearance of *Homo*.[8]

The Eurasian continent is a slightly messier case; there the extinctions took place over a long period of time and may have been driven in part by the reforestation which followed glacial retreat and destroyed open grazing lands. But in Australia, New Guinea, and Oceania, the extinctions began at the time migrating humans arrived. In North America, the arrival of big-game hunters from Asia, the "Clovis" people (named for an archeological site near Clovis, New Mexico), about 11,500 years ago was followed by the disappearance of thirty-five entire classes of mammals.[9] As in other venues, the small animals were spared; but most of the large herbivores that humans would have favored as game were decimated within perhaps 1,000 years or less, along with the carnivores that fed on them. Among their bones, archeologists have found the distinctive fluted spear points of the Clovis hunters.

To the extent that humans were responsible for the animal holocaust of the late Ice Age, they may not have been motivated entirely by hunger. In North America, the human population on the eve of the extinctions was probably well under one million, while the large mammals numbered from 50 to 100 million.[10] The biomass slaughtered—even assuming that half of a carcass by weight is waste—appears to have been well beyond the capacity of human appetite.[11] One speculation is that humans caused much of this damage unwittingly, by spreading a microbial disease that specialized in killing large mammals other than humans.[12] But another possibility is that humans simply killed far more than they needed to, as suggested by Paleolithic mass kill sites in which only the top layer of animal carcasses appears to have been utilized as food.[13] This is what the paleontologists call "overkill," and it must have been, to those humans who engaged in it, a dramatic proof of human predatory prowess.

In human cultures, hunting is seldom a matter of mere food acquisition anyway. It is usually a highly ritualized activity, tied into local systems of prestige and religious authority. Prehistoric hunters, like contemporary hunter-gatherers, probably observed prescribed rites and taboos before and after the hunt and during the distribution of meat and the disposal of bones. In many cases, the hunt itself may have been as much a ritual as a food-gathering errand. Humans have hunted, in part, for the same reasons they have sacrificed living creatures or terrified their children with nightmarish rites of initiation: as a way of reenacting the primal transformation from prey to predator.

In defense of humankind, we should note that no other animal, at least none that I have been able to discover, has experienced the kind of evolutionary role reversal achieved by our species within just a few hundred thousand years. A million years ago, lions (or something very like them) were lions and antelopes were antelopes, and one the prey of the other, pretty much as they are now. Only the line of *Homo* made a decisive advance up the food chain, learning to band together in highly organized ways, to augment their strength with fire and sharpened stones, and to enrich their strategies with verbal memories of past exploits. Our victory over the other animals was a brilliant achievement, but clearly it took its toll. The kindest thing one can conclude about the long record of human carnage is that it may have been only through the compulsive repetition of acts and spectacles of violence—the hunt, the sacrifice, the initiatory ordeal, and eventually the war—that our ancestors were able to reassure themselves that they were, in fact, no longer prey.

At some point, inevitably, there were no longer enough wild animals to satisfy either the hunger or the anxiety of the human race. Even at very low human population densities, the productivity of hunting is eventually limited by the supply of animals to hunt. Most human cultures reached this point about 10,000 years ago, immediately following the extinctions of the late Ice Age. There was nothing to do then but turn to agriculture—and to war.

The Neolithic "revolution," which is usually depicted as an epochal advance and triumph of human ingenuity, may be more accurately described as a desperate adaptation to ever shrinking stocks of game.[14] Hunting continued to be a favorite sport and a supplementary food source, but for the most part humans switched from preying on wild animals to preying, usually with far greater restraint, on ones that they "owned." The only economically significant version of "hunting" which survived into the Neolithic was raiding, in which bands of men, and eventually armies, attempted to steal one another's herds. In his study of Siberian reindeer economies, anthropologist Tim Ingold writes:

> as the live animal resource passes into the domain of human property relations, competitive strength is redirected from the interaction between men and animals to the interaction *between men* in respect of animals. The pastoralist becomes a predator on his own kind.[15]

Under these new conditions, the predator beast, which had seemed to rule the world at one time and to personify, as deity, the violence of nature, becomes little more than a pest. The human obligation to the animals they owned and ate was to protect them from wild predators, like wolves and lions, whose status in the human scheme of things declined accordingly. Wolves running wild, hunting other wild things, held a mystic power for human hunting peoples.[16] But the wolf that robs the chicken coop or drags off the newborn lambs comes to be seen by humans as a hateful competitor, if not a parasite, and subject to exterminatory measures. At an earlier stage of human evolution, the roles had been reversed: Humans were the scavengers, animal predators the "providers" of meat. Nature as a whole loses some of its mystic power, Ingold speculates, when "the power of disposal over a wild animal resource . . . passes from the spirits to men."[17]

Historians of a materialist bent have tended to locate the beginnings of war—or what they dignify as "real" war, that is, as opposed to mere raiding—near the time of the rise of agriculture, when human societies began to possess things, like land and stores of grain, that were worth risking death to capture. Some of the earliest Neolithic settlements unearthed, like that at Jericho, were surrounded with thick walls clearly meant to discourage human intruders.[18] According to the scenario laid out by Robert L. O'Connell, "real," systematic war arises as nomadic herding peoples discover that raiding settled, agricultural communities can be a more efficient way to make a living than patiently nurturing one's own food supplies. The settled communities, in turn, develop armed defenses, and these are, soon enough, employed offensively against neighboring settlements.[19]

But there are at least two problems with this account. One is that it discounts the evidence for war in the Mesolithic period, that is, before the emergence of agricultural civilizations. In *War Before Civilization*, anthropologist Lawrence Keeley makes a convincing argument that the scholarly tendency to see "primitive" war as somehow less "real" than the "civilized" kind is little more than a condescending bias. In historical times, "primitives" have fought as seriously and effectively as have the highly organized armies of modern nation-states—the Sioux and Cheyenne victory over Custer at Little Bighorn offering one familiar example. Furthermore, the archeological record strongly suggests that Mesolithic wars between hunter-gatherers were frequent and deadly: More than half the fifty-nine men, women, and children buried about 12,000 years ago at Gebel Sahaba in southern Egypt appear to have died violently, most from stone projectile points, and many show fractures indicative of injuries inflicted in earlier encounters.[20]

The other problem with the standard account is its assumption that people will not fight (or perhaps I should say "really" fight) unless there are vital material resources—such as the potential loot generated by agricultural communities—at stake. This view slights the widespread conflicts over "goods" which serve little function except as badges of prestige and warrior prowess: scalps and skulls; severed heads,[21] hands, penises, and other portable body parts; captives for rituals of human sacrifice. Just as prehistoric humans probably killed animals for reasons other than hunger, they no doubt killed one another for purposes other than gain—such as the accumulation of a particularly imposing collection of severed heads. As Keeley points out, there is evidence for prehistoric head-hunting in numerous sites,[22] suggesting that early wars may have been motivated in some cases by factors other than hunger.

So we may be in better conformity with the facts to say that war arises in the Mesolithic epoch—a time of diminishing game and predator populations—and that it arises, at least in part, as a new source of prestige for men who might otherwise have been employed as hunters and as defenders against wild animals. Which is to say that war served not only to enrich the victorious community as a whole, but to enhance the status of a specific group within it: the men who fought or led the fighting.

Recall that the Mesolithic—the epoch when war, or at least warlike raiding, apparently begins—was the time when, generally speaking, communal hunting had given way to the strategy of stalking individual animals, most likely undertaken by small groups of male hunters. In the scenario first suggested (as far as I can tell) by historian Lewis Mumford, there is a direct continuity of personnel between the male hunting sub-band and the first warrior bands. The earliest warriors we know through recorded literature, the Sumerian hero Gilgamesh and his companion Enkidu, were not only warriors but hunters and battlers of killer beasts.[23] So, as mentioned earlier, were the Greek chieftains who fought at Troy. In their homelands, in times of peace, they had battled lions and wild boars. According to the French classicist Pierre Vidal-Naquet, "the 'culture heroes' of the Greek legends are all hunters and destroyers of wild beasts."[24]

With the decline of wild predator and game populations, there would have been little to occupy the males who had specialized in hunting and anti-predator defense, and no well-trodden route to the status of "hero." What saved the hunter-defender male from obsolescence or a life of agricultural toil was the fact that he possessed weapons and the skills to use them. Mumford suggests that the hunter-defender preserved his status by turning to a kind of "protection racket": pay him (with food and social standing) or be subject to *his* predations.[25]

Eventually, the presence of underemployed hunter-defenders in other human settlements guaranteed a new and "foreign" menace to defend against. The hunter-defenders of one band or settlement could justify their upkeep by pointing to the threat posed by their counterparts in other groups, and the danger could always be made more vivid by staging a raid from time to time. As Gwynne Dyer observes in his survey of war, "pre-civilized warfare . . . was predominantly a rough male sport for underemployed hunters."[26]

In small-scale societies, not only "unique heroes" like Enkidu but the majority of adult men would have found themselves in need of some substitute for the hunter-defender role. As encounters with wild animals (both game and predators) became less central to human survival, so, potentially, did adult males become less central to the survival of women and children. Women could grow crops, and certainly do so almost single-handedly in horticultural societies today. Women—and children—could care for domesticated animals (although armed men would still be more effective at defending the herds against wild predators). There was no indispensable and uniquely male occupation left.

In their engaging study of warfare among southwestern American Indians, anthropologists Clifton B. Kroeber and Bernard L. Fontana propose that war may indeed have arisen to fill the void. One by one, they eliminate the various materialist theories—involving land and access to water—which have been offered to explain these peoples' perpetual wars, and propose instead that war persists because it is a prestigious thing for men to do, that it is an exciting and even "religious" undertaking. In their account, the rise of agriculture is important to the history of war only insofar as it signals the decline of hunting and the decreasing economic contribution of the male sex. They quote from a study of the Navajo:

> A relative decrease of available game animals . . . threatened the status of men. Worldwide, this has produced secret men's associations which artificially tried to maintain the old glory and comradeship which formerly existed during hunting expeditions.[27]

And what better way to maintain the "old glory," Kroeber and Fontana suggest, than to recast the "men's association" as an army and replace the hunting expedition with war?

I should remind the reader that a theory of the origin of war is not the same as a theory of war. To say that war may have begun as a substitute activity and source of prestige for male hunters is not to say that all wars ever since serve the same function. Something does not necessarily persist for the same reasons it begins. But the notion that war initially served the interests of a particular human subgroup—adult males or the specialized hunter-defenders among them—is at least consistent with the fact that war has been, in historical times, almost universally the business of men and men alone.

Masculinity and War

War is, in fact, one of the most rigidly "gendered" activities known to humankind. So nearly exclusive is the connection between war and manhood that some scholars of war, typically male, have felt little need to mention the existence of a sex alternative to their own. A 1990 anthology on the anthropology of war, written entirely by males, contains no index entries on "gender" or "masculinity," and mentions women fewer than a dozen times (as wives, captives of war, and participants in cannibal feasts).[28] Other writers, typically female, are so struck by the link between masculinity and war that they find in masculinity—or even mere biological maleness—a satisfyingly complete explanation of war. In this view, war becomes an inevitable outgrowth of male aggressiveness, with the weaponry, the thrust of spears and missiles, the piercing and explosions, all mimicking the phallic side of sex.

The "gendering" of war goes far deeper than that of, say, the weaving Hektor recommends to Andromache:

> Go therefore back to our house, and take up your own work,
> the loom and the distaff, and see to it that your handmaidens
> ply their work also; but the men must see to the fighting.[29]

Probably invented by women, weaving has been, in certain periods and places, inextricably tied to notions of womanhood[30]—hence, for example, the notion of women's realm as the "distaff" side of human affairs. But in other situations, or with new technologies, weaving has been just as securely a manly thing to do. Similarly, many other roles and occupations—that of religious leader, healer, farmer, fisher, pottery maker—have been shared at times or fought over by men and women.

In the case of war, history offers no such alternations between the sexes. Certainly there are instances of female warriorship, but except for the female regiment maintained by Dahomeyan kings in west Africa, these are usually mythological, like the Amazons, or aristocratic, like the ancient British warrior queen Boadicea.[31] More commonly, women who have wanted to become warriors have had to first become "men." Among the many examples historian Julie Wheelwright offers of women who have dressed as men in order to fight is Deborah Sampson, who transformed herself into "Robert Shirtluff" and enlisted in the American revolutionary army. There she served with distinction until a shoulder wound gave her sex away. How she managed urination and menstruation up until that time remains a mystery; we know only that she "preserved her chastity inviolate by the most artful concealment of her sex."[32]

Not only have women had to dress as men to become warriors in many cultures, men who failed as warriors have been reviled as "women." Anthropologist of war Maurice Davie relates that

> when the Iroquois denationalized the Delawares and prohibited them from going to war, the latter were, according to the Indian notion, "made women," and were henceforth to confine themselves to pursuits appropriate to women. Among the Pomo of California, when a man became too infirm to be a warrior, he was made a menial and required to assist the squaws. This was true in Cuba and Greenland, with the additional degradation of wearing female dress.[33]

Or consider the Fang people of the Congo, where a man unarmed was not considered a true man and was told to "go and rear children."

When a group of Fang men shot someone down in an ambush, they came home shouting, "We are real men, we are real men, we have been to town and shot a man, we are men, real men."[34]

Thus war-making is not simply another occupation that men have monopolized. It is an activity that has often served to *define* manhood itself—which is exactly what we would expect if war in fact originated as substitute occupation for underemployed male hunter-defenders. In historical times, one of the acknowledged purposes of war has often been to make men "men," that is, to give the adult male something uniquely "manly" to do. The archaic Greeks waged what the French historian Yvon Garlan called "ritual wars" for the purpose of initiating young men into manhood, meaning also warriordom.[35] Tacitus reported a similar function for war among the ancient Germans:

> Many noble youths, if the land of their birth is stagnating in a protracted peace, deliberately seek out other tribes, where some war is afoot. The Germans have no taste for peace; renown is easier won among perils, and you cannot maintain a large body of companions [young warriors serving a chief] except by violence and war.[36]

Among the traditional cultures encountered by nineteenth- and early-twentieth-century anthropologists, the passage from boyhood to manhood often required successful participation in war, meaning often the killing of an enemy. Davie tells us that

> a Masai is not supposed to marry until he has blooded his spear. The Karamojo youth must distinguish himself in war before he may marry. Among the natives of Papuan Gulf, a man must be initiated as a warrior before he is free to enter the marital state. The Naga warrior has to bring home a scalp or skull before he is qualified to marry.[37]

Similarly, among the Kaoka speakers of Guadalcanal,

> a young man had to take part in a campaign and shed blood before he was eligible for marriage or the office of priesthood. Legendary stories relate that, after a long period of peace, villagers would deliberately send insults to one another to provoke a fight.[38]

We find the same theme among American Indians:

> A Creek might be famous for oratory, stoicism under trial, or wisdom in council, but if he had not been on a war party, he bore no title and was classified as a boy.[39]

Nor is the notion of war as the portal to manhood confined to "primitives." After the U.S. invasion of Panama in 1989, the press hailed President Bush for succeeding in an "initiation rite" by demonstrating his "willingness to shed blood."[40] Male leadership, just like adult male status in general, must be proved with blood.

Women could, potentially, have been warriors in far greater numbers than they have been. The female disadvantage in the realm of muscular strength was mitigated long ago with the invention of the bow and arrow, not to mention that great leveler of our own era, the gun. Nor, as Jean Bethke Elshtain emphasizes in her study of women and war, do women have any innate inhibition against fighting and shedding blood. Revolutions and insurrections have again and again utilized women in combat roles, if only because revolutionary forces are generally less formal and tradition-bound than the armies of nation-states. One can also find plenty of examples of less high-minded collective violence on the part of women. In 1677 a mob of women in Marblehead, Massachusetts, stormed through the cortege guarding a pair of Indian prisoners, leaving the poor captives with "their flesh in a manner pulled from their bones."[41] More recently, on July 12, 1993, four members of the overseas press were pulled from their car and "torn apart" by a crowd of vengeful Somali women.[42]

Even as "noncombatants," women have played lethal roles in

men's wars. According to a nineteenth-century ethnographer, Polynesian women had the job of selecting and cooking defeated enemies for postbattle feasts:

> They pick out the good bodies of the slain for the oven, and throw the bad away; they tie up a captive to a tree, dig a hole, and kindle a hot stone-oven for his body before his very eyes. The women go to battle, they keep to the rear, and attend to the *commissariat*! Whenever they see one of the enemy fall, it is their business to rush forward, pull the body behind, and dress it for the oven.[43]

Among some Amerindian tribes, it was the business of women to torture enemy captives. And, for what it's worth, Kipling warned his fellow Britishers in Afghanistan to shoot themselves rather than fall into the hands of the female enemy:

> If you're wounded and left out on Afghanistan's plains
> And the women come out to cut up what remains,
> Just roll to your rifle and blow out your brains,
> And go to your death like a soldier.[44]

So there is no compelling biological or "natural" reason why men have so exclusively starred in the drama of war. Men make wars for many reasons, but one of the most recurring ones is to establish that they are, in fact, "real men." Warfare and aggressive masculinity have been, in other words, mutually reinforcing cultural enterprises. Warmaking requires warriors, that is, "real men," and the making of warriors requires war. Thus war becomes a solution to what Margaret Mead termed "the recurrent problem of civilization," which is "to define the male role satisfactorily enough."[45]

This particular way of "defin[ing] the male role" inevitably had disastrous consequences for the female one as well. Their exclusion from warriordom did not mean that women were excluded from the terrors of war, safely consigned to the role of bystanders and baby makers. If war made men predators, it tended to make women into slaves—prizes of war much like grain stores and cattle. As Gerda Lerner concludes from her study of gender in the ancient Middle East:

> There is overwhelming historical evidence for the preponderance of the practice of killing or mutilating male prisoners and for the large-scale enslavement and rape of female prisoners.[46]

To survive as a captive—and help ensure the survival of her captive children—a woman had to be, at least superficially, submissive and compliant. In *The Trojan Women*, Euripides has Hecuba advise her daughter-in-law Andromache, widow of the Trojan hero Hektor:

> . . . you must forget
> what happened with Hector. Tears will never save you now.
> Give your obedience to the new master; let your ways
> entice his heart to make him love you. If you do
> it will be better for all who are close to you.[47]

But it is not only the captive women who would have been ground down by the practice of enslaving female prisoners of war. A woman within the victorious society might see her husband return from war with an attractive young captive or two, just as Clytemnestra saw Agamemnon return from Troy with the Trojan princess Cassandra. And even without sexual competition between women of the victorious and defeated groups, the practice of treating women as booty may well have encouraged misogyny in the victors.[48] In the situation Lerner describes, where enemy males were killed and enemy females enslaved, the only surviving adult representatives of the defeated enemy would of course be female, and the psychological equation would have been established, over time, between femaleness and the enemy "Other."

Could the male role be defined in ways that are more peaceable and less damaging to both sexes? Yes, certainly. War is not the only way of establishing a division of labor, or even a hierarchy of power, between men and women. There have been societies or subgroups within societies where men grow up, not to fight, but to take on a distinctive role as herders of animals, plowers of the soil, or salary-earning office workers. But even in these settings, the warrior usually still holds pride of place as a masculine ideal—the hero of epic tales and, in our own time, the star of Hollywood action movies.

Arguably the primordial male hunter-defender deserved whatever special status he was accorded within his culture. In battling wild animals—predators or fierce ungulates like the aurochs—he risked and often sacrificed his life to serve the human group. But the warrior who evolved from the hunter-defender was not so clearly deserving of the prestige he won at spear point. He too might give his life for the group in campaigns portrayed as thoroughly justified and defensive, but insofar as war is something "man-made," insofar as it can be considered an artifact of human culture, he was on potentially far shakier ground than the battler of wild beasts. Someone, some real-life Lysistrata or analog of the much maligned Clytemnestra, might notice the circular logic linking masculinity and war—that men make war in part because war makes them men—and conclude that men *could* stop.

But could they? To say that the practice of war may have begun as "something for men to do"—a system for allocating prestige analogous to that of the male sub-band's hunt—does not mean that it can be seen forever after as men's *fault*. War is not just a product of human impulses, a crime repeated fresh in each generation. Once unleashed, it has a furious power of its own, which human cultures ignore at their own peril. The warrior's business may first have begun as a "protection racket," but as soon as there was a real external threat to protect against—the incursions of "foreign" tribes or empires—the male warrior may indeed have earned his status as a local hero.

Is it not wonderful for a man, having been born a man, to die at the hands of another man and then, with his quiver and bow at his side, lie on the ground as a corpse?[1]

—MONGOLIAN PROVERB FROM THE TIME OF GENGHIS KHAN

8
FEARFUL SYMMETRIES

However and wherever war begins, it persists, it spreads, it propagates itself through time and across space with the terrifying tenacity of a beast attached to the neck of living prey. This is not an idly chosen figure of speech. War spreads and perpetuates itself through a dynamic that often seems independent of human will. It has, as we like to say of things we do not fully understand, "a life of its own."

Biological metaphors for war are popular among those who study war abstractly, through the grid of mathematics.[2] Normally we think of war as a product of human volition—an activity, a habit, perhaps an "institution"—growing out of human needs and cultural proclivities. And of course it is that: Take away human whims and passions, and there is no war, or at least no human versions of it. But if we consider war abstractly, we see that something else is going on. As the Dutch social scientist Henk Houweling points out, the mathematical study of outbreaks of war and of national decisions to participate in wars shows "strong indications of epidemicity":

> By using methods of epidemiology we do not suggest, of course, that wars are transmitted by bacteria or by common exposure to some causal variable in the environment. Our analysis does not reveal the *cause* of war. But it does suggest that one of the causes of war is war itself.[3]

If war is analogous to a disease, then, it is analogous to a contagious disease. It spreads through space, as groups take up warfare in response to warlike neighbors. This may seem obvious, but statistical studies show that warfare is indeed more intense and frequent in the vicinity of warlike groups.[4] War has another way of spreading, too, and that is through time. Ineluctably, the insults inflicted in one war call forth new wars of retaliation, which may be waged within months of the original conflict or generations later. Even the conditions of peace may serve as a springboard to new wars, as the modern world learned from the Treaty of Versailles; among the Central Enga of New Guinea, unpaid indemnities from one war are a common excuse for the next one.[5] So, to continue the epidemiological metaphor, if war is regarded as an infectious "disease," it is caused by a particularly hardy sort of microbe—one capable of encysting itself for generations, if necessary, within the human soul.

Stated in more conventional terms, war spreads from band to band and culture to culture because it is a form of contact that no human group can afford to ignore or disdain. If outsiders show up hoping to woo mates or trade goods or induct you into their religious practices, you can always tell them to go away. But, as Andrew Bard Schmookler argues in his brilliant exploration of human power relationships, *The Parable of the Tribes*, you can no more brush off a war party than you can tell a mugger who demands your money or your life that, frankly, you'd rather keep both and continue peaceably along your way.[6] If the other tribe harbors a corps of thuggish aggressors, so must yours—or fall prey to those who thought up thuggery first. No warlike instinct, greedy impulses, or material needs are required to explain why war, once adopted by some, must of necessity be adopted by all. Peaceable societies will survive only in isolated or marginal locales—the deep forests of the Mbuto, the snowfields of the Inuit. Everyone else is swept up into the dynamic of war. As Schmookler writes:

> Among all the cultural possibilities, only some will be viable. . . . The warlike may eliminate the pacificistic; the ambitious, the content. . . . Civilized societies will displace the remaining primitives, modern industrial powers will sweep away archaic cultures. The iron makers will be favored over those with copper or no metallurgy at all, and the horsemen will have sway over the unmounted. Societies that are coherently organized and have strong leadership will make unviable others with more casual power structure and more local autonomy. . . . What looked like open-ended cultural possibilities are channeled in a particular, unchosen direction.[7]

In other words, as it spreads from place to place, war tends to stamp a certain sameness on human cultures. At the most obvious level, it requires that each human society be as war-ready as the other societies it is likely to encounter; that spears be matched with spears, fighting men matched with the men of potential enemy groups; and that in all groups, similar proportions of energy and resources be dedicated to destructive ends. No doubt there are other directions in which human cultures might have evolved—toward greater emphasis on the arts, for example, or philosophy, or more lighthearted games and rituals. But war, once chosen by some, quickly became the "unchosen direction" imposed on all.

Most scholars have paid little attention to the homogenizing effects of war. The enemy, after all, is always the fearsome and wicked

Other. "The occasions for each particular war will vary perhaps," Robin Fox has written,

> But ultimately "we" fight "them" because they are different, and their difference is threatening in its challenge to the validity of the ideas we live by.[8]

Similarly, Ruth Benedict argued that the problem arises from what is basically a cognitive confusion: Our fellow humans often look to us like animals. Give the other tribe a strange accent, a peculiar religion or unusual style of body paint, and, in our provincialism, we take them for a different species. In "primitive" societies, she wrote,

> human beings are merely one's own little tribe; the rest are nonhuman like the animals. Killing animals is of course acclaimed, and nonhuman bipeds of the neighboring tribe are equally objects of prey. Their death proves my strength just as a successful lion hunt does.[9]

Left unexplained in this account is why *Homo sapiens*, being so famously intelligent in other respects, should alone of all the species be unable to recognize its own kind. In fact, there is reason to believe that diverse cultures have been capable of peaceful interaction for many thousands of years, meaning that they were also capable of recognizing one another as human. For example, the vast distribution of "Venus" figurines throughout the Eurasian continent would seem to attest to cultural contact and exchange among presumably quite different peoples as early as the Upper Paleolithic. By the Neolithic, goods like obsidian were being traded across thousands of miles in the Mediterranean and Near East—again presumably among people who recognized one another as human beings.[10] Even the most parochially minded Paleolithic bands were probably exogamous, that is, disposed to pick mates from outside the band rather than risk incest within.[11] Diversity is endemic to the human race, which would have had to realize long ago that the stranger may be next year's trading partner, or kin.

Conversely, warfare is hardly confined to groups that differ strikingly in culture, language, and appearance. On the contrary, anthropologist Lawrence H. Keeley observes that "ethnographers have frequently encountered tribes that intermarried and traded with one another but were also periodically at war."[12] Peaceful trading and socializing may alternate with vicious warfare—a pattern observed among certain Inuit, North American Indian, and Brazilian tribes. To quote Keeley:

> When the Sioux came to trade at Hidatsa villages along the Upper Missouri, a truce was in force only within sight of the villages; once the [Sioux] nomads passed out of sight by climbing over the bluffs, they might steal horses or kill Hidatsa and were themselves subject to attack. The Mae Enga of New Guinea asserted, "We marry the people we fight."[13]

But the notion that war arises, basically, from ignorance and provincialism has persisted because it is in many ways an optimistic one: If war represents a failure to recognize human diversity, then all we have to do to end it is to learn to see through the local variations in language, culture, religion, and so forth and rediscover our common humanity. In this view, the flaw that leads humans into war is not a moral but a cognitive one and can be cured through the kind of education that engenders an enlightened tolerance of human differences.

Now, from the point of view of any particular side, in any particular war, the enemy may indeed be seen as a repulsively different Other. But the differences are often almost imperceptible to an outsider—as between Protestant and Catholic Irish people, for example, or Serbs and Croats, or one subtribe of Yanomamo Indians and another—and over time they will be overshadowed by the common and overarching imperatives of war. Certainly this is true at the level of technology, where failure to mimic the enemy can be fatal. An American commentator observed of the Cold War:

> All things Communist remain anathema, but the slightest word of some new development in Russia is sufficient to set in motion investigations by several congressional committees and private foundations to find out why we are not doing the same thing.[14]

But the symmetry between enemies goes beyond the instruments of war. During the Cold War, the ostensibly democratic United States developed the permanent bureaucracy of the "national security state," parallel to that of the Soviets and including government agencies dedicated to rooting out and suppressing domestic dissent. In general, as Israeli military historian Martin van Creveld explains:

> Given time, the fighting itself will cause the two sides to become more like each other, even to the point where opposites converge, merge, and change places. . . . The principal reason behind this phenomenon is that war represents perhaps the most imitative activity known to man.[15]

There is a mechanism—almost a human reflex—that guarantees that belligerents will in fact be "given time" for this convergence to occur, and that mechanism is revenge: A raid or attack or insult must be matched with an attack of equal or greater destructive force. One atrocity will be followed by another; and no matter how amicable the two sides may once have been, they will soon be locked together in a process from which no escape seems possible. To the warrior, the necessity of revenge may be self-evident and beyond appeal:

> The Jibaro Indian is wholly penetrated by the idea of retaliation; his desire for revenge is an expression of his sense of

> justice. . . . If one reprehends a Jibaro because he has killed an enemy, his answer is generally: "He has killed himself."[16]

The "necessity" of revenge may well be another legacy of our animal-fighting, prehistoric past. Revenge has a pedagogical purpose, whether the enemy is animal or human: It teaches the intruder to stay away. Conversely, the creature that does not fight back marks itself as prey. At the Paleolithic kill sites where early humans battled competing scavengers, some version of revenge may have been essential to establishing the human claim to meat. Like modern dogs, canine intruders could have been taught to keep their distance by being struck or stoned. Similarly, many wild predators have learned that the price of human meat can be gunshots, spear wounds, or fiery sticks waved in their faces, and they seem to have passed the lesson along to their young. In the face of nonhuman enemies, retaliation makes sense: The animals will not counterretaliate at some later time but, being sensible, will slink away.

But no matter how often we are told that some human enemy must be "taught a lesson," the impulse to revenge is by no means entirely rational. In traditional societies, wars may be started for no other purpose than to overcome grief. The Kwakiutl of the Pacific Northwest often followed up natural deaths with retaliatory head-hunting raids:

> The dead relative might equally have died in bed of disease or by the hand of an enemy. The head-hunting was called "killing to wipe one's eyes," and it was a means of getting even by making another household mourn instead.[17]

Among South American Indians living near the Putumayo River, even damage caused by a thunderstorm could be an excuse for a retaliatory raid, since "every ill that befalls a man they set down to the evil intent of an enemy."[18] Similarly, the Miyanmin of New Guinea lacked the concept of a "natural" death, so that all adult deaths were viewed as "political acts carried out by the enemy." Every death, then, was an insult, which had to be avenged by going to war:

> After a period of mourning (marked by violence and brawls) the hamlet may be abandoned, as if the survivors of the deceased were war refugees, and/or retaliatory attacks on other hamlets (on whom blame has been assigned by ritual).[19]

Grief, depression, helplessness—these are the experiences of *prey*. The obvious way out, the way our species learned through a million years of conflict with larger and stronger animals, is to assume the stance of the predator: Turn grief to rage, go from listless mourning to the bustling preparations for offensive attack. This, more or less, is what Achilles does in the *Iliad*: He recovers from the paralysis of hurt feelings and grief through his spectacular revenge for Patroklus's death. Animals secure in their predator status know nothing of revenge. But humans are hardly secure; our triumph over the other species occurred not that long ago, and childhood, for each of us, recapitulates the helplessness of prey. For purely emotional reasons, then, human antagonists readily find themselves caught up in the well-known "cycle of violence," taking turns as prey and predator, matching injury with injury—bound together as powerfully as lovers in their bed.

The dance of action and reaction engenders a symmetry between belligerents which warriors recognize and sometimes consciously enhance. To defeat an enemy, you must know that enemy and learn to think as he thinks. Before Achilles can kill Hektor he must become as much like him as possible, spending books 18 to 20 of the *Iliad* mimicking him and usurping his identity as a hunter. Conversely, if someone is so truly and incomprehensibly different as to be subhuman in the sense Ruth Benedict suggests, he may never achieve the status of a genuine "enemy." Nineteenth-century European aristocrats refused to duel with their social inferiors, nor did Europeans always bother to dignify their campaigns against indigenous peoples with the word "war." The clashes of British against French or French against Prussian were "wars," recalled with definite names and dates, but—with a few exceptions like the Zulu Wars—their fiercely resisted incursions against Africans and Asians tend to be lumped together indiscriminately under bloodless phrases like "imperialist expansion."

At the level of the individual, the symmetry of war may even be expressed as a kind of love. Enemies by definition "hate" each other, but between habitual and well-matched enemies, an entirely different feeling may arise. Sometimes this love is reserved for the trophies created from the bodies of dead enemies, their shrunken heads or scalps:

> The scalp of an enemy was of remarkable importance for the Cocopa warrior. He brought the object back with him and soon retired to a place isolated from other people where he spent several nights and days in communion with the scalp. During that time it talked to him, "especially at night, telling him how to be a great warrior and giving him special powers."[20]

Or the dead enemy may be incorporated by his killer's tribe as a kind of honorary kinsman. The practice of naming a child after a particularly valiant enemy was once widespread, from New Guinea[21] to the North American plains.[22] Genghis Khan's birth name, for example, was Temu-jin, taken from a tribal enemy his father had vanquished and captured.[23]

There have been, in some instances, ritual occasions for the face-to-face expression of love between enemy combatants. When an Aztec warrior subdued an opponent in battle, he formally reassured his prisoner that he would not be eaten, and "considered his captive as his own flesh and blood, calling him son, while the latter called him father."[24] Or consider what Richard Barber, the historian of medieval European knighthood, called "the curious custom of fighting in mines." The besiegers of a fortress often dug mines under the fortress walls; the besieged would dig countermines in order to get out and harass the besiegers. If a mine met a countermine, a fight might ensue, conducted by torchlight and according to the rules of the tournament. The odd part is that, merely by participating in this underground combat, enemy knights were transformed into "brothers-in-arms," meaning that their personal enmity was dissolved and they were henceforth "bound to one another in such a way, that each will stand by the other to the death if need be."[25]

The symmetry forged by war echoes the peculiar symmetries often found in sacrificial rites. In Aztec ritual, the sacrificial victim was sometimes dressed to impersonate the god or goddess who was the intended recipient of the sacrifice. In Christian imagery, which reflects far earlier traditions, Jesus is both the sacrificial "lamb" and, through the mystery of the Trinity, the deity to whom the lamb is offered. Hubert and Mauss noted the extreme and complicated "doubling" in ancient Greek sacrificial rites. The great Dorian festival of the Karneia, for example, celebrated in honor of Apollo Karneios, was supposedly instituted to expiate the sacrificial killing of the soothsayer Karnos, who is himself Apollo Karneios.[26] These symmetries may reflect humankind's primordial experience of being both prey and predator—an experience faithfully re-created in every battle.

War, then, is not simply a clash of Others, made possible by an ignorant horror of difference. The warrior looks out at the enemy and sees men who are, in crucial respects, recognizably like himself. They are warriors, too, and whatever differences they may have, whatever long-standing reasons for hatred, they share the basic tenets of warriordom: a respect for courage, a willingness to stand by one's comrades no matter what, a bold indifference to death. Even when divided by race and vast cultural differences, enemies may admire each other for their conduct as warriors. To the medieval European Crusaders, for example, the

> enemy was not a priori an object of hatred. . . . The Saracen, strong, brave, and fierce and always vanquished in the end, was the ideal adversary in the medieval warrior's imagination.[27]

More ambivalently, a British colonel wrote of the West African Asantes he had helped to defeat: "It was impossible not to admire the gallantry of these savages."[28] In a sense, warriors everywhere constitute a tribe unto themselves, transcending all other tribes and nations.

Certainly, and especially in our own time, warring cultures have sought to magnify their differences for propagandistic reasons—witness the demonization of the "Huns," "Japs," and "gooks" Americans have fought against. But at the same time, as Schmookler observed, war also works to flatten out many of the differences—of culture, if not, of course, of race or language—that distinguish tribes and nations. Trade does this, too, imposing similar tastes and fashions on people who may share little else, but war does it in a highly specific way. For one thing, the concentration of the weapons and prestige of war in the hands of men reinforces male supremacy, which is in itself a nearly universal characteristic of human societies. Certain common patterns of gender relations have been observed, for example, among warlike, small-scale horticultural societies, whether they are in the Amazon basin, New Guinea, or parts of Africa. In these societies women are valued largely as prizes of war or as prestigious possessions accorded to victorious warriors, and have little or no voice in group decision-making. As anthropologist William T. Divale observes:

> Primitive warfare is part of a syndrome which also includes female infanticide, polygyny, and marriage alliances. The almost universal occurrence of this syndrome in primitive cultures plus its important ecological role has led to the conclusion that the syndrome constitutes the basic structural framework or template of primitive social organization.[29]

In addition, the maintenance of warriors itself imposes certain disciplines and forms of organization: Weapons must be manufactured, sometimes out of raw materials gathered from distant sites, and potential warriors must be instructed in their use. The use of metal weaponry in particular demands a complex division of labor and, usually, a centralized command system to coordinate the mining and transport of ore and the manufacture of the weapons. In the ancient world, the imperatives of weapons manufacture and warrior maintenance often went along with despotism and the formation of highly centralized, dynastic states. But not always: The ancient Greeks fought on foot, in a phalanx formation that stressed equality and interdependence, and, as historian Victor Hansen has convincingly argued, this mode of warfare was compatible with the limited democracy of the city-state. In general, the early-twentieth-century sociologist Stanislaw Andrzejewski argued, militarism has a decisive influence on forms of political organization, but whether it favors democracy or despotism depends on the particular mode of warfare practiced.[30]

So there is no single cultural pattern stamped by war on all human societies, everywhere and at all times. We can say, though, that similar technologies and styles of warfare place similar demands on human cultures, and that these demands tend to impose a kind of sameness in areas of social endeavor that are seemingly remote from the business of war. Contrary to Marx, it is not only the "means of production" that shape human societies, but "the means of destruction,"[31] and for much of human history the means of destruction have favored societies ruled by warriors themselves.

> Do you not know that I live by war and that peace would be my undoing?[1]
>
> —Sir John Hawkwood, English Free Company captain during the Hundred Years War

9
The Warrior Elite

Nothing more clearly illustrates the power of war as a culture-shaping force than the eerie parallels between feudal Japan and feudal Europe. Both societies rested on the labor of relatively unfree peasants, and both were ruled by hereditary warrior classes—knights in Europe and *bushi*, or samurai, in Japan—representing, or at least serving, the landed aristocracy. If, through some magical transposition, a medieval knight and a samurai had met on the same road, they would have immediately recognized each other as kin. Both wore helmets and armor, fought on horseback, rallied to flags emblazoned with dynastic symbols or totems, invested their swords with mystic power, and subscribed to a special warrior ethic—chivalry in Europe, *bushido* in Japan—which codified, for its adherents, a kind of religion of war.

In her study of the *bushi* tradition, Catharina Blomberg lists these parallels, only to dismiss them as "entirely fortuitous"[2] since, after all, there had been no contact between medieval Europe and Japan. What she misses is the entirely unfortuitous effect of the means of destruction which these two cultures shared: Both employed metal blades to cut human flesh and horses to transport warriors to and about the battlefield. This technology leads to, and even seems to require, the kind of social arrangement we know as feudalism, which has been defined as an "essentially military . . . type of social organization designed to produce and support cavalry."[3] A very similar pattern emerged in precolonial western Africa: a social and economic elite of mounted, knightlike warriors, subscribing to a quasi-religious warrior ethic.[4]

The knight and the samurai are in some ways special cases, preferring, as they did, to fight at close range with their cherished swords. Other warriors of the pre-gun era, no less proud and individualistic, fought from a distance with metal-tipped arrows propelled by compound bows. The European knight was again and again shocked to encounter, during the Crusades and the various incursions of nomadic Asian "hordes," highly skilled mounted warriors who announced their attacks with a hail of arrows and used their bladed weapons primarily to dispatch the wounded. But all—swordsmen and archers alike—were part of a system of warfare that depended on the synergy of metal and muscle. The metal could be worked to a point as an arrow tip or pounded to a cutting edge as a sword. The muscle could be that of the human arm alone or that of the arm reinforced by the speed and strength of the horse. Either way, the metal-and-muscle approach to warfare imposed certain common themes on the cultures that engaged in it, whether they did so reluctantly or with zest.

The most obvious and fundamental commonality was that the metal-bearing warrior depended on the labor of other, nonwarrior men. In small-scale horticultural societies, such as those of New Guinea or the Amazon Valley, all men are warriors, and the induction to warrior status coincides with the male initiation rite to which all boys are subjected. To be a man, a "real" man, is to be a warrior; ideally the two conditions are indistinguishable. But as the tools of war evolve and become more costly, warrior status narrows to an elite set off from other men as well as women. The Yanomamo warrior made his own weapons and required no "underclass," beyond that represented by his wives, to do his planting and hoeing and cooking. Behind each knight or samurai, however—or, for that matter, each mounted archer—stood a small army of food-producing peasants of both sexes, plus grooms and other servants, as well as miners and craftsmen to manufacture his weapons and armor.

For more than 5,000 years, from the beginning of recorded history to A.D. 1500, and over a huge geographical range, the means of destruction centered on this combination of metal and muscle. Bronze weapons and armor first appeared in Mesopotamia at about 3500 B.C. and cheaper iron weapons came into use about 1,300 years later. Horses made their battlefield debut early in the second millennium B.C., pulling sturdy chariots from which men shot arrows and hurled spears. Within a few centuries, the metal-and-muscle-based means of destruction had spread south to northern Africa, west to Europe, and eastward to India, China, and Japan.[5] Lacking horses and the appropriate metals, the warring Mesoamerican civilizations depended on obsidian weapons, wielded by men on foot. But obsidian, no less than iron or copper and tin for bronze, had to be mined, transported, and worked into shape by loyal underlings.

There were two possible ways for warrior groups to resolve the problem of their dependence on large numbers of other men. One is represented by stratified societies in which a warrior elite is supported by a nonwarrior class (or classes) and, in return, undertakes to protect this subpopulation from the incursions of other warrior groups—an arrangement often described, roughly speaking, as "civilization." Alternatively, the warrior group might not bother to maintain or protect its own laboring class and sources of materials; it might "live off the land," fulfilling its needs through constant raids and conquests, that is, armed robbery. This approach, utilized by the nomadic fighters who repeatedly harassed settled agricultural communities in both ancient and medieval times, was generally seen by civilized people as a kind of "barbarianism."

The Mongol warriors who fought under Genghis Khan, for example, had little need for a permanently subjugated population to support them. In many ways, they constituted one of the most self-sufficient armies ever fielded. Their tough little mares were not only a means of transportation but a source of food, in the form of milk. And unlike the larger horses that bore the weight of armored knights, the Mongol horses grazed on the grass around them, even grass buried under snow, and needed no supplies of special fodder. But for anything else, such as the metal parts of his weaponry, as well as luxuries like bread and wine, the Mongol warrior was utterly dependent on the people whose towns and farms he burned and sacked.

The difference between the "civilized" and the "barbarian" approach to warfare was clearly not as great as practitioners of the former liked to think. Although the warrior within a settled society might not extort every meal at sword or spear point, his dominance over the mass of toiling underlings who grew his food and forged his weapons was maintained, ultimately, by force. The exact causal links between the rise of large-scale warfare and the emergence of class societies are still a subject for debate, but it seems unlikely that large numbers of people would submit to lifelong labor on limited rations unless inspired, now and then, by the threat of death. At least we can say, echoing Andrzejewski, that the means of destruction employed in war have again and again done service as the means of domestic repression.[6]

Thus a certain brutal logic underlies the "civilized" warring states of the ancient and medieval worlds: The warrior depends for his superior weapons (among other things) on the labor of others, and at the same time, it is his weaponry that enables him to exploit the labor of others. No mob of peasants armed with pitchforks could, for example, hope to topple the armored and mounted knight, who could mow them down with his lance or hack them from on high with his sword. Such a commanding figure must be treated with deference, even with the abject obeisance otherwise reserved for gods. In feudal Japan, a commoner encountering a samurai on the road was expected to dismount, bow deeply with his eyes averted, and pray that he would not become a victim of *tsuji-giri*, or "crossroads cutting," in which a samurai would use some random common person as material on which to test his sword blade.[7]

There is another way, too, in which the "civilized" warrior resembled the "barbarian" raider: The lower class, on whose labor he depended, was very often made up of people different from himself in language and culture, people whose own warrior elite had been previously defeated in war. While the nomadic warrior preyed briefly on each set of victims, looting, destroying, and then moving on, his settled counterpart might prey on the same subjugated people for generations, even eventually becoming genetically intermixed with them. In one stratified society after another, the lower class turns out to be composed wholly or partly of a defeated people or their descendants, ethnically different from the ruling class: the Messenians within Sparta, Israelites within Egypt, Gallic peoples within Roman Europe, African agriculturalists within kingdoms ruled by the descendants of conquering Hamitic pastoralists, Saxons within Norman England.[8] Thus, class divisions have been, in many settings, a product of war. From the point of view of the common people, the "civilized" warrior might be almost as much a "foreign" enemy to his own people as was the dreaded nomad raider from the hinterlands.

But at the deepest level, the resemblance between the free-ranging barbarian warrior and his civilized counterpart can best be expressed with a biological metaphor: Both were *predators* on human life and culture. Historian William H. McNeill describes warrior elites as "macro-parasites," analogous to micro-parasites like bacteria and viruses,[9] and offers the example of the third millennium B.C. Mesopotamian king Sargon, who maintained his army of fifty-four hundred men by constant predation on the surrounding countryside:

> To keep such a force in being also required annual campaigning, devastating one fertile landscape after another in

> order to keep the soldiers in victuals. Costs to the population at large were obviously very great. Indeed Sargon's armies can well be compared to the ravages of an epidemic disease that kills a significant proportion of the host population yet by its very passage confers an immunity lasting for several years.[10]

The elite warrior must be fed and, in part because of the bursts of muscular energy required by his way of fighting, fed far better than those who grow the grain. He must be clothed and quartered somewhere. His horses, too, if he possesses them, must be fed and quartered and groomed. But he himself neither sows nor reaps, and from the vantage point of the ordinary people, he can be counted on to be a producer of only ruin and death. Cretan warriors from the ninth century B.C. sang—proudly, we may imagine, or perhaps with a wink:

> My wealth is spear and sword, and the stout shield which protects my flesh; with this I plough, with this I reap, with this I tread the sweet wine from the grape, with this I am entitled master of the serfs.[11]

Sometimes the elite warrior understood his predatory relationship to the rest of humankind, and may even have felt a vague unease on account of it. In his book *The Code of the Warrior*, Rick Fields quotes the seventeenth-century philosopher-samurai Yamaga Soko as wondering:

> The samurai eats food without growing it, uses utensils without manufacturing them, and profits without buying or selling. What is the justification for this?

But Yamaga Soko quickly answers himself:

> The business of the samurai consists in reflecting on his own station in life, on discharging loyal service to his

> master if he has one, in deepening his fidelity in associations with friends, and . . . in devoting himself to duty above all.[12]

The samurai deserved his special status, in other words, because he was a samurai and ultimately needed no more justification for his predations than, say, a wolf or lion would.

In fact, the elite warrior epitomized the human status as predator. He must even have looked to his fellow humans like a member of some far better endowed species. His horse gave him superhuman height, his armor acted as a glittering exoskeleton from which bladed weapons protruded like tusks or claws, while his heraldry might announce his kinship with lions, leopards, eagles, or other threatening animals.

Fictive Families

If war itself is thought of as something other than human—an abstract system that is "alive" in some formal, mathematical sense and preys on human societies—then warrior elites are the human form it takes. Through much of history it is they, and not the mass of ordinary people, who have made war, sought war, and celebrated war as a heroic, and even religious, undertaking.

To the nonwarrior—the peasants, for example, who so often found themselves in the way of thundering warrior hosts—war can be a catastrophe on the scale of plague or famine. To the warrior, though, it is the very condition of life, of a good life, anyway, which women and peasants can never fully share. In war he finds adventure, camaraderie, searing extremes of emotion, proof of manhood, possibly new territory and loot, and always the chance of a "glorious death," meaning not death at all but everlasting fame. In between wars, he keeps the memory of these things alive with recited epics and chansons de geste, reenacts them as duel or tournament, and celebrates them in warlike pageantry. Elite warriors going back to ancient times would have felt well represented by the words of a young German *Freikorpsmann* who wrote, shortly after World War I, "People told us that the War was over. That made us laugh. We ourselves are the War."[13]

In generalizing about warrior elites, we are, of course, gliding recklessly over vast cultural differences and historical changes. Within the European tradition alone, the notion of a warrior elite embraces both the rough-and-tumble men-at-arms of the early Middle Ages and the dandified aristocrats of a much later time. It includes the knight, who fought in a more or less undisciplined, individualistic manner, as well as the officer within a huge bureaucratized army, who may never have fought at all but commanded scores of lesser men to do so. It includes mercenaries who fought for whatever prince could pay their fee, as well as idealists who fought for their god or, later, nation. It includes, too, men who would hardly seem to qualify as members of an elite: poor knights, second sons forced off the ancestral land by primogeniture, men like Don Quixote, for example, who were sometimes little more than beggars bearing arms.

If there is any excuse for generalizing about warrior elites, it is that they themselves have freely done so. Their members have again and again understood themselves to be part of one long, unbroken tradition linking father to son and, more generally, the fighting men of one time to those of another. In their own minds, they form a special kind of lineage—of which General Douglas MacArthur's famous image of a "long gray line" of West Point alumni is one fragmentary example—stretching back thousands of years. It is from this notion of lineage that the warrior derived his most exalted and mystic sense of who he was: not merely a mortal individual, "born of woman," but a link within a far superior tradition, analogous to a priesthood and composed exclusively of men, meaning often only "noble" men.

Charioteers and mounted fighters were the founding patriarchs of the lineage, and the "mystique" or "romance" of war still reverberates with their hoofbeats, clashing blades, and hissing storms of arrows and hurled spears. Well into the era of the gun, when chemical energy had decisively replaced the power of human—and eventually even equine—muscle, warriors clung to the spirit and even the paraphernalia of the pre-gun era. Civil War General Stonewall Jackson ordered a thousand pikes (the medieval weapons) for his men.[14] (Whether they were delivered or not, I do not know, but they would hardly have been an effective defense against Union artillery.) The European officer corps entered the First World War expecting to fight on horseback and made only a slow and grudging adaptation to motor vehicles. Similarly, metal blades—except for bayonets—were abandoned only recently and with much sorrow and ceremony: In World War II General George Patton claimed that "the saddest moment in his life came when he stood at attention, weeping, as his cavalry regiment marched past to stack their sabers for the last time."[15]

In the mind of the warrior, the idea of a warrior lineage stretching back thousands of years is hardly an abstraction. Certainly it was very real to Patton: His family featured generations of distinguished military men; his childhood heroes included Julius Caesar and Alexander the Great; he believed he was the reincarnation of dead heroes, both Confederate and Viking. At a visit to a Civil War battleground sometime in the 1920s, he got into an argument about where exactly a certain general had been standing. The argument was resolved by an elderly veteran, who claimed to have participated in the battle as a boy. "Yes," Patton responded, "I was here too."[16]

Patton may be an extreme case, but elite warriors are generally encouraged to locate themselves within a transnational warrior lineage. West Point's Washington Hall confronts the cadets with a giant mural depicting

> more than two millennia of military exploits in a mass of spears, arrows, muskets, gas masks, siege engines, and elephants: Cyrus at Babylon, William at Hastings, Meade at Gettysburg, Joffre at the Marne.[17]

Where the tradition is historically vague or insufficiently uplifting, imagination has filled in. Nineteenth-century Prussians, for example, saw themselves as the successors of the Spartans and the Assyrians, or rooted their pedigree in medieval times, sometimes describing themselves as "crusaders."[18] Medieval knights, in turn, sought roots in ancient times, through a twelfth-century genre of romances which described the heroes of the Trojan War as if they were medieval knights themselves, complete with suits of armor.[19] Addressing the cadets at West Point, General MacArthur conjured up a ghostly succession of American warriors who were to serve as the superegos of the young. Were the cadets ever to fail in their duty, "a million ghosts in olive drab, in brown khaki, in blue and gray, would rise from their white crosses, thundering those magic words: Duty, honour, country."[20] For imaginative reach, though, no one has matched the German Nationalist science of "aryanology," which sought to trace the Wehrmacht's ethnic and spiritual lineage back thousands of years to the prehistoric Indo-European armed male band, or *Männerbund*. These pseudoscholarly efforts to construct a continuous bloodline of German-Aryan warriors no doubt played a role in Hitler's conception of himself as a member of a "race of Aryan god-men."[21]

There has been, at various times and places, a real basis for the warrior's notion of a warrior lineage: Metal-and-muscle technology tended to favor a hereditary warrior elite, with warrior status passed on from father to son, largely because of the cost of equipping each fighting man, especially if he required armor and horses. In medieval Europe, for example, a single knight's equipment was worth the equivalent of about twenty oxen, or the plow teams of ten peasant families.[22] Thus warriors had to be wealthy compared with average people (or, in the case of mercenaries, employed by wealthy men), and wealth took the form of land, which was inherited through the blood lineage, or noble family. Many acres of land, cultivated by peasants, were required to maintain a noble household with its corps of knights and squires; conversely, the extreme social inequality characterizing feudalism could be maintained only by employing armed force, from time to time, against the resentful peasantry. "Feudal aristocracy existed by war and for war," Toynbee wrote; "its power had been founded by arms, and by arms that power was maintained."[23]

Much of Europe's warrior elite persisted as an unbroken blood line for centuries, well into the age of guns. To take the case of Prussia, a warrior society par excellence: As late as 1871, 96 percent of officers promoted to the rank of brigadier general were from the landed nobility; by 1914, 58 percent were still men of the landed aristocracy, almost half of them holding titles that dated back to before 1400.[24] Similarly, the pre–World War I British officer corps was rooted in the landed aristocracy, a regimental position being one of the few occupations deemed suitable for a young man of relative wealth and leisure. Thus, right up into the twentieth century, armies have been led disproportionately by men whose surnames included the "de" or "von" of feudal entitlement, whose male relatives had led armies before them, and who took up the sword or the gun as a matter, more or less, of birthright.

A Lineage of Men

But there is a problem with hereditary lineages based on real blood ties: They consist, by necessity, of two sexes. In the era of muscle-based fighting, few women could have hoped to achieve warrior status, even if custom had not frowned upon such "unwomanly" aspirations. They had little to contribute, from a warrior's point of view, except wombs in which to incubate the next generation of fighting men. According to anthropologist Nancy Jay, the patriarchal imagination has long sought to expunge any other female contribution and construct a lineage of men alone. In Aeschylus's play *The Furies*—to take a particularly clear-cut example—the young, "modern," Olympian gods Apollo and Athena argue that mothers are not truly parents, but only vessels for the father's seed. In the Bible, the long lists of "begats" link male names alone, with only an occasional, almost parenthetical reference to a mother, wife, or sister. Similarly, medieval knights and samurai entered battle prepared to announce their noble antecedents to all potential combatants, but these recitations would normally have included only male names.

The suppression of women within warrior elites goes beyond the usual patriarchal imperative of ensuring the orderly transmission of property from father to son. Within warrior elites, marriage was usually politically motivated and used as a means of building alliances between sometimes hostile clans or states. Thus a bride entered her husband's household as a representative of an erstwhile or potential enemy group. She might in fact be treated as an enemy herself, as in this unsettling tale from anthropologist June Nash's study of gender relations among the precontact Mexicans:

> Shortly after the Aztecs arrived in Chapultepec . . . the Aztecs asked the chief of the Calhuacans, Coxcox, for his daughter in marriage to their chief. According to the Ramierez codex, the god Huitzilopochtli declared that she should be sacrificed. Her father was invited to the wedding party but was appalled when he went into the chamber and found the priest dressed in his daughter's skin. . . . [This was] an attempt both to assert and [to] validate the combative stance of the Aztecs in the heavily populated valley where they had chosen to live.[25]

Or a bride might choose to act as an enemy, a kind of fifth column within her husband's household. Japanese history is filled with stories of loyal daughters serving as treasonous wives or vice versa: brides who were expected to spy on their new family or who were used by their husbands to carry disinformation back to their fathers and brothers. An aphorism attributed to the sixteenth-century daimyo (samurai lord) Takeda Shingen advised that "even when husband and wife are alone together, he should never forget his dagger."[26] Nothing, though, underscores the dilemma of the woman within a warrior elite as strikingly as the myth of the princess Signy in the Norse saga of the Volsungs. Forced by her father to marry a hostile king, Siggeir, she bears him two sons, but she knows them to be potential enemies who might eventually battle her own father and brothers. So, ever the good daughter, Signy arranges for her sons to be killed by her brother. Then, with the help of a sorceress, she assumes a new shape, sleeps with her brother, and bears a son she can finally love: the hero Sinfjotli.[27] If the solution seems drastic, so too was the problem: Exogamy—the requirement that one marry outside one's own immediate clan or blood line—too often condemned a women to life behind enemy lines.

The untrustworthiness of women as wives limited even the role they could play as mothers. In any case, practically speaking, warriors are made, not born, and the making of new warriors has been an exclusively male business—a form of "reproduction" in which women play no part at all. In medieval Europe, boys of noble family were taken from their mothers at the age of about seven, to begin their training as pages and then as squires. When a young man was ready to be "girded with the sword" or initiated into knighthood, his father did the honors (until sometime in the twelfth century, when the church took on this role).[28] In the samurai's initiation rite of *genbuko*, performed at age fifteen or sixteen, an older male relative placed the boy's formal *bushi* robes on him.[29] To the extent that initation rites represent a rebirth, as much ethnography suggests, it is a rebirth to males, obliterating the earlier biological birth from a woman's body.

But whatever ceremonies take place in moments of peace, the warrior's true rite of initiation can only be battle itself, and this has been, almost universally, the exclusive business of men. Through his first kill, a young man "earns his spurs," "bloods his spear," or even, as was said by Americans in Vietnam, "loses his virginity," thus marking his rebirth into the world of grown-up men. Informed that his son was hard pressed by the French at the battle of Crécy, King Edward III refused to send him reinforcements, commanding that the English nobles "let the boy win his spurs."[30] Thus, the chronicler Jean Froissart implies, did a loving father ensure his son's ascent to warrior status.

Some men are so altered by the experience of battle that they can never again be at ease in the mundane world which women also inhabit. They will become permanent warriors: Crusaders who, on returning from the Holy Land, devoted themselves to battling European heretics; English knights who refused to stop fighting during truces in the Hundred Years War but remained in France as freebooting marauders; Civil War veterans who left the battlefields of the American East to battle Indians in the West; German officers who, after the First World War, led the reactionary Freikorps that terrorized the German working class—and who went on to form the corps of Hitler's brown-shirted storm troopers, the S.A.* As the German literary scholar Klaus Theweleit's study of the Freikorps men makes clear, a major attraction of their way of life was that it was virtually woman-free. He quotes, for example, from a fascist novel in which a Freikorps commander is described admiringly as having "no idea there are such things as women."[31]

War is not the only way, of course, that men have sought to create lineages free of women. Priesthoods and certain professions or crafts have often served the same function, with skills and lore being passed from one generation of males to the next, often through special ceremonies of initiation. Property, too, has usually been transmitted from man to man, and, according to Jay, one function of blood sacrifice in ancient religions was to define, through ritual, the male-only lineage required for inheritance: "What is needed to provide clear evidence of social and religious paternity is an act as definite and available to the senses as childbirth." In her account, this act was sacrifice, with the right to participate in the sacrifice marking the boundaries of true kin for the purposes of inheritance. "Sacrificing," she wrote, "produces and reproduces forms of intergenerational continuity generated by males, transmitted by males, and transcending community through women."[32] Or, to quote a Hindu text, the Maitrayani-Samhita, "In truth man is unborn. It is through sacrifice that he is born."[33]

---

*In our own time, too, the laid-off warrior can be a constant menace, often to his own people as well as to his erstwhile enemies. Afghani men, inducted into warriorhood during their nation's war with the Soviet Union, stock the world's supply of Islamic terrorists. American veterans of recent wars have found ways to extend their warrior days by joining right-wing militias and, in a few notorious cases, engaging in domestic terrorism.

Jay died at the peak of her career, but if she had lived to consider the postsacrificial era, she would no doubt have observed that the rite that eventually came to define an elite male lineage was not the slaughter of animals at the altar, but the slaughter of men in war. The battle itself has often been conceived as "one great sacrificial action,"[34] according to classicist Walter Burkert, with the mounds of the dead sometimes serving as the "meat" meant to feed the gods. Among some ancient northern European tribes, the dead of both sides were viewed as sacrificial offerings, and the ravens who ate them were seen as representatives of the deity to whom the sacrifice was offered.[35] In the oldest Hindu epic, the Mahabharata, the final battle becomes a sacrificial ritual presided over by the god Krishna: "Trembling and quivering, they were slain like animals in a sacrifice."[36]

If battle is a kind of sacrifice and sacrifice is, according to Jay, a kind of birth, we can infer that battle has served at times as a peculiar means of reproduction. Battle makes a warrior out of a boy; and his rebirth as a warrior, no less than his original birth, is marked by the shedding of blood.

In extreme, or perhaps ideal, cases, warriors dispense with biology altogether and reproduce themselves entirely through the mechanism of war. The Janissary armies that fought for Muslim princes in the fourteenth and fifteenth centuries were celibate, at least in regard to women, as were the medieval European warrior-monks, the Knights Templars and Knights Hospitalers. Shaka, the nineteenth-century Zulu king and military genius, did not allow his men to marry until they reached middle age, and threatened to kill any of his concubines who became pregnant.[37] Such pure and dedicated warriors need no heirs except the young men they initiate through battle, no family but the half-imagined warrior lineage. Warriors make wars, but it is also true that, in what has so far been an endless reproductive cycle, war makes warriors.

> The soldier of Christ kills safely; he dies the more safely. He serves his own interests in dying, and Christ's interests in killing! Not without cause does he bear the sword![1]
>
> —SAINT BERNARD

10
The Sacralization of War

Warriors do not come automatically to a transcendent, or religious, sense of their occupation, any more than do professional chefs or athletes. The only traits universally valued in fighting men are courage and loyalty to one's band or leader, and these values they share with street gangs and organized-crime syndicates. Within the limits of acceptable warriorlike behavior, there is plenty of room for bullying and loutishness of all degrees—and not only toward the enemy of the moment. Gilgamesh, the first warrior-hero of recorded history, had to be distracted from his predations on his own people, who open the story by complaining that "his arrogance has no bounds by day or night. . . . His lust leaves no virgin to her lover."[2]

History offers plenty of warnings about the dangers of underemployed warriors to the civilian population that supports them. In ancient Sparta, young men in a *krypeia*, or secret male society, honed their warrior skills by going to live secretly in the countryside, emerging at night to kill any helots, or serfs, they could find.[3] Rape has been endemic wherever warriors rule and was even legalized in medieval Europe as the feudal lord's droit du seigneur. Knights did not necessarily appear "in shining armor" but sometimes in the guise of the predator, like the spectacularly evil Raoul de Cambrai in the *chanson* of the same name. In the story, Raoul attacks a nunnery, pitches his tent right in the chapel, with his bed at the altar and his hawks mewed to the crucifix, and ends up burning the nuns alive in response to an imagined insult.[4] Similarly bad behavior was not unknown among real-life knights: An early fourteenth-century list of thirty-one sins common among knights includes pillaging, killing priests, and "puff[ing] themselves up with pride."[5]

The European warrior elite, perhaps more than any other, was given to drunkenness and brawling, with unpleasant consequences for the civilian population. Evidence for the role of strong drink goes back to prehistoric times: The distinctive "beakers" left by the mounted warriors who swept through Europe in the third millennium B.C. contained a flavored version of mead.[6] In early Greece, warrior culture centered on the feast, held in the hall of a warrior leader, and featuring long bouts of drinking and boasting.[7] This tradition was carried on by the medieval knighthood, whose castle halls served as both dining rooms and dormitories for the assembled men-at-arms—both barracks and barroom, in other words.

Wherever knights gathered there was the possibility of general violence. Tournaments, so stately and elegant in Hollywood depictions, often degenerated into riots,[8] and the Church tried vainly to ban them. Even church property was not exempt from the effects of knightly high spirits. The noble participants at the knighting of Louis d'Anjou and his brother Charles at a monastery in 1389 were, according to a contemporary chronicler, "driven by drunkenness to all such disorders, that . . . several of them sullied the sanctity of the religious house, and abandoned themselves to libertinage and adultery."[9]

Yet warrior elites, for all their lapses into thuggery, have long sought to make war into something sacred and worthy of general respect. Encouraged, often, by the religious authorities themselves, warrior elites have borrowed all that they could from established religions, ransacking them, as it were, for glorious rationales and colorful fragments of ceremony. Even wars undertaken for no other purpose than loot, or for no purpose at all other than the initiation of a fresh cohort of warriors, achieve a mystic status when fought in the name of the true cross, the Ark of the Covenant, a relic of the Prophet, or the honor of the fatherland. To the true member of the warrior elite, every war can be a holy one.

One of the most direct and obvious ways to sacralize war was to use it as a means of capturing victims for human sacrifice. Here the Aztecs remain the best-studied example. As a nation of warriors and craftsmen, they were dependent on the peoples they conquered for much of their food, for slaves, and for luxury items like gold and decorative feathers. But the gratification of material needs was apparently not enough, by itself, to justify the Aztecs' perpetual campaigns against their neighbors. What made war seem legitimate and just was its contribution to the religious rite of sacrifice. In Aztec Mexico, as in the nineteenth-century west African kingdoms which also practiced the ritual sacrifice of war captives,

> the public sacrifice of war captives advertised military success and the obligation to provide victims for sacrifice supplied a justification for the waging of war.[10]

Historically, war may have gained religious legitimacy in other cultures, too, by putting itself in the service of ritual human sacrifice. It is impossible, especially in retrospect, to sort out the religious excuses for war from its other functions, such as the taking of loot or the perpetuation of a warrior subgroup. The tribute the defeated were required to pay might itself take the form of human sacrificial material. Athens, according to myth, had to send "seven youths and seven maidens" annually to Crete, to be devoured by the Minotaur.[11] And if we ever doubt the human capacity for absolutely disinterested destruction, there were Celtic tribes that, according to the Romans, not only hanged all captured enemies as sacrificial offerings, but killed the enemies' horses, hacked them to pieces, and threw them into a river or lake, along with all the enemies' weapons and gold. This could be dismissed as myth if piles of valuable booty had not been recovered from Danish peat bogs, more or less as described.[12]

In time human sacrifice lost its power to confer sanctity on war—or on anything else, for that matter. There is evidence of moral revulsion against human sacrifice among some of the very peoples who are presumed or known to have practiced it. The Aztec pantheon included not only the bloodthirsty warrior god Huitzilopochtli, but the gentle figure of Quetzalcoatl, who, in some versions of the Aztec mythology, opposes human sacrifice.[13] In Greek mythology, the gods sometimes demand human sacrifice, and sometimes punish humans for practicing it. Ambivalence about the rite shows up, for example, in the various literary treatments of Iphigenia's death. In Aeschylus's version, the girl struggles and pleads, making her death so appalling that even the Chorus must avert its eyes. But in Euripides' play, she is a willing victim—in fact, less a sacrifice than a suicide:

> I have been thinking, mother—hear me now!
> I have chosen death: it is my own free choice.[14]

The abandonment of human sacrifice has often been taken as evidence that humans are capable of moral progress. But the difference between those who fought wars to capture sacrificial victims and those who fight them for more "rational" reasons is, in the end, a rather niggling one. War consists of both fighting and killing, which ordinarily go on far from civilians' view. What distinguishes the practitioners of human sacrifice is that they were able to partially separate these two activities: The fighting would go on on the battlefield, but at least part of the killing would go on later, far from the battlefield, when the prisoners were sacrificed in public view. It is not that the Aztecs were a particularly bloody-minded people; by European standards, their battles seem to have been rather courteous affairs. But they did believe in separating out part of the killing and saving it up, so to speak, for a spectacular event to be witnessed by all.

The use of war to gain sacrificial victims conferred a special religious status on the warriors themselves, but it also served the interests of civilians, who would have had reason to fear a lawless warrior subgroup in their midst. Putting war to work in the service of religious ritual was a way of reminding the warriors that they were still bound by the rules and rituals of the group, that they were not free to deploy their destructive skills at home. In particular, the handing over of captives to a "civilian" sacrificer was a way of stating that while warriors might fight, the power to kill still resided in the group as a whole.

War and the Postsacrificial Religions

Some religions are, of course, more compatible with war and warrior elites than others. Ancient religions such as that of the Greeks had no principled objections to war; they were themselves sacrificial religions, centered on the act of killing. Among the Greeks, notions of morality were largely a secular invention; the gods themselves were amoral and sometimes fomented human wars for the fun of it. Even the Jehovah of the Pentateuch, who was so obsessive about matters of diet and hygiene, was essentially a warrior god: "I will make mine arrows drunk with blood," he thunders at one point, "and my sword shall devour flesh."[15]

But the new religions that arose between the fifth century B.C. (when Siddhartha, who became the Buddha, lived) and the eighth century A.D. (the time of Mohammed) offered an entirely new perspective on life, death, and the shedding of blood—and one that was often hostile to war and all other forms of intrahuman violence. For one thing, the practice of these religions was not centered on ritual bloodletting. Christianity, for example, only recalls the tradition of human sacrifice; it does not literally act it out. Abjuring the "grand aesthetic ceremonial" of the public sacrifice,[16] the new religions demanded individual participation in the form of ethical behavior as well as ritual observances and prayer.

And the new religions defined ethical behavior far more broadly than had the old. One of the reasons historian Karl Jaspers describes them as "post-axial"—implying an advance past some critical watershed—is that the new religions were *universalistic*: They postulated a deity (or, in the case of Buddhism, a far more abstract spiritual entity) who presided over all humans and not just a particular tribe or nation. Even the foreigner now contained some spark of the divine essence, and could not be killed without potentially incurring God's wrath. Thus, at least officially, Buddhism and Christianity condemned the practice of war, while Islam allowed it only against the not-yet-converted.

Why these religions arose in widely separate parts of the civilized world, in roughly the same millennium, is something few historians venture to explain. One factor may have been that animal sacrifice, on the scale demanded by the ancient religions, was simply becoming too costly. Human populations were growing, making herd animals too precious for the old ostentatious displays of piety. In India, according to D. D. Kosambi, the ancient herding economy had given way to agriculture by the time of Siddhartha, and Buddhism sensibly ratified the change by forbidding the slaughter of animals for the purpose of religious display.[17] A similar distaste for sacrifice appears within Judaism at the time of the prophets, perhaps in part for the same underlying reason, and Zoroastrianism, arising between the ninth and sixth centuries B.C., was in some ways a revolt against a "herder priesthood that thrived on performing animal sacrifices."[18]

Another, more frequently cited factor favoring the new religions was the rise, all over the civilized world, of a merchant class.[19] Trade differs from war in that it channels greed into the *nonviolent* acquisition of wealth, and hence requires traits not usually valued by the old warrior elite: truthfulness, reliability, and a capacity for rational deliberation—rather than the warrior's traditional hotheaded impetuosity. Conveniently, the post-axial religions provided a common ethical framework within which commerce could flourish. To again draw on the insightful Kosambi:

> Truth, justice, not encroaching upon the possessions of others show that a totally new concept of individual prop-

> erty had arisen. . . . Without such a morality, taken for granted today, trade would have been impossible. The staunchest of the Buddha's lay followers were traders.[20]

As was, of course, Mohammed himself.

A third factor favoring the new religions was the growth, within complex societies, of a lower class composed of the representatives of militarily defeated peoples. As Karl Luckert writes, these new religions were "movements on behalf of ordinary people" and often explicitly disapproving of warrior elites.[21] Constant warfare, followed by the disenfranchisement or enslavement of the losers, had produced markedly stratified and heterogeneous societies whose lower ranks often seethed with resentment of their conquerors. Like so many other peoples, the Greeks and Israelites within the Roman Empire, the Dravidians in Aryan-ruled India, were subject to ruling castes which had come to power through military force. It makes sense that defeated peoples would be drawn to religions that were inclusive of the lowliest individual, that valorized mercy, and that explicitly condemned the warlike.

The problem of defeat looms large in the Old Testament from Ezekiel on: How to explain a God who allows the wicked and idolatrous Philistines, for example, to triumph over his chosen people.[22] In the New Testament the issue is resolved through a profound renunciation of victory itself. Glory no longer belongs to those who triumph by force but to those who are triumphed over. Revenge ceases to be a temptation, since those who suffer defeat in this world—the poor, the meek, the downtrodden and unarmed—will triumph in the next. God, in fact, came to earth as a poor man and a member of a defeated nation, and he came in order to suffer torture and humiliation at the hands of the conquerors. In the image of the crucified Christ, the values of the ancient warrior elite are inverted: The ruler of the universe assumes the posture of ultimate defeat. God is no longer the beneficiary of sacrifice but the victim, not the predatory Jehovah of the Pentateuch but the prey.

Fittingly, at some point in Christian Europe, a new character comes to play the part of the predator beast, and this is the very antithesis of the deity: Satan.

> In medieval Christian thought the dragon and the serpent were often connected with Satan. Cast from heaven, Satan is depicted in medieval art as a voracious monster who angrily consumes his victims.[23]

Or hell itself, as Burkert reports, was pictured as "a huge devouring animal with yawning jaws."[24]

It is easy to see how a victim-centered religion would appeal to the poor and even to women of higher social rank—both groups that often originated in militarily defeated populations. But it is not so clear why warriors themselves would want to adopt a religion professed by women and other social inferiors. The Roman army of the late empire had gone its own way, in terms of religion, becoming a hotbed of Mithraism—a militaristic, sacrifice-centered religion not shared by Roman civilians and certainly not by women.[25] Presumably, the European warrior elite of the post-Roman era could have remained loyal to their pre-Christian warrior gods, like Mithra or Wotan, while leaving the victim-god Jesus to the poor and the weak. It was the warriors, after all, who were in a position to enforce their beliefs. Yet something very different happened, most clearly in Europe, where the warriors came to worship, and even co-opt as a new kind of warrior god, an earlier warrior elite's most exalted victim.

Christianized War

A merger of warrior values with the religious notions held by common people occurred in other places, too. Islam gave the warrior an honored role (at least when he restricted his hostilities to infidels), and even Buddhism was co-opted by the samurai as a source of power and self-mastery. But in matters of war a certain Eurocentrism may be justified, given the success of Europe's global predations from the sixteenth century on. This eventual burst of expansionism was powered, in no small part, by the remarkable merger of religion and militarism which took place in the Middle Ages, and which has been described by historian Philippe Contamine as both a militarization of the church and a "sacralization of war."[26]

Most historians, Contamine included, tell the story of the merger of Christian and military values from the point of view of the church, in part because the church left a carefully recorded story to tell. It is not on the whole an edifying tale. To its credit, the church made numerous attempts to rein in the warrior elite. An edict issued by the Council of Narbonne in 1045 illustrates the church's attempt to carve out some space, quite literally, for itself and noncombatants generally, decreeing that

> there should be no attacks on clerics, monks, nuns, women, pilgrims, merchants, peasants, visitors to councils, churches and their surrounding grounds to thirty feet (provided that they did not house arms), cemeteries and cloisters to sixty feet, the lands of the clergy, shepherds and their flocks, agricultural animals, wagons in the fields, and olive trees.[27]

At the same time, though, the church was, bit by bit, abandoning its own original commitment to pacifism. Arguably, it had little choice. By the fifth century A.D., when Augustine propounded his doctrine of the "just war"—essentially a defensive war, led by recognized authorities and conducted with a modicum of Christian restraint—the notion of "turning the other cheek" must have seemed either foolhardy or quaint. In the centuries after the fall of Rome, Europe had been harassed by wave after wave of Viking, nomadic Asian, and Muslim Turkish invaders, and the church often emerged as the only institution in a position to organize resistance. A truly Christian, that is, pacifist, church could hardly have survived as an institution in a world otherwise ruled by the sword.

But the church's growing tolerance of violence soon extended to Europe's endless internecine wars, and by the middle of the tenth century mere tolerance was giving way to active participation. In the chaos following the breakup of the Carolingian Empire in the ninth century, historian Alan E. Bernstein reports, "new prayers evolved for armies, for warriors, for swords: 'Lord . . . destroy the enemies of your people!'"[28] The church began to make itself useful to the warrior elite by providing ritual blessings for military banners, swords, and other weapons.[29] By the middle of the next century, the church had largely taken over the ceremony of knighting.[30] Church decor began to feature armored heroes as well as the usual tortured saints.

Even the hard-and-fast rule that clerics themselves must abstain from war could be breached with a wink. In the year 1000, Bishop Bernard led the army of the Saxon emperor Otto III to battle, but this sin was mitigated by the inclusion, within his lance, of a few nails from the true cross.[31] The Archbishop of Mainz in 1182 is said to have killed nine men in battle, but since he used a club instead of a sword, he was not guilty of shedding blood. After the battle he donned his pontifical robes and said mass while "a choir of nuns sang sweetly *Gaudeamus*."[32]

For its part, the warrior elite happily adopted the language and trappings of Christianity, if not exactly the spirit. The fifth-century Frankish king Clovis vowed to his Catholic wife, Clotilda, that he would convert if he succeeded in battle against the Alamanni. Victorious, he was baptized, along with three thousand of his army, and resumed his career of conquest.[33] But whatever it did for a knight's military prowess, Christianization no doubt enhanced his credibility among the common people, making him seem and sometimes behave much better than a mounted thug. And for all the literary emphasis on the individual, highborn combatant, the knight was utterly dependent on the contributions of his social inferiors, from peasants to burghers. The brilliant contribution of Christianity was that it provided a worldview uniting the highborn knight and the lowly serf, the oppressor and the oppressed.

Chansons and other contemporary accounts have little to say about the common man's role in medieval warfare, which was invariably portrayed as the thunderous clash of individual mounted knights. But, as I emphasized in the last chapter, someone had to forge the knight's weapons and armor,[34] care for his horses, and assist him in various ways once he was weighed down by his gear. In myth and legend, the knight's sword often has a mystical provenance; in reality, craftsmen sweated over the forge for days at a time to temper the steel. Then there were the various auxiliaries who accompanied a knight to battle: three to five men, including a mounted squire and a few lightly armed "boys" on foot.[35] Long campaigns required retinues of craftsmen and laborers—blacksmiths, for example, and miners to dig under the walls of besieged cities. In addition, there were large numbers of peasant foot soldiers: archers, pikemen, and lightly armed men whose tasks included creeping beneath the horses of enemy knights and stabbing them in the belly, as well as dispatching the enemy wounded.[36] These were risky jobs, requiring initiative and motivation. It helped, therefore, that commoners shared a mystic belief system with the warrior elite, and that campaigns were often led by one of the warrior saints, like Saint Michael or Saint George, or by Jesus himself.

The peculiar story of Joan of Arc illustrates Christianity's power to bridge social inequalities for the sake of war. As a girl of peasant birth, Joan was doubly excluded from the adventure of war (though certainly, as a resident of northern France during the Hundred Years War, not immune from its depredations). Yet when she reported having been instructed by saints to lead the French army against the English, no one seemed to find this claim laughable. The only question, both for the Dauphin and for the clerics who cross-examined her, was whether her visions were indeed inspired by saints as opposed to, say, witchcraft or madness. Once their authenticity had been established to everyone's satisfaction, the seventeen-year-old girl was indeed given an army to lead, or at least lead in a symbolic fashion. To the royalty and nobility of France, as well as the peasantry, it went without saying that the Christian deity would find a way to intervene in the military affairs of mortals.

Christianization also had a practical impact on the warriors' relationship to commoners. "Chivalry," as the Christianized warrior code is known, required that knights be defenders of the weak, meaning women and the unarmed generally, as well as of the church. The late-twelfth-century poem *L'ordene de chevalrie* drew an analogy between the knight's relationship to the common people and his relationship to his horse. He leads them; they, in turn, support him[37]—and no doubt they supported him more willingly if he refrained from raping their daughters and snatching their pigs and cows.

But the warriors also found in Christianity a source of emotional sustenance beyond anything the earlier, "pagan" religions had to offer. Victory was always glorious, but the religion of a defeated people, originally hostile to war, made it glorious even to die in defeat. Those who fell in battle could be seen as martyrs analogous to Jesus, like the legendary knight Roland, who chooses a martyr's death rather than bother his uncle Charlemagne for reinforcements. In the *Chanson de Roland*, the famous knight bleeds to death slowly and beautifully, an inspiring example for Christian warriors everywhere and a sure prelude to eternity in heaven. Christianity glorified the fallen warrior by highlighting the ancient symmetry between sacrificer and sacrifice, which in turn recalls the dual human experience as both predator and prey. As Zoé Oldenbourg writes, the Christian God was

> made more terrible and interesting by the fact that he was also the sacrificial lamb, the victim of the Crucifixion. The invincible warrior and the eternal martyr God, inspiring pity of the most uplifting kind, were one and the same.[38]

The merger of church and military transformed each battle into a religious rite. Flags on both sides were likely to be embroidered with religious images and texts, with the cross itself serving as an emblem for the English, French, Bretons, and others. Before the battle, the rites of confession, communion, and mass were observed.[39] As they charged at one another, the knights uttered war cries invoking the warrior saints: Saint George! for the English, Saint Denis! for the French. Throughout the battle, clergy were kept busy behind the lines praying for their respective sides. Finally, when the battle was over, the victor might, out of gratitude, make an offering of captured armor to the church or dedicate a chapel to the helpful saints.[40]

The apotheosis of Christianized militarism—and militarized Christianity—was the Christian *war*. In 1095 Pope Urban II called on European knighthood to capture the Holy Land from the infidel Saracens, making it clear that a major purpose of the crusade was to deflect the knights' predatory impulses away from Europe itself:

> Oh race of the Franks, we learn that in some of your provinces no one can venture on the road by day or by night without injury or attack by highwaymen, and no one is secure even at home.

We know he is not talking about common, or lowborn, criminals because it emerges in the next sentence that the solution to this problem is a reenactment of the "Truce of God," meaning voluntary restraint on the part of the knights, whose energies are now to be directed outward toward the infidels:

> Let all hatred depart from among you, all quarrels end, all wars cease. Start upon the road to the Holy Sepulchre to wrest that land from the wicked race and subject it to yourselves.[41]

Militarily, the Crusades were largely a disaster for the Christians, but they did serve to cement the fusion of the cross and the sword. The church's concept of the "just war" had always been something of a grudging concession to reality. Here, though, was a war that was not only "just" but necessary and holy in the eyes of God, Christendom's first *jihad*. Those who participated in Europe's internal wars were often required to do penance for the sin of killing; but participation in a crusade had the opposite effect, cleansing a man from prior sin and guaranteeing his admission to heaven. It was the Crusades, too, that led to the emergence of a new kind of warrior: the warrior-monk, pledged to lifelong chastity as well as to war. In the military monastic orders of the Knights Templars and the Knights Hospitalers, any lingering Christian hesitations about violence were dissolved. The way of the knight—or at least that of the chaste and chivalrous knight—became every bit as holy as that of the cloistered monk. And by dispensing with even the sexual and reproductive services of women, the warrior-monks achieved, at least for a few centuries, the ideal and perfect lineage of men.

Even more strikingly than the Crusades against the Saracens, the crusades against European heretics represented the ultimate fusion of church and military. The "heretics" targeted by Pope Innocent III at the beginning of the thirteenth century were among the last European adherents of the original Christian doctrine of nonviolence. The Cathars, as they were called, held that all were criminal and that "the soldier obeying his captains and the judge pronouncing sentence of death were both nothing but murderers."[42] For this and other doctrinal errors, the Cathars were punished with extermination. In return for an offer of indulgences, northern French knights "flayed Provence [home of the Cathars], hanging, beheading, and burning 'with unspeakable joy.'" When the city of Béziers was taken and the papal legate was asked how to distinguish between the Cathars and the regular Catholics, he gave the famous reply: "Kill them all; God will know which are His."[43]

Historians have often attributed the military success of the Muslim Turks (including the "Saracens" encountered on the Crusades) to Islam's supposedly unique affinity for war. It could be argued, though, that Christian Europe went much further in the sacralization of war. Islam, after all, was serious about its prohibition on war between Muslims—a stricture eventually overcome by the use of slave armies for intra-Islamic battles. In the end it did not matter that Mohammed had been a warrior as well as a merchant, while Jesus had been an advocate of nonviolence. It was Christian Europe that was to go on, starting in the sixteenth-century, to conquer most of the world, obliterating indigenous societies or converting them at sword point to the potent combination of Christianity and European-style militarism.

But there was one great flaw in the synthesis of militarism and religion that emerged from medieval Europe: It was ultimately the spiritual property of the warrior elite, and even the church could not reliably and consistently bridge the bitter class divisions that separated this elite from the mass of ordinary people. If wars led by kings and nobles constitute the familiar side of medieval history, class wars—waged by haphazardly armed peasants—make up its "underside." Feudal societies were shaken by sporadic peasant uprisings, called *ikki* in Japan,[44] *jacqueries* in France (for the humble sort of man, "Jacques," who led them). In fourteenth-century England it was a radical priest, John Ball, who instigated a near-revolution by reviving Christianity's original message to the downtrodden:

> In what way are those whom we call lords greater masters than ourselves? How have they deserved it? Why do they hold us in bondage? If we all spring from a single father and mother, Adam and Eve, how can they claim or prove that they are lords more than us, except by making us produce and grow the wealth which they spend? . . . They have shelter and ease in their fine manors, we have hardship and toil, the wind and the rain in the fields. And from us must come, from our labour, the things that keep them in luxury.[45]

It is difficult to gauge the depth of resentment illiterate peasants felt for their warrior overlords. But if Froissart is to be believed (and he may have exaggerated to conform to the prejudices of his wealthy patrons), the participants in peasant rebellions were often no less brutal than the nobles they sought to overthrow—burning down the castles and homes of knights and squires, raping the fine ladies, and "killing and robbing wherever they went."[46] Conventional wars, too, may have provided the peasant foot soldiers with an opportunity to vent their anger at their social superiors—or at least those serving on the other side. While enemy knights commonly treated one another with care, if only because a captured knight could be held for ransom, Froissart reports that the French foot soldiers moved in on the downed Flemish knights at Roosebeke "with no more mercy . . . than if they had been dogs."[47] And it is hard not to see an element of class vengeance in the English bowmen's slaughter of unhorsed French knights at Agincourt:

> Dirty, ragged and wildly excited, they threw themselves upon the men-at-arms and swinging their arms above their heads brought the heavy blades and leaden spikes down with fearful force upon the armour of the men-at-arms . . . hack[ing] at their faces and the weak joints in their armour.[48]

For their part, the nobles had little respect for the peasant foot soldiers who accompanied them to battle. French knights tended to be particularly snobbish, seeing their foot soldiers as "the scum of the people"[49] and sometimes refusing to serve with them at all.[50] At the battle of Crécy, the French king, disappointed by the performance of his (lowborn) Genoese archers, commanded his knights: "Quick now, kill all that rabble. They are only getting in our way!"[51] Instead of being honored for their contributions, lowborn men might well be punished for intruding on their betters' sport. In 1078, the southern German peasants who had taken up arms in defense of their emperor, Henry IV, were, after their defeat, castrated by their feudal overlords for being so presumptuous as to have taken up arms at all.[52] Even the deaths of the poor were laughable; after the battle of Senlis in 1418, "there was a captain who had a crowd of foot-men who all died, and there was great laughter because they were all men of poor estate."[53]

So the religion of war, as conceived by feudal warrior elites, held little room for the common man, much less the common woman. Theoretically, knight and foot soldier fought under the aegis of the same God and ascended together to the same blessed afterlife. But the knight had more ancient and pagan dreams to fulfill: He fought to achieve personal glory, just as Achilles had, and to uphold the honor of his noble lineage. Neither of these uplifting possibilities would be accessible to the common person until the invention of a new type of warfare and, with it, a new kind of god: the nation.

> Happy the blest ages that knew not the dread fury of those devilish engines . . . [which] made it easy for a base and cowardly arm to take the life of a gallant gentleman.[1]
>
> —CERVANTES

11

GUNS AND THE DEMOCRATIZATION OF GLORY

War, ultimately, has no great affection for the men who love it most. General Douglas MacArthur might have preferred to combat the enemy one on one, saber in hand, just as Don Quixote pined for the days before guns, when the joust had determined everything. But no tradition is so sacred to a warrior elite that it cannot be swept aside by new and more effective methods of death-dealing. In the centuries between 1500 and 1800, European warfare changed in ways that fundamentally challenged the primacy of the old warrior elite, and eventually, in some times and some places, the very notion of an elite of any kind. The foot soldier, whose role in medieval warfare had usually been of an auxiliary and janitorial nature—cleaning up, with axes and pikes, after the glorious charges of knights—moved to center stage, while the knight sunk to his present status as the quaint symbol of a romanticized past.

Two "military revolutions" swept Europe between the sixteenth and nineteenth centuries, the first consisting largely of technological and organizational changes—in weaponry, in command structures, in the means of raising and provisioning armies—and the second overlapping with the *political* revolutions of the late eighteenth century. The earlier of the military revolutions reduced the common man to the level of a tiny precision component within that larger engine of war, the bureaucratized army; the later one invested him with the kind of glory once reserved for the warrior elite. Readers wanting more on the purely military side of these changes are referred to the experts I have relied on.[2] Here we will be more concerned with the accompanying transformation of the passions of war, which were, in effect, diffusing downward from the elite to the average soldier and citizen. In the new era, the sacralization of war would depend less on established religions like Christianity, and more on the new "religion" of nationalism.

The gun is usually credited with being the weapon which overthrew the old elite style of fighting, but the change began centuries before the widespread employment of firepower. A prescient observer would have glimpsed the coming transformation of European warfare in 1346, at the battle of Crécy, where the French nobility was mowed down by the arrows of English peasant longbowmen. The principle, in the case of both the gun and the bow, is of action at a distance: Where the elite warrior's goal was to close with an individual enemy and defeat him in single combat, now the bow or the gun propelled inanimate missiles at an enemy whose features might never be visible. The killer and the killed could be many yards away from each other, even crouched, unheroically, behind bushes or rocks.

One crucial feature of the missile-propelling weapons was that they were far cheaper than the ponderous equipment of the old-time knight. Each peasant could fashion his own bow, if necessary, and handheld guns became increasingly affordable at the end of the eighteenth century when mass-production methods began to be applied to their manufacture. Guns and bows were also far easier to learn how to use than the knight's complex armamentarium; a knight began his training in boyhood, but a bowman or a gunner could be readied for combat in months or weeks. Cheap weapons and cheaply trained men almost guaranteed that the size of fighting units would rise—from tens of thousands of men in the sixteenth century to hundreds of thousands by the eighteenth.

Missile-based warfare favored mass, sub-elite armies in another way, too: It made killing an impersonal business, requiring little motivation on the part of the individual gunner or bowman. The missile-bearing foot soldier did not meet his enemy with a shouted *défi*, or challenge, in which each announced his noble lineage; he did not have to meet him at all, since he barely had to see him to make him a target. The victim might be a nobleman of intimidating stature and wealth, or he could be a peasant foot soldier like oneself. The archer or gunman might never know which individual had been doomed by his arrow or bullet, might never be able to separate the screams of pain his weapons had occasioned from the general din of battle. "Would to God," one French nobleman complained of the gun,

> that this unhappy weapon had never been devised, and that so many brave and valiant men had never died by the hands of those . . . who would not dare look in the face of those whom they lay low with their wretched bullets.[3]

Only slowly, and with great reluctance, did the European warrior elite adapt to the new regime of killing-at-a-distance. Even after their efficacy had been repeatedly demonstrated, no knight would think of taking up the bow and arrow, which had been seen by the European warrior elite as cowards' weapons since the time of the Trojan War. "Cursed be the first man who became an archer," declared one *chanson de geste*; "he was afraid and did not dare approach."[4] Real warriors, in the knightly tradition, sought the intimacy of close combat, nobleman on nobleman, and refused to crouch, as archers often did, for cover. Death and defeat were preferable to the slightest loss of social standing.

No story of elite resistance to technological change is more baffling or pathetic than that of the French knighthood in the Hundred Years War with England. As if in a state of collective psychological denial, the French repeated the disaster of Crécy by riding to their deaths in a hail of arrows again at Poitiers in 1356 and once more, in 1415, at Agincourt. Their eventual acceptance of a peasant girl as a military leader is probably best understood in the context of this technological crisis and the profound demoralization it occasioned. Since the charge of armored knights, which had been the tactic of choice for more than five hundred years, no longer seemed to work, Archbishop Jacques Gélu had advised the king that "God might well have chosen a peasant girl to save France in order to 'humble the proud' who had failed."[5] Once ensconced in her command, Joan was able to cut through the technological conservatism of more experienced warriors in another way: For all her otherworldliness, she was a pioneer in the use of artillery in battle and helped establish gunpowder as a routine tool of war.[6]

It was the gun that most decisively leveled the killing fields,* causing warrior elites almost everywhere to hold out against its explosive power for as long as they could. In Egypt, the elite Mamluk warriors disdained the gun. In Italy, one sixteenth-century condottiere ordered the eyes plucked out and the hands cut off of any enemies caught with firearms.[7] Japan went the furthest, with the central government actually banning the gun a few decades after its introduction by Europeans in 1543. As Noel Perrin has written, the Japanese warrior elite had been quick to grasp the gun's potential threat to their entire social system: "It was a shock to everyone to find out that a farmer with a gun could kill the toughest samurai so readily."[8]

---

*The replacement of the bow and arrow by the gun is not as obvious an improvement as one might think. At the beginning of the sixteenth century, when many localities were making the conversion, a well-trained archer could shoot far more rapidly and accurately than a man with an harquebus. One attraction of the gun, though, was that it took less training (Parker, *Military Revolution*, p. 17). But firearms also held a less rational fascination, McNeill suggests, because of both the noise they made (probably at that time the largest man-made noise ever) and their sexual symbolism (McNeill, *Pursuit of Power*, p. 83).

Elite resistance to the gun underscores a contradiction inherent in the very notion of a warrior *elite*. The point of war is to win, but elite warriors have another aim, too, which is to preserve their status as an elite. For long periods of time, these aims may be completely consistent, since members of hereditary warrior elites are likely to be the best trained and best suited to command. In times of technological change, though, the elite's status-consciousness often takes the form of a deep and fatal conservatism, a tendency to cling to favored weapons and methods well into their obsolescence. The Japanese samurai class could indulge themselves in two more centuries of sword-fighting only because of their geographical isolation. But on the vast and heterogeneous European land mass, such vainglorious traditionalism could not be maintained for long. Eventually, the imperative of winning had to assert itself over the cherished perquisites of class.

The way in which the European warrior elite adapted to missile warfare was by attempting to forge large numbers of armed men into a single mega-weapon—an army—which could be effectively wielded by a small number of men at the top. Medieval wars had been fought not by "armies" in any recognizable, modern sense but by loose collections of men, often under little or no central command. The relatively small size of medieval forces—numbering in the thousands or, at most, tens of thousands of men—made a certain amount of anarchy tolerable. But one of the first results of missile warfare was to increase the number of troops assembled at any engagement. The sniper's occasional well-aimed bullet or arrow would not suffice; a veritable rain of lethal arrows or bullets was required. As a French observer noted in the late fifteenth century, "The supreme thing for battles are the archers, but let them be by the thousands, for in small numbers they are worth nothing."[9]

Once one political entity had upped its numbers of troops, others were required to follow suit. Arguing for an increased military budget, a speaker in the English Parliament complained in 1733 that "the eighteen thousand men proposed bears no proportion to the numbers kept up by our neighbors."[10] By that time, most European states had gone well beyond the old practice of recruiting foot soldiers or mercenaries in an ad hoc manner for each war as it came along. Standing armies, in which thousands of men were kept in combat-ready condition even in times of peace, became the rule in most places in the seventeenth century.

The sheer size of the new armies necessitated rigid systems of discipline and command. For one thing, members of the old military elite could hardly trust a huge assemblage of lowborn men—all of them probably unwilling conscripts, and each of them equipped with lethal firepower—unless these troops had been beaten into a condition of slavish docility. Within the new armies, the old warrior elite gave up the heroic combat role of the knight and assumed the bureaucratized leadership role of the officer—whose power of the individual officer over his men was so absolute that, as historian Hans Delbrück observed of the Prussian military, "the soldier had to fear his officer more than the enemy."[11] A seventeenth-century French military manual details the punishments an officer could apply at his own discretion: Officers down to the level of sergeant major were entitled to kill recalcitrant underlings with their swords; captains could strike with the flat of the sword; sergeants could beat their men with the "shaft of the halberd," though not with the sword; and so on.[12]

But punishment implies a prior breakdown of discipline. There were methods developed at the end of the sixteenth century to ensure that discipline was so thoroughly internalized that no one would think of disobeying an order—that, ideally, no one would think at all. A Dutch prince, Maurice of Nassau, came up with the idea of the drill. Instead of being trained once and then trusted to use their skills on the battlefield, troops were to be trained incessantly from the moment of induction to the very eve of battle. They were to form ranks, march, and manipulate their weapons, over and over, in any kind of weather, as a full-time occupation. One point of the drill was to speed up cumbersome operations like the loading of muskets, which, in a remarkable foreshadowing of twentieth-century industrial Taylorism, was broken down into thirty-two separate steps that were to be repeated in unison by those performing the drill.[13] At the same time the drill also served to eliminate any "downtime" during which troops could lapse into sedition or brawling, as well as any vestige of individual initiative. Even as elite a warrior as Frederick the Great, whose role in the drill was surely a commanding one, could write home wearily: "I come from drill. I drill. I will drill—that is all the news I can give you."[14]

Ideally, the resulting "clockwork army," to borrow Manuel de Landa's phrase,[15] could be rolled out onto the battlefield as if it were a single, huge instrument of war. Little was required of the human units of this machine except that they stand their ground and fire on command. Aiming was not expected[16] or originally even worth the effort, given the inaccuracy of early firearms like the musket and arquebus. The idea was simply to direct volley after volley of bullets at the enemy until one or the other side ran out of men. Thus, for the average soldier, courage was less in order than fatalism and a kind of stolid passivity. As O'Connell writes:

> The system required him to stand imperturbably at point-blank range, disdaining all cover, and fire methodically into enemy ranks until either small arms, cannonball, or cavalry saber cut him down.[17]

Needless to say, mortality rates were shockingly high, with probably one out of four or five soldiers dying in each year of active service. "Enlistment," as historian Geoffrey Parker observes, "in effect, had become a sentence of death."[18]

Such high rates of military "wastage" reinforced the need for ever larger armies. The bigger the army, the greater the need for systematic methods of discipline and control, and with better methods of discipline and control, the bigger the army could be. Thanks to a general increase in the European population, the only limits on this dynamic were the difficulties of paying and provisioning standing armies that were now often the size of major cities. By the late eighteenth century, Prussia was spending approximately 90 percent of its revenue on the military, while France was devoting two thirds of its budget to its army alone.[19]

One consequence of the increase in army size was the emergence of a new form of social organization: the modern bureaucratic state. In Delbrück's words:

> As a prerequisite, or perhaps we should say a side effect, of the great change in the army, there developed a new administration of the state, a bureaucracy whose mission was to collect the taxes required to maintain the army.[20]

Other factors were also militating toward the formation of bureaucratic states—most notably, the rise of commerce, which required that there be some central authority to enforce contracts and impose uniform systems of currency and weights and measures. But the needs of armies no doubt outweighed the convenience of merchants. Prussia, for example, as historian Michael Howard has written, "was not so much a State which possessed an army as an army which possessed a State," and was created by the Hohenzollern dynasty "primarily to provide an army to support their power."[21] In the age of mass armies, the unit of militarism could no longer, obviously, be a small-scale feudal holding, a duchy or a barony. It had to be a centrally administered land mass containing sufficient productive resources to feed and lodge tens or hundreds of thousands of essentially nonproductive males at all times—that is, a nation-state.

The preeminence of war as a factor leading to the formation of bureaucratic states is nicely illustrated by an example from a very different time and place: China in the third century B.C. In ancient China's "military revolution," aristocratic charioteers gave way to massed infantry armed with swords and spears. The old style of warfare had involved forces of no more than ten thousand men per battle, while the new mass armies numbered ten times that. As a result, Parker notes, the old rough-and-ready style of governance would no longer do:

> Naturally, military changes of this magnitude presented chronic problems of supply and command which forced the warring states to reshape their political structure; and so most governments changed from something resembling a large household, with most important offices in the hands of the ruler's relatives or leading noblemen, into an autocratic state run on behalf of a despotic prince by a salaried bureaucracy.[22]

Just as the elite style of warfare had called forth feudalism in settings as different as medieval Europe and Japan, mass armies everywhere led to the bureaucratic state. The means of destruction, as we have observed, play a decisive role in the shaping of human cultures.

But the emergence of the nation-state as an administrative unit tells us nothing about the beliefs or passions of the people who called it their own. For our purposes, the most important consequence of the mass army was that an ever larger proportion of the male population was undergoing a wholly new kind of experience which would lay the basis for a new kind of passion: that of nationalism.

Well before notions like "France" or "Italy" or "the fatherland" had the power to stir and uplift people, soldiers in the new mass armies were experiencing directly what it meant to feel like "part of something larger than oneself." Armies were still often multinational groupings, bringing together men of different dialects and languages. But it was in these armies, as George L. Mosse has written, that "most volunteers, but many conscripts as well . . . experienced a new kind of community held together by common danger and a common goal."[23] The spreading imposition of uniforms, along with the relentless drilling, necessarily helped heighten this new sense of community in the average soldier. A member of the old warrior elite derived his identity from his place in a noble lineage of warriors; a soldier in the new armies derived his from his membership in a living mass of warriors capable of marching, working, and fighting as one.

This was not, of course, an experience that most men welcomed or sought out. Given the barbarous discipline and the high chances of dying in battle, men went to great lengths to avoid conscription or, once conscripted, to escape. Desertion rates were astronomical by present-day standards; "at certain times," Parker tells us, "almost an entire army would vanish into thin air."[24] For a lower class which had not yet experienced the discipline of the factory, whose members would not ordinarily participate in any collective endeavor on a scale greater than a harvest, army life must have been a rude and terrifying ordeal.

But there were also the first stirrings of something else—if not yet nationalistic fervor, then something far more basic. We have no records of the feelings and impressions of ordinary soldiers in this period,[25] but William H. McNeill has drawn on his own experience in World War II to provide a firsthand insight into the psychological effect of drill. The "movement of the big muscles in unison," he writes, "rouses echoes of the most primitive level of sociality known to humankind." A rhythmic bonding of individuals develops, which, he speculates, is linked to the dance and to the noisy, foot-stamping confrontations of prehistoric humans with animals.[26]

The technical term for this experience is "phase entrainment": the process through which a number of individuals synchronize their movements or activities. Humans voluntarily seek entrainment by, for example, dancing in circles or lines, participating in parades and precision marching teams, or, as sports spectators, chanting and performing synchronized movements like "the wave." So far as I can determine, psychology has little to say about this desire to achieve rhythmic conformity with our fellows. But whether sought freely or imposed by a drill sergeant, entrainment can provide a deeply satisfying, and often uplifting, experience of "boundary loss," which leads, in its extreme form, to ecstatic trance.[27] Through such forms of "muscular bonding," McNeill conjectures, we catch a glimpse of the long lost "primary community" of the prehistoric human band.[28]

It was not, of course, a fully functioning human community that was being shaped in the mass army of early modern Europe. Armies do not produce goods or reproduce human beings; in fact, the despotically controlled armies of the time could not even feed themselves, since the danger of desertion ruled out the foot soldier's traditional right to wander off and forage for himself. If such an army can be analogized to a living thing, it was a huge, slow-moving, predatory creature that had somehow lost the ability to ingest its own prey. It was a complex beast, as McNeill writes, with its rigid command structure serving as "a central nervous system, capable of activating technologically differentiated claws and teeth,"[29] but a beast whose only function was to kill.

But this beast, which more and more of Europe's young men were now finding themselves part of, was still at a very primitive stage of evolution. Its central nervous system worked in only one direction: from the top down, general to officer and officer to men, meaning from nobleman to commoner. Frederick the Great wanted his men to understand that their every act "is the work of a single man," namely, their commander. Among the rank and file, he wrote, "no one reasons, everyone executes."[30] In no way, then, was the early modern mass army designed to exploit the fact that its ultimate sub-units were themselves sentient beings capable of taking in information and making decisions for themselves. Not expected to aim and seldom trusted to scout, the individual soldier hardly needed sense organs at all, just the habits of repetitive motion established by the drill. The next stage of the mass army's evolution would initiate a much fuller exploitation of the soldier's human capacities, including his emotions as well as his skills. But this would require another, and more far-reaching, kind of revolution.

Revolution from Below

The American Revolution was Europe's first confrontation with an armed force which had no use for the elite etiquette of war. Rather than standing in formation and firing on command, the colonists hid behind trees and stone walls, aiming at carefully selected targets. Mostly farmers, they delighted in picking off the aristocratic British officers, who, on a European battlefield, might still have expected to be treated with the deference appropriate to their class.[31] From the British point of view, the Americans had no notion of honor at all. They were not above dressing in red coats in order to sneak behind enemy lines or, on occasion, pretending to surrender only to get close enough to fire a punishing volley. Whereas the troops commanded by the British (many of them Hessian mercenaries) had been trained to shoot, the Americans knew how to *kill*.

The American advantage derived not only from the rebels' higher morale but, as O'Connell suggests, from their more direct and primitive relationship to nonhuman life.[32] Late-eighteenth-century Europe offered the common man little experience of the hunt; game animals were largely confined to aristocratic estates, where mounted noblemen pursued them for sport. America, in contrast, was still relatively rich with game, and the average farmer was a deer stalker who came to the battlefield armed with a hunting rifle and a hunter's skills. If he had fought humans before, they were in most cases Indians, who were themselves in the habit of fighting men as if they were animals: by stalking and shooting from cover. The Indian warrior became the colonists' tutor. As one New Englander wrote in 1677:

> In our first war with the Indians, God pleased to show us the vanity of our military skill, in managing our arms, after the European mode. Now we are glad to learn the skulking way of war.[33]

In part, then, the transformation of war-making in the nineteenth century was spurred by Europe's contact, via the America revolutionaries, with what were essentially Stone Age methods of killing.

It took more than a decade for the lessons of the American Revolution to be applied to the European battlefield. The European officer corps was still overwhelmingly aristocratic, addicted to its rituals and distrustful of its troops. Historian Alfred Vagts provides a pointed example of the Europeans' unwillingness to learn from the Americans:

> When it was proposed on the Continent in the 1790's to dull the luster of firearms [in order to make them less obvious targets], as had been found advisable in the American war, a military author protested: the soldier would then have too little to polish, and "lose his *point d'honneur* of cleanliness."[34]

Before Europe could make use of the new form of warfare pioneered (or, we might say, rediscovered) in America, a revolution on European soil had to overthrow the ancient and ossified relationship between noble and commoner or, as they were known in the new mass armies, officer and enlisted man.

The French Revolution, following on the heels of the American one, had profound effects at both ends of the military hierarchy. At the lower levels, it meant that the average soldier no longer saw himself as the subject of a king but as the citizen of a nation. This sudden elevation of his perceived status made him less willing to die in the old way, by standing in stiff lines and firing volley after volley on command. But it also made him more willing to "give his life," if that was required, because he now had something to give it for: the nation, conceived as *his* nation. Before the revolution, according to Mosse, no effort had been made "to encourage the soldiers to identify with the aims of [the] war. It was assumed that they had no interest in them." After the revolution, however, "the soldier no longer fought merely on behalf of a king, but for an ideal which encompassed the whole nation under the symbols of the Tricolor and the *Marseillaise*."[35] As historian J. Christopher Herrold writes, the soldiers of the revolutionary French army were

> the first European soldiers in more than a century who could regard the cause for which they were fighting as their own, the first commoners permitted to distinguish themselves by such acts of personal initiative and heroism as until then had been tolerated only in the noble-born.[36]

At the same time, the effect of the French Revolution was to disperse, discredit, and destroy the upper levels of the military hierarchy—some of whom were executed or exiled as royalists while others deserted to the armies of the European allies who had rushed in to suppress the revolution. With the old French warrior elite in disarray, the way was open for a ruthless and brilliant newcomer, Napoleon Bonaparte, to harness the military possibilities unleashed by both revolutions, American and French.

In contrast to the aristocratic commanders he replaced, Napoleon had only one objective in war: total victory, meaning the total defeat of his adversaries. Members of the traditional military elite had always been saddled with the often conflicting priority of maintaining their power within their own armies and societies. But Napoleon, an obscure Corsican propelled to power by the spirit of *liberté, égalité, fraternité*, had no conservative social agenda to distract him from the business of winning. He could dispense, for example, with the slow-moving supply trains that often literally paralyzed conventional armies—both because his officers did without the luxuries usually attendant on officer status (his men even did without tents)[37] and because his troops could be trusted to run loose and forage for food on their own.[38]

Nothing better illustrates the new autonomy and status of the French citizen-soldier than Napoleon's attitude toward desertion. In the classically precise, obsessively drilled Prussian army, desertion was to be prevented "by avoiding camping near a forest; by having the men visited often in their tents; by having [mounted] hussar patrols ride around the camp . . . by not allowing soldiers to fall out of ranks . . . by having hussar patrols move along on the side when the infantry is passing through a wooded area."[39] Prussian soldiers, in other words, were treated more or less like prisoners of war by their own officers. Napoleon, in contrast, instructed his officers to rely on peer pressure:

> The commanders will urge the soldiers to feel that those men [deserters] are shameful, for the greatest punishment

in a French army for not having participated in the dangers and the victories is the reproach that is directed to them by their comrades.[40]

It was on the battlefield, though, that the new citizen-soldier proved himself an irresistible military innovation. The revolutionary nobleman Lafayette had attempted to introduce American tactics to the French military, but credit for "Americanizing" European warfare goes to Napoleon. His troops did not simply stand and deliver clockwork volleys like a single giant unit of artillery; they skirmished, as the American colonists had, overwhelming the relatively inert armies of their enemies with swarms of self-mobilizing sharpshooters. Where old-regime armies were slow-moving and, for all practical purposes, blind beasts whose brains were concentrated entirely in a few top commanders, Napoleon's army was one that moved fast, fed itself on the ruins of its prey, and derived its intelligence and sensory input from hundreds of thousands of individual mobile units. And everywhere Napoleon's ambitions drove him—throughout Europe, deep into Russia, even south into Egypt—the old-regime armies gave way before this new and more highly evolved form of predator beast.

The French and American revolutions are, of course, best known for their effects in realms unrelated to the business of killing. They shattered the centuries-old structures of aristocratic and dynastic domination, thereby opening up an entirely new sense of the possible—not only to the middle-class (and, in the American case, often wealthy) men who led them, but to the poor and, eventually, to that perennial lower class, women. The French Revolution in particular revised the calculus of human hope and despair, convincing some that real change for the better is within reach, and others that no real change is ever possible, only a bloody reshuffling of the people on top.

But from a military point of view, the effect of the revolutions was brutally simple: They made possible, for the first time, the full exploitation of the killing power of the gun. The potential had always been there, but it could not be utilized in old-regime societies with their rigidly old-regime armies, in which the use of the gun had been reduced to a ritual of drill. The promise (and horrific menace) of the gun could be fulfilled only by a gun bearer who was capable of seeing and moving and taking aim on his own—and this was the new revolutionary citizen-soldier.*

Inevitably, such a drastic change in the practice of war had to affect the passions men brought to war. In the new era, notions of glory and sacrifice could no longer be confined to a narrow hereditary class of warriors, because the new method of fighting made every man a warrior in the old-fashioned sense. Like the highborn knight or samurai, the citizen-soldier was expected to display initiative, make lightning judgments, and perform acts of heroism. At the very least, he in turn could expect to share in the "glory" of war—the renown and tangible marks of esteem formerly reserved for valorous members of the warrior elite. The first step in the crafting of a new, mass religion of war was, accordingly, what we might call the democratization of glory: In the American and French revolutionary armies, honors and distinctions such as medals and stripes were awarded, for the first time, to ordinary soldiers.[41]

The effect of this was to undermine the ancient association between "nobility" and hereditary wealth. In the medieval hierarchy of values, qualities such as courage and altruism were almost inseparable from membership in the economic elite, so that words like "noble" and "base" referred to both character and social standing. Noblemen, in the economic sense, were expected to be courageous and self-sacrificing in war, but no one "expected to find moral qualities in the lower classes who made up the soldiery—neither courage,

*Writing later in the nineteenth century, Karl Marx expected socialist revolution to bring human social relations into line with the technological promise of the newly industrialized means of production. Obviously, human relationships could not remain stuck in, say, the feudal era, at a time when production was taking place in steam-powered factories. What Marx did not notice is that the "bourgeois" revolutions, French and American, had already succeeded in bringing the "social relations" of war into line with "the means of destruction."

nor loyalty, nor group spirit, nor sacrifice, nor self-reliance."[42] The presumed character defects of the average foot soldier had long been recognized as a military handicap. In the very first European revolution, that of the English in 1660, Oliver Cromwell had written to his cousin and fellow revolutionary John Hampden:

> Your troops are mostly old, worn-out serving men, wine bibbers, and similar riff-raff. On the other hand, the enemy's troops are sons of gentlemen and young men of position. Do you believe that the courage of such miserable and common fellows will ever be equal to that of men who have honor, courage, and resolution in their hearts? You must seek to raise men of a single spirit and—do not begrudge me what I am saying—of a spirit that is equal to that of gentlemen.[43]

If the mass armies of the early modern period had proletarianized the foot soldier, reducing him from the status of peasant to that of a cog in a machine, the revolutionary armies of the late eighteenth and nineteenth centuries now "noble-ized" him. He too had a shot at glory; he too had "honor" to defend; and he too possessed what had once been the trappings of the nobly born—a flag, for example, which now symbolized a vast population rather than a single dynasty. According to Vagts, "The tricolor [flag of France] gratified emotions previously enjoyed only by the nobility. In short, the whole nation had become the nobility."[44]

The trade-off for this elevation in status was that the average male now risked a much higher chance of dying in battle than had his peasant ancestors in the era of knightly combat. Napoleon was particularly wanton in his squandering of men as "cannon fodder," expecting them not just to stand and shoot but to charge fearlessly at the enemy's artillery positions. He fielded the largest armies Europe had ever seen, numbering in the hundreds of thousands, and lost a total of 1.3 million to 1.5 million of his own men in the course of his conquests—enough to leave a lasting dent in the population of the nation whose interests he supposedly fought to advance.[45] In exchange for being "noble-ized" by the new revolutionary ethos, the soldier was expected to more willingly "give" his life; and in exchange for giving his life, he would be given a share of glory.

But the "democratized glory" accessible to the average soldier was a strangely depersonalized version of the glory sought by members of the traditional warrior elite. The knight or samurai wanted glory for himself as an individual, or at most for his noble lineage. It was his own name that he announced in his battlefield challenge to the enemy, his own name that he hoped would be remembered forever in epics and *chansons*. But the kind of glory held out to men in the armies of George Washington, Napoleon Bonaparte, and all military leaders since their time need have no name attached to it at all. Democratized glory can be thoroughly anonymous glory, of the kind celebrated in the peculiar institution of the tomb of the "unknown soldier." As Benedict Anderson writes:

> No more arresting emblems of the modern culture of nationalism exist than cenotaphs and tombs of Unknown Soldiers. The public ceremonial reverence accorded these monuments precisely *because* no one knows who lies inside them, has no true precedents in earlier times.[46]

This new kind of glory attached not to the individual but to a new kind of entity, the hypothetical collectivity which the French revolutionaries heralded as *la nation*. If the revolutionary armies encouraged individual initiative, they were still mass armies, like those of the old regime. Revolution may have empowered the individual, but the revolutionary armies were still a far cry from being collections of knights, each charging off on his own pursuit of personal glory. Napoleon understood the difference and reserved the notion of "glory" for the old knightly tradition; modern soldiers were not to confuse "love of fatherland" with "love of glory."[47] To one of Napoleon's admirers, the Prussian philosopher Hegel, "true valour" was not "knightly valour" but, rather,

> the true valour of civilized nations is their readiness for sacrifice in the service of the state, so that the individual merely counts as one among many. Not personal courage, but integration into the universal is the important factor here.[48]

And "the universal," meaning the nation and, for Hegel, even more mystical entities beyond that, was in the first instance the modern mass army.

> Behold, the people shall rise up as a great lion, and lift up himself as a young lion: he shall not lie down until he eat of the prey, and drink the blood of the slain.
>
> —NUMBERS 23: 24

12
AN IMAGINED BESTIARY

"The nation" is one of the most mysterious categories of modern thought. It is, most citizens of nations would agree, something that people are willing to die for. But anyone seeking a more precise and scientific definition will be plunged into a swamp of turgid scholarship, which gets even more deeply frustrating if the quest is expanded to include the passions inspired by nations, or *nationalism*. There are not many things people are willing to die for that they cannot point to or touch or even adequately put into words.

One historical reason for the mystery of nations and nationalism is that the great social theorists of the nineteenth century were transfixed by something far removed from the thought of glorious and voluntary death. After the hideous bloodletting of the Napoleonic Wars, Europe lapsed into a period of peace and economic development. It was the capitalist market economy, burgeoning throughout much of

Europe since the early 1800s, that fascinated Karl Marx and Adam Smith. As John Keegan writes, Marx put all his emphasis on the market economy

> largely because, at the time when he wrote, finance and investment overshadowed all other forces in society, and the military class—exhausted by the Napoleonic wars and dispirited by the defeat of its interests in Russia in 1825 and in France in 1830—was at an unnaturally low ebb of self-confidence.[1]

The rise of the market favored a new "materialist" view of humanity—as rational, calculating individuals seeking to advance their individual interests. In fact, the phrase "the Wealth of Nations" in the title of Adam Smith's 1776 volume is a misnomer; only individuals, or corporations, were the possessors of the wealth that built factories and harnessed the power of steam. "Nations" were of little interest to Smith or to Marx, and in the harsh capitalist world their theories described, there was no possible motive for *giving* anything, perhaps especially one's life. In the Marxist paradigm that has played such a large role in Western social thought, nationalism could only be a form of "false consciousness," a seemingly irrational distraction from the class struggle through which working people, banding together, would advance their true interests.

For a long time, the puzzle of nations and nationalism could be sidestepped by assuming that nations are "natural" groupings analogous to biological families. If there were indeed significant genetic commonalities among, say, French people or Germans, then it could be argued that a soldier giving his life for one of these nations is, in some small measure, acting in his own genetic self-interest. But even the most venerable nations turn out to be mongrels. France has its Bretons, with their distinct language and traditions; Britain its Scots and Welsh; Spain uneasily embraces the Basques and Catalonians. Furthermore, most of the world's nations are hardly venerable but are newcomers like Uganda or, for that matter, Italy. Instead of being rooted in fixed bloodlines, nations are fairly arbitrary agglomerations, forever being shaped and reshaped, like Russia or Yugoslavia, by the vicissitudes of politics and war.

In Benedict Anderson's memorable phrase, nations are not natural but "imagined communities," whose imagining has taken a great deal of conscious effort. In the European cases, intellectuals had to resurrect the folklore and epics which could be used to give people a sense of a common past. The printing press, along with the new market in what we now call "information," had to publicize these findings to increasingly literate publics. State-sponsored schools had to impose a common vernacular language on what was often a hodgepodge of dialects and then educate people to literacy in it. Equally strenuous efforts were required in the third world, where national boundaries had often been laid down arbitrarily, for the convenience of the European colonialists.

The work of Anderson, and of historian Eric Hobsbawm, has much to tell us about the creation of nations as a purely cognitive undertaking: How do people come to believe there is such a thing as Serbia or France? What these scholars fail to explain, however, are the passions that attach themselves to the idea of the nation—the emotions of nationalism. In *Imagined Communities*, Anderson seems to promise at the beginning to explain the religious power of the nation over its citizens, but we are quickly immersed in the relatively bloodless business of "imagining"—the construction of common languages and "traditions," and so forth. The reason for this oversight, it seems to me, is that these writers, like most who owe something to the Marxist tradition, pay almost no attention to *war* as a factor shaping human societies. But what is France if not as defined against England or Germany? What is Serbia if not as defined against Germany or Croatia? "From the very beginning," as the military historian Michael Howard has written, "the principle of nationalism was almost indissolubly linked, both in theory and practise, with the idea of war."[2]

The immediate forerunner of nationalism, as we have seen, lies in the experience of community engendered in the mass armies of prerevolutionary (and prenationalist) Europe. In these armies, the individual soldier knows that he is threatened by distant forces, foreigners who wish him dead. He knows too that he is, as an individual, helpless in the face of this threat. But he is not just an individual; he is a unit—as the constant drilling, if nothing else, convinces him—of something far larger and more powerful than himself. What he feels, as a result, is very different from the anomic sense, common to mass societies, of being only "one of many," because in this case the many add up to something greater than the sum of the parts. What he feels is the confidence drawn from collective strength, which can amount, even in the face of death, to a kind of joy.

If group living arose among hominids as a response to predation, it seems at least likely that the human capacity for intense feelings of group identification arose in the same kind of situation. Long before hominids had developed a technology of offense and defense—sharpened sticks or spears, axes and slings—they would have discovered the value of a collective defense: standing together, making noise, brandishing sticks, throwing stones. As I suggested in chapter 5, there may have been, over many thousands of years, natural selection for those humans or hominids who were particularly enthusiastic about the rituals of collective defense—who derived a pleasurable thrill from it, that is—as opposed to those, for example, who abandoned their fellows and ran for the nearest tree. Tree climbers still abound among us, but there is something in the experience of confronting danger as a group—an army, for example, or a mob—that can arouse a kind of exhilaration in almost anyone.

Nationalism, however, is experienced not only by soldiers in armies. It is experienced, and often more strongly, by civilians who are far from any real danger and who have never drilled or fought. Nazi "philosopher" Alfred Rosenberg understood the connection between civilian nationalism and the intense community forged in armies, writing in 1937:

> The German nation is just now about to find its style of life for good. . . . It is the style of the marching column, regardless of where and for what purpose this marching column is to be used. . . . It is a mark of the German style of life that no German wants nowadays to feel himself a private person.[3]

In the age of nationalism, patriotic ceremonies began to be designed, consciously or not, to give civilians the feeling that they, too, constituted a kind of "army," united by common danger and bonded by rhythmic activities analogous to the drill. George L. Mosse observes that the nineteenth century saw "the introduction of rhythm into all ceremonies—marches, parades, and festivals—in order to transform the undisciplined masses into a disciplined crowd." The "Marseillaise" was the first national anthem set to a marching beat; in imitation, other nations began to sing their anthems to similarly infectious and militant rhythms. By "joining in the national liturgy [and] singing national anthems," Mosse writes, large numbers of people now had the experience of "sublimating themselves to the greater national community."[4]

Other developments, too, were encouraging the civilian to participate in the thrill of collective defense—from his or her armchair, in most cases. The various factors which Anderson identifies as preconditions for nationalism: a common language, a sense of common traditions and history, and organized media to engage the citizens' attention. The civilian who reads, on a wall poster or in a newspaper, that the Austrians are marching on Paris or the French are marching on Moscow—that all that is "French" or "Russian" now lies in peril—has been drawn into the alarms and thrills of collective defense. The function of the media in this case is *emotional* entrainment: Just as the drill causes men to move in the same way at the same time, the media are capable of arousing the same or similar feelings in large numbers of civilians at the same time. And as large numbers of people become aware of feeling the same thing at the same time (perhaps only because the media are quick to tell them what everyone else is supposedly feeling), they come to share in the soldier's exalted sense of being part of something larger than themselves.

This awareness of "something larger" into which the individual might merge is repeatedly expressed in nineteenth-century philosophical writings. Where economically oriented thinkers like Marx saw only the isolation and anomie induced by the capitalist economy, others, like Hegel before him and the philosopher J. G. Fichte, saw the emergence of a new collective identity through which, as Fichte put it, "each single person becomes part of an organized whole and melts into one with it."[5] No doubt the two perspectives are, as Marx might say, dialectically connected: As the average citizen experienced an ever greater economic reality of individual isolation, he or she became more open to—and perhaps even eager for—the feeling of submergence within some larger community, no matter how vague and imaginary that community might be.

It is time now to look more closely at this "larger whole" that the individual "melts into." For the soldier it is, in the most literal sense, the army. The first modern armies, starting in the seventeenth century, went to great lengths to strip from each soldier all sense of individual uniqueness and to impress on him that he had no will or ambition other than that which the army allotted to him. Beginning in the late eighteenth century, though, in the era of revolution, the "larger whole" takes on a far less literal meaning, as the nation, which potentially embraces civilians, too. What *is* this new entity that men—and women, insofar as they also achieve the status of citizens—profess themselves willing to die for?

The first clue is that the nation is not a static community, but one that is imagined as existing in time. As Anderson puts it, rather ornately, the nation is "a sociological organism moving calendrically through homogeneous, empty time."[6] It has a past; it is nothing, in fact, without a past. Even brand-new nations attempt to situate themselves within some long-standing tradition (the human struggle for freedom and self-determination, for example) or recurring necessity ("When, in the course of human events . . ."). Much of the work of "imagining" the nation as a community lies in the effort to resurrect or invent a national past, and this past is in most cases defined by war: Serbs look back to the battle of Kosovo in 1389; Americans look to Lexington and Bunker Hill. As Michael Howard has written:

> France *was* Marengo, Austerlitz and Jena: military triumph set the seal on the new-found national consciousness. Britain *was* Trafalgar—but it had been a nation for four hundred years, since those earlier battles Crécy and Agincourt. Russia *was* the triumph of 1812. . . . Italy *was* Garibaldi and the Thousand. . . . Could a Nation, in any true sense of the word, really be born without a war?[7]

The nation, then, is our imagined link to the glorious deeds—or the terrible atrocities still awaiting revenge—that were performed by others long ago.

To put it another way, the nation is a warrior lineage in which everyone can now claim membership. With the democratization of glory, every citizen is encouraged to think of himself or herself as a member of a noble bloodline. "The French" replace the Bourbons. And as every noble lineage had its special heraldry, every nation has its flag. The exaltation that a patriotic citizen feels at the sight of his or her flag is, in part, pride in the imagined lineage to which every citizen now belongs: "Those who came before us" and "those who gave their lives so that . . ."

A similar upgrading of the common person occurred in Japan in the nineteenth century, after the Japanese had reembraced the gun and created a modern mass army. According to Edwin O. Reischauer:

> Modern mass education had quickly spread the strong nationalism of the upper classes of the late Tokugawa period to all Japanese, but more remarkably, it had soon convinced the descendants of peasants, who for almost three centuries had been denied swords and other arms and had been exploited by a military caste above them, that they too were members of a warrior race.[8]

But a lineage is still a lifeless abstraction compared to what we think of as a nation. A lineage cannot act except through its individual representatives, whereas nations "act" all the time: They enter into alliances, issue statements, make treaties, and, most decisively, make war. Even more anthropomorphically, one commonly reads of nations "mourning," "remembering," "risking," and "daring." To thinkers like Hegel and the even more overtly nationalist writers who followed him, the nation was a living being—the "organism" Anderson refers to, only not merely "sociological," but with an occult sort of life of its own. As Hegel put it, substituting "state" for "nation":

> Predicates, principles, and the like get us nowhere in assessing the state, which must be apprehended *as an organism*, just as predicates are of no help in comprehending the nature of God, whose life instead must be intuited as it is in itself[9] (emphasis added).

Even the least philosophical patriot understands the nation as something that "lives," at least in the sense that it will "live on" after him. Hence the readiness, even eagerness, of the patriot to die for his country: If the nation is an immortal being and he is part of it, then, in dying to defend it, he is in fact participating in that immortality. Just as, in ancient religions, blood sacrifice had a fructifying, generative function, helping to make the crops grow and herds increase, so too the sacrifice of oneself for the nation can be construed as a life-giving act. "The Gallipoli campaign has been described as 'the most glorious failure in military history,'" the Sydney *Morning Herald* observed in 1922:

> But was it a failure to Australia? It has made us a nation. Was the price worth paying? Are not nations like individuals? If the nation is to be born, if the nation is to live, someone must die for it.[10]

In the opinion of Hegel and the later theorists of nationalism, nations need war—that is, the sacrifice of their citizens—even when they are not being menaced by other nations. The reason is simple: The nation, as a kind of "organism," exists only through the emotional unity of its citizens, and nothing cements this unity more decisively than war. As Hegel explained, peace saps the strength of nations by allowing the citizens to drift back into their individual concerns:

> In times of peace civil life expands more and more, all the different spheres settle down, and in the long run men sink into corruption, their particularities become more and more fixed and ossified. But health depends upon the unity of the body and if the parts harden, death occurs.[11]

Meaning, of course, the death of the nation, which depends for its life on the willingness of its citizens to face their own deaths. War thus becomes a kind of tonic for nations, reviving that passion for collective defense that alone brings the nation to life in the minds of its citizens. Heinrich von Treitschke, the late-nineteenth-century German nationalist, put it excitedly:

> One must say in the most decided manner: "War is the only remedy for ailing nations!" The moment the State calls, "Myself and my existence are at stake!" social self-seeking must fall back and every party hate [partisan hatred?] be silent. The individual must forget his own ego and feel himself a member of the whole. . . . In that very point lies the loftiness of war, that the small man disappears entirely before the great thought of the State.[12]

Considered as a living being or "organism," the nation is clearly both awesome, like a deity, and at the same time far less admirable, in the sense of being constrained by any kind of morality, than the individuals it comprises. Ordinary citizens must refrain from violence, from theft and other crimes; but the nation, acting in an arena of other nations, is governed by no higher law or (judging from the impotence of institutions like the United Nations and the World Court in our own time) by none worth mentioning. Citizens who have a dispute to settle must seek the judgment of the courts; nations are more likely to duke it out on the field of battle. Citizens who brawl on the streets are punished; nations that go to war are feared and often respected. If the nation as organism has a personality, it is that of the mounted warrior of old: impetuous, belligerent, touchy about all matters of "honor," and in a state of readiness, at all times, for war.

At a more archaic level of the imagination, the nation-as-organism becomes something more, or less, than human. Here is a "creature" that, according to Hegel, requires blood in order to sustain its life—the blood of actual human beings. We recognize, in this view of the nation, another version of humanity's primordial enemy and original deity: the predator beast. And in fact, it is only in the era of nation-states that Europeans routinely came to see the enemy as a monster or beast. In the premodern European warfare of warrior elites, the ties of class and kinship that linked elite combatants on both sides made it difficult to think of the enemy as anything other than human. By the twentieth century, though, newspaper cartoons and propaganda posters routinely represent the other side as a serpent, a vampire, a rat, or even a shark.[13]

But it is not only the enemy nation which comes to resemble a nonhuman threat to human life. Predatory creatures play a major role in the flags, coats of arms, and less formal symbols that various nations adopt for themselves: the eagle for the United States, Germany, Mexico, Poland, and Spain; the lion for Britain, Czechoslovakia, Finland, Kenya, the Netherlands, Norway, and Iran; the hawk for Egypt;[14] the bear for Russia. What we become, when we merge into that "something larger than ourselves" that the nation represents, is what our species has most deeply feared and passionately longed to be.

> The idealization of war by peoples become primitive again is no sign of moral decadence, but on the contrary the sign of a new hero-worship and sacrificial spirit.[1]
>
> —COUNT KEYSERLING

13

THREE CASES OF WAR WORSHIP

Lofty feelings directed toward an intangible, superhuman being: Most people of our own time would recognize these as the ingredients of a religion. The analogy between nationalism—and I mean, of course, "secular" nationalism—and religion has been drawn many times. Benedict Anderson admits nationalism's "strong affinity with religious imaginings."[2] Toynbee went further, seeing nationalism as a replacement for Christianity, which had been vitiated by a soulless capitalist economy. But for the most part the relationship between nationalism and religion has been left as a sort of decorative analogy. Few, if any, have pressed the issue or found it useful to pursue the notion of nationalism *as* a religion, complete with its own deities, mythology, and rites.

One reason we hesitate to classify nationalism as a kind of religion is that nationalism is a thoroughly "modern" phenomenon. It emerges in Europe in the nineteenth century and is spread throughout the third world—largely in reaction to European imperialism—in the twentieth century. Our own modernist bias convinces us that things which are recent must also be "modern," in the sense of being rational and "progressive." On one side of that great historical divide identified as the Enlightenment lie superstition, oppression, and fanatically intolerant religions. It is on the other side, along with science and a faith in progress, where we locate nationalism. To acknowledge that nationalism is itself a kind of religion would be to concede that all that is "modern" is not necessarily "progressive" or "rational": that history can sometimes take us "backward," toward what we have come to see as the archaic and primitive.

It is in times of war and the threat of war that nationalism takes on its most overtly religious hues. During the temporary enthusiasms of war, such as those inspired by the outbreak of World War I, individuals see themselves as participants in, or candidates for, a divine form of "sacrifice." At the same time, whatever distinctions may have existed between church and state—or, more precisely, between church-based religions and the religion of nationalism—tend to dissolve. During World War I, for example, secular authorities in the United States devised propaganda posters in which "Jesus was dressed in khaki and portrayed sighting down a gun barrel."[3] For their part, religious authorities can usually be counted on to help sacralize the war effort with their endorsements. During the feverish enthusiasm of World War I, the Bishop of London called on Englishmen to

> kill Germans—to kill . . . the good as well as the bad, to kill the young men as well as the old. . . . As I have said a thousand times, I look upon it as a war for purity, I look upon everyone who dies in it as a martyr.[4]

But if nationalism is to be more than a temporary passion whipped up by war, it has to find ways to sustain and institutionalize itself apart from more conventional religions. It must, in other words, assume some of the trappings of a conventional, church-based religion itself. Uplifting myths are required, special holidays, and rituals that can be enacted by people who may not feel, at the moment of enacting, any great passion at all. Such rituals and myths keep nationalism alive during times of deprivation and defeat—even during interludes of peace—just as, say, Christian ritual preserves the faith in people who may only occasionally, or once in a lifetime, experience genuine spiritual transport.

It was World War II that saw the full flowering of institutionalized "religious" nationalisms, designed to maintain the fervor of whole populations for months and years at a time. In many ways, the Second World War was a continuation of the first, growing out of grievances implanted by the first war and featuring some of the same alliances and forms of war-making. The tank, the submarine, and the airplane, for example—which did so much to distinguish World War II from the wars of previous centuries—were all first deployed in World War I. So the two wars may be seen as a continuum analogous to the Thirty Years War—a "double war" that could not find a way to stop.[5]

But World War II was distinct in ways that required the *sustained* emotional mobilization of the participant populations. First there was the sheer size of the armies involved. The armed forces of the United States, which had numbered about 5 million in World War I, reached over 16 million at the height of World War II, and other belligerents put similar proportions of their populations into uniform. More important, though, was the fact that this was a "total" war. In World War I, there had still been some inhibitions against the targeting of civilians, who ended up accounting for 15 percent of the fatalities. By World War II, the destruction (and exploitation) of civilians was deliberate policy on all sides. The British used air power to "de-house" the German population; the U.S. bombed the civilian populations of Hiroshima, Nagasaki, and Dresden; the Germans and Japanese destroyed cities and exploited defeated populations as slave labor. As a result, in World War II the civilian share of fatalities, including Holocaust victims, shot up to 65 percent of the total.[6]

Air power made the mass bombings of civilians possible, but it was the huge involvement of civilians in the industrial side of war that made it seem strategically necessary. In the culmination of a trend under way since the beginning of gun-based warfare, millions of civilians were now enlisted in the business of manufacturing weapons and otherwise supplying the increasingly massive armies. In this situation, there were no "innocent" civilians, except possibly children, and the war took on a genocidal character unknown to the more gentlemanly conflict of 1914–18. Nowhere was this clearer than in the U.S. confrontation with the racially different Japanese. William Halsey, the commander of the United States' naval forces in the South Pacific, favored such slogans as "Kill Japs, kill Japs, kill more Japs" and vowed, after the Japanese attack on Pearl Harbor, that by the end of the war Japanese would be spoken only in hell.[7]

In its relentless appetite for "manpower," World War II even challenged the traditional male exclusivity of war. Women not only filled in for missing males in munitions factories and other vital industries; they were invited into the U.S. and British armed forces as clerical and administrative workers, issued uniforms, and allowed to participate in the pageantry, as well as the risks, of war. Soviet women, or at least some of them, briefly achieved full warrior status, "flying combat missions, acting as snipers, and participating in human-wave assaults."[8] In a war in which a civilian faced nearly the same chance of dying as a soldier, there was no "protected" status for females anyway. War was everywhere, and everyone was a part of it.

The distinctively religious nationalisms that emerged around the time of World War II drew heavily on familiar religious traditions but inevitably rendered them more "primitive" and parochial. Recall Karl Jaspers's classification of religions as "pre-" and "post-axial," with the "axis" being that ancient equivalent of the Enlightenment, the heyday of classical Greece. The pre-axial religions were tribalistic, postulating deities with limited jurisdictions and loyalties, while the post-axial religions were, at least in theory, universalistic and addressed to all people alike. Thus all the participants in the bloodbath of World War

II were adherents of, or at least familiar with, creeds that held out some notion of the "brotherhood of man": Christianity in the case of the Americans and Europeans, Buddhism in the case of the Japanese, and, if it can be counted as a kind of "religion," the atheistic ideology of international socialism in the case of the Soviets.

But nationalism is nothing if not tribalistic and cannot, by its very nature, make the slightest claim to universalism: No one expects Poles to offer their lives for Peru, or goes proselytizing among Canadians to win their allegiance to the flag of Nigeria. In the religion of nationalism, the foreigner is always a kind of "heathen" and, except in unusual circumstances, unsusceptible to conversion. To the extent that nationalism replaced the universalistic (post-axial) religions, as Toynbee saw it doing, human beings were abandoning the bold dream of a universal humanity and reverting to their tribalistic roots.

Nowhere was this clearer than in the Soviet Union, where the war prompted Stalin to abandon the universalistic ideology of communism for a narrow and quasi-religious nationalism. Nationalism, he observed, was "the key to maintaining civilian morale,"[9] and he exhorted his people to follow the example of "our great ancestors," a category in which he now listed not only Lenin but such counterrevolutionary figures as tsarist generals, feudal landlords, and even a saint of the Russian Orthodox church.[10] At the same time, the Soviet government displayed a sudden friendliness toward the traditional Russian Orthodox religion, halting anti-religious propaganda and permitting the church to reestablish a Holy Synod. In 1944 the glaringly anachronistic "Internationale" was replaced with a new, more suitably parochial anthem.[11]

Here we will look briefly at three examples of the kinds of religious nationalism that were associated with, or grew out of, World War II: Nazism in Germany, State Shinto in Japan, and the ritualized "patriotism" that emerged in the postwar United States. Each of these served its adherents as a "religion" by offering an entire worldview, justifying individual sacrifice and loss and mobilizing the uplifting passions of group solidarity. And as religions, each has reached back—past Christianity or, in the Japanese case, Buddhism—to more ancient, "pre-axial" kinds of religion: pre-Christian European religion in the case of Nazism, Shinto itself in Japan, and Old Testament Judaism in the case of American nationalism.

Nazism

Nazism may be the closest thing there has been to a freestanding religion of nationalism, unbeholden and even hostile to church-based religions. Historian Arno Mayer observes that

> nazism had all the earmarks of a religion. Its faith and canon were institutionalized in and through a political movement which bore some resemblance to a hierarchical church. The self-appointed head of this church, the führer, exercised strict control over a ranked political clergy, as well as over a select order of disciples, with all the initiates wearing uniforms with distinct emblems and insignias. During both the rise of nazism and the life of the Nazi regime, this clergy acted as both the celebrants and the congregations for a wide range of cultic ceremonies, some of which took place in sacred shrines and places. Most of these ceremonies were conspicuously public and massive, their purpose being to exalt, bind, and expand the community of faithful.[12]

Hitler would have agreed with Mayer. "We are not a movement," he told his followers, "rather we are a religion." The purpose of his Ministry of Propaganda and Enlightenment was to communicate not information, he remarked, "but holy conviction and unconditional faith."[13] Nazism had its own prophet, the Führer; its own rituals of mass rallies and parades; even its own "holy days." According to historian Robert G. L. Waite:

> The Nazi holidays included 30 January, the day [Hitler] came to power in the year he referred to as "the holy year of our Lord 1933," and 20 April, his own birthday and the day when the Hitler youth were confirmed in their faith. The holiest day . . . was 9 November, celebrated as the Blood Witness [*Blutzeuge*] of the movement.[14]

Ordinary citizens found many ways to participate in the new religion. They displayed *Mein Kampf* in their homes in the place of honor once reserved for the Bible; they even addressed prayers to the Führer. The League of German Girls, for example, developed its own version of the Lord's Prayer: "Adolf Hitler, you are our great Leader. Thy name makes the enemy tremble. Thy Third Reich comes, thy will alone is law upon earth," and so on.[15] Ceremonies of Nazi oath-taking consciously paralleled religious rites of confirmation, as this account from a Nazi newspaper makes clear:

> Yesterday witnessed the profession of the religion of the blood in all its imposing reality . . . whoever has sworn his oath of allegiance to Hitler has pledged himself unto death to this sublime idea.[16]

Raised as a Catholic himself, Hitler drew heavily on Christian imagery for his religious fantasies. He often compared himself to Jesus or, in a more Jewish formulation, to the promised Messiah; he thought of the SS as his own version of the Society of Jesus.[17] But he and his followers had no use for Christianity's claims to universalism, nor of course for its appeal to mercy, and took measures to restrict the role of the German churches. A more congenial religious foundation for Nazism could be found in the pre-Christian Germanic beliefs that nationalist intellectuals had dug up and imaginatively reconstructed during the nineteenth and early twentieth centuries. According to Guido von List, a leading popularizer of such *volkisch* ideology, Christianity, with its gospel of love, had been a disaster for the ancient

German people, leading to "the debilitation of Teutonic vigour and morale."[18] Nazism represented a return to the unsullied warrior culture associated with the ancient, tribal Germans. Its swastika was lifted from the mythological Aryan repertory of images, and its state was meant to recall the pagan male warrior band, or *Männerbund*.

Hitler himself was a fanatical devotee of war and nationalism-as-the-religion-of-war. As Keegan argues, much of his outlook and ambition was shaped in the trenches of the western front, where he served as an infantryman from 1914 through 1917 in a regiment which, like so many others, lost more than 100 percent of its initial troop strength. Again and again, young Hitler survived artillery bombardments that left his comrades piled up dead around him,[19] only to see their replacements similarly dispatched. No doubt he owed some of his messianic sense of himself to these narrow escapes, and it may be also that the relentless, industrialized slaughter of trench warfare served as psychological preparation for the annihilation of the Jews and other undesirables at home.

There is no question, though, that the war was for Hitler an experience of religious intensity. He wrote in *Mein Kampf* of being "overcome with rapturous enthusiasm" at the outbreak of the war.[20] On the train ride to the front, when the troops spontaneously burst into "Die Wacht am Rhein," Hitler recalled, "I felt as though I would burst."[21] He was a brave and dedicated soldier, though prone to annoy his comrades by lecturing them on politics or the evils of smoking and drinking. Thoroughly puritanical in his devotion to war, he later described the trenches as a "monastery with walls of flame."[22]

Thus the Nazis did not rely on the traditional Christian rationale—vengeance for the killing of Christ—for their genocidal treatment of the Jews. In the Nazi theology, a major crime of the Jews was to have betrayed their country in *war*. Never mind that German Jews had served loyally in the First World War; never mind that they were, by the thirties, more thoroughly assimilated into gentile society than they had ever been. To Hitler they were a hateful, even mocking, reminder of defeat. In the Nazi imagination, Jews were prominent among those responsible for the famous "stab in the back" that supposedly prevented German victory in the First World War. For the Germans to regain their archaic purity as warriors, all traces of this "foreign" evil had to be expunged. Only then could the nation rise up, as a single organism, from the humiliation of defeat to the status of global predator.

There is a tantalizing detail in Waite's study of Hitler: his fascination and identification with wolves. As a boy he had been pleased to find that his given name was derived from the Old German "Athalwolf," meaning "noble wolf." He named his favorite dog Wolf, called the SS his "pack of wolves," and believed that crowds responded so rapturously to him because they realized "that now *a wolf has been born*."[23] Mimi Reiter, a teenaged Austrian girl who was briefly involved with Hitler in 1926, recalled a curious outburst in a cemetery, where they had gone, at Hitler's request, to visit Mimi's mother's grave:

> As he stared down at her mother's grave he muttered, "I am not like that yet! [*Ich bin noch nicht so weit!*]" He then gripped his riding whip tightly in his hands and said, "I would like you to call me Wolf."[24]

This incident, assuming it was correctly remembered, bespeaks a worldview divided into the most archaic categories of all: not Aryan vs. non-Aryan or gentile vs. Jew, but predator vs. prey. Hitler had seen too much "like that," too many comrades reduced to meat. To be dead is to be vanquished is to be prey. But in Hitler's worldview there is no middle ground, no mode of existence apart from this bloody dichotomy. Those who do not wish to be prey must become predators. Conversely, those who are not predators are prey. To have survived (the First World War, in Hitler's case) is to have achieved the status of the wolf. The ancient European warrior sought to transform himself into a wild carnivore; so too Hitler transcended the failed art student he had been as a youth, survived the war, and became what was, in his own mind, the only thing he could be: a predator beast.

State Shinto

By the time of the Second World War, Japan already boasted a fifty-year tradition of secular nationalism, promulgated relentlessly through every institution of Japanese life. Public education, which reached 90 percent of Japanese children by 1900, included military training for boys and the systematic inculcation of militarism and emperor worship for both sexes. Arithmetic classes did calculations based on battlefield situations; science-class topics included "general information about searchlights, wireless communication, land mines and torpedoes."[25] A reading text offered the story of an unsufficiently enthusiastic sailor, whose mother admonishes him:

> You wrote that you did not participate in the battle of Toshima Island. You were in the August 10 attack on Weihaiwei but you didn't distinguish yourself with an individual exploit. To me this is deplorable. Why have you gone to war? Your life is to be offered up to requite your obligations to our benevolent Emperor.[26]

Among the institutions enlisted to the aims of Japanese imperialism was Shinto, the traditional religion. One of the world's oldest surviving religions, Shinto features thousands of deities, or *kami*, which are worshipped in private homes and at thousands of shrines around the country. Until the Meiji period, in the late nineteenth century, Shinto seems to have been largely apolitical and not even, by the overheated standards of the West, very "religious." It coexisted peaceably with Buddhism, concerning itself with the maintenance of the shrines, the observance of festivals, and the performance of domestic rituals and weddings. It is no wonder that so many of the samurai had preferred Buddhism, with its austere metaphysic and magnificent indifference to death.

But the samurai were a tiny elite, and their Zen Buddhism never attracted a numerically significant following.[27] With the militarization of Japanese society that began near the turn of the twentieth century, it was the ancient "folk religion," Shinto, that was conscripted to the nationalist cause. Japan's victories in the First Sino-Japanese War (1894–95) and the Russo-Japanese War (1904–05), followed by the annexation of Korea, transformed the once reclusive island nation into one of Asia's leading military powers. Shinto priests were now expected to inculcate patriotism along with more ancient forms of piety and to preside over nationalistic rituals, such as the veneration of the emperor's portrait.[28] In return, the Shinto priesthood was given public money for the training of priests and the maintenance of shrines, as well as state support in its growing rivalry with Buddhism. By the eve of World War II, Shinto had become, for all practical purposes, the state religion.

The aim of State Shinto was what historian Helen Hardacre calls a "nationwide orchestration of ritual": the entrainment of the entire population through simultaneous ritual observances. Children began the school year with patriotic celebrations in which the emperor's official statement on education served as "a sacred object" of worship.[29] Passengers on streetcars were "required to stand and bow reverently" when passing the Imperial Palace or important Shinto shrines.[30] Older Shinto rituals were also recruited to the nationalist cause; many of these, according to Ruth Benedict, were benign enough and certainly ancient:

> On the frequent days of rites official representatives of the community came and stood before the priest while he purified them with hemp and paper streamers. He opened the door to the inner shrine and called down the gods, often with a high-pitched cry, to come to partake of a ceremonial meal. The priest prayed and each participant in order of rank presented . . . a twig of their sacred tree with pendant strips of white paper.[31]

What was new about State Shinto was the *synchronization* and centralization of ritual, so that the same ceremonies were now observed by everyone at the same time, from the emperor at a central shrine to peasants at their *yohaisho*, or "place to worship from afar."[32] No one, Christian or Buddhist, was exempted from what Hardacre calls this "daring attempt at social engineering."[33]

To escape charges of religious totalitarianism, state authorities took the position that Shinto was not a "religion" at all but something both more secular and more deeply rooted in Japanese life: the "national spirit" itself. At the metaphysical core of the new nonreligion, and overlapping more traditional Shinto concerns, was the notion of *kokutai*, meaning, literally, nation-body.[34] *Kokutai* parallels the European intellectuals' notion of the nation-as-organism; it was the mystical living entity which arose from the fusion of individual citizens into a single and devoted mass. Symbolized by the emperor and the Shinto shrines, *kokutai* demanded absolute fealty from the citizenry, including a willingness to give their lives. As with European nationalist ideology, dying was no tragedy if one's death strengthened the nation-body, or nation-as-organism. A document published by the Japanese Ministry of Education in 1937 makes an argument that could have been lifted from Hegel:

> Offering our lives for the sake of the emperor does not mean so-called self-sacrifice, but the casting aside of our little selves to live under the august grace and the enhancing of the genuine life of the people of a State.[35]

For all its continuities with the past, State Shinto by no means reflected some preexisting Asian willingness to submerge the individual in the collective whole. "*Kokutai*" may have been an ancient word, but the "Kokutai Cult" arose only in the 1930s. The whole notion of the nation as a mystical "body" or organism centered in the actual body of an individual leader was a phenomenon of the modern era—the era of mass armies. In the era of a mounted warrior elite, Japan had nurtured an elite ethic of war: the samurai code, or *bushido*, analogous to the European knights' Christianized "chivalry." But in the era of gun-based mass armies, *bushido* had to be democratized to include the masses, who were now free, as once only their superiors had been, to experience a "glorious" death in war.[36] Just as European nationalism represented a democratization of an older, elite warrior ethos, State Shinto was *bushido* for the masses.

Like European nationalisms, State Shinto saw war as a sacred undertaking. The popular writer Tokutomi Iichiro described the Second World War in the ritual language of Shinto purification ceremonies: "For the Japanese," he wrote, "the Greater East Asia War is a purifying exorcism, a cleansing ablution."[37] Other influential intellectuals—professors of history and philosophy at Kyoto Imperial University—added that war "is eternal" and should be recognized as being "creative and constructive."[38]

Japanese religious nationalism outdid its European counterpart in one respect: the glorification of the war dead. Europeans honored their fallen soldiers with monuments and holidays; the Japanese worshipped them, and still worship them, as gods. Almost 2.5 million are so honored at the Yasukuni Shrine in Tokyo—not only kamikaze pilots but less distinguished soldiers and even army nurses. At the shrine, which is filled with photos and other memorabilia of the deceased, worshippers leave small plaques inscribed with their prayers. It was in the knowledge that they would become *kami*, and be appealed to by ordinary citizens for intervention in such mundane matters as high school grades, that six thousand young Japanese volunteered for suicide missions in World War II. A poem found on the body of one Japanese soldier after the battle of Attu in the Aleutians was translated as saying: "I will become a deity with a smile in the heavy fog. I am only waiting for the day of death."[39]

American Patriotism

In the American vernacular, there is no such thing as American nationalism. Nationalism is a suspect category, an ism, like communism, and confined to other people—Serbs, Russians, Palestinians, Tamils. Americans who love their country and profess a willingness to die for it are not nationalists but something nobler and more native to their land. They are "patriots."

In some ways, this is a justifiable distinction: If all nations are "imagined communities," America is more imaginary than most. It has no *Volk*, only a conglomeration of ethnically and racially diverse peoples, and it has no feudal warrior tradition to serve as a model for an imaginary lineage the average citizen might imagine himself or herself a part of. But at the same time, there can be no better measure of America's overweening nationalist pride than the fact that we need a special "American" name for it. Nationalism, in contemporary usage, is un-American and prone to irrational and bloody excess, while patriotism, which is quintessentially American, is clearheaded and virtuous. By convincing ourselves that our nationalism is unique among nationalisms, we do not have to acknowledge its primitive and bloody side.

Americans might well take pride in their uniquely secular civic tradition: The Founding Fathers were careful to separate church and state, not only because they feared the divisiveness of religious sectarianism, but because they did not want to sacralize the state. Their aim was to ensure, as John Adams wrote, that "government shall be considered as having in it nothing more mysterious or divine than other arts or sciences."[40] But war inevitably wore down the wall between church and state, between government and the "divine." In the late nineteenth century, America's imperialist ventures abroad helped infuse American patriotism with a new, quasi-religious fervor. Then, during the Cold War that immediately followed World War II, American nationalism began to invoke the dominant Protestant religion, to the point, often, of seeming to merge with it. Patriotic Americans countered the official atheism of the enemy nation with a proud fusion of "flag and faith." The point "was not so much religious belief as belief in the *value* of religion," historian Stephen J. Whitfield has argued, and above all "the conviction that religion was virtually synonymous with American nationalism."[41]

But for all its debts to the Protestant tradition, American nationalism does not depend on any particular religion for its religious dimension. It is, practically speaking, a religion unto itself—our "civil religion," to use American sociologist Robert Bellah's phrase. In some of its more fervent and sectarian versions, American nationalism makes common cause with white supremacy, anti-Semitism, and Christian millenarianism and even adopts Nazi symbolism. But my concern here is with the more mainstream form of nationalism, which is thought to unite all of America's different races, classes, and ethnic groups. Compared to the blood-soaked rhetoric and rituals of Nazism, this civil religion is a bland and innocuous business—perhaps especially to someone who was raised within its liturgy of songs, processions, prayers, and salutes. It is, nonetheless, an extension and a celebration of American militarism, and no less bellicose in its implications than State Shinto or Nazism.

American patriotism, like the nationalisms of other nations, is celebrated on special holidays, and these are, in most instances, dedicated to particular wars or the memory of war. The Fourth of July, Memorial Day, Flag Day, and Veterans Day all provide occasions for militaristic parades and the display of nationalistic emblems and symbols, especially the flag. On these and other occasions, such as commemorations of particular wars or battles, bugles are blown, wreaths are ceremoniously laid on monuments or graves, veterans dress up in their old uniforms, and politicians deliver speeches glorifying the nationalistic values of duty and "sacrifice." Through such rituals and observances of nationalism as a "secular religion," historian George L. Mosse has written, war is "made sacred."[42]

But the "religion" of American patriotism is also distinctive in at least two ways. First, it features a peculiar kind of idolatry which can only be called a "cult of the flag."* Just as the wartime Japanese fetishized the emperor's portrait, Americans fetishize their flag. A patriotic pamphlet from 1900 declared in unabashedly religious terms

---

*Other comparable, English-speaking nations—the United Kingdom, Canada, and Australia—do not indulge in flag worship. According to the *Wall Street Journal* (Nov. 7, 1996), British efforts to create a mass market for Union Jacks have fallen flat: "Many don't like what it stands for. A fair number aren't sure when, or if, the law lets them unfurl it. Quite a few haven't the foggiest idea of which side of it is up."

that the United States "must develop, define and protect the cult of her flag, and the symbol of that cult—the Star Spangled Banner—must be kept inviolate as are the emblems of all religions."[43] Early twentieth-century leaders of the Daughters of the American Revolution held that "what the cross is to our church, the flag is to our country," and, in more overtly primitive terms, that the flag had been "made sacred and holy by bloody sacrifice."[44]

The American flag can be found in almost every kind of public space, including churches, and it must be handled in carefully prescribed, ritual ways, down to the procedure for folding. It is "worshipped" by displaying it, by pledging allegiance to it, and, occasionally, by kneeling and kissing it.[45] It is the subject of our national anthem, which celebrates a military victory signaled by the survival, not of the American soldiers, but of the American flag, when

> the rockets' red glare,
> the bombs bursting in air,
> Gave proof thro' the night
> that our flag was still there.

And anyone who still doubts that the American flag is an object of religious veneration need only consider the language of the proposed constitutional amendment, narrowly defeated in the Senate in 1995, forbidding the "desecration" of flags.

The other distinctive feature of American nationalism-as-religion, at least as compared to those of more secular-minded nations, is its frequent invocation of "God." We pledge allegiance to a nation "under God," our coins bear the inscription IN GOD WE TRUST. This was not just a concession to America's predominant Christianity, as Bellah explains, because the God being invoked is not exactly the Christian God:

> The God of the civil religion is . . . on the austere side, much more related to order, law, and right than to salvation and love. . . . He is actively interested and involved in

> history, with a special concern for America. Here the analogy has much less to do with natural law than with ancient Israel; the equation of America with Israel . . . is not infrequent.[46]

Put more bluntly, this is the Old Testament God, short-tempered and tribalistic. And it is not so much "order, law, and right" that concern Him as it is the fate of his people—Americans, that is, as his "chosen people"—in war.* "If God is on our side," Moral Majority leader Jerry Falwell observed confidently in 1980, "no matter how militarily superior the Soviet Union is, they could never touch us. God would miraculously protect America."[47]

In fact, every aspect of America's civil religion has been shaped by, or forged in, the experience of war. Memorial Day and Veterans Day honor the soldiers, both living and dead, who fought in past wars, and war veterans are prominent in the celebration of Independence Day and in promoting the year-round cult of the flag. The cult itself can be dated from the Spanish-American War, which signaled America's emergence as a global imperialist power. It was on the day after the United States declared war on Spain that the first statute requiring schoolchildren to salute the flag was passed, by the New York State legislature, and in the wake of World War I, eighteen states passed similar statutes.[48] And it was in the 1950s, at the height of the Cold War, that the coins and the pledge of allegiance were modified to include the word "God." At the middle of a century that included American involvement in two world wars and military incursions into

*Though I am borrowing some of his insights, I should make it clear that Bellah's concept of the American "civil religion" is quite different, and does not explicitly involve nationalism or militarism. He imagines it as some vague, generic type of religion that "actually exists alongside of and rather clearly differentiated from the churches" and serves to provide a transcendent framework for our notion of America. Only when he observes that "the civil religion has not always been invoked in favor of worthy causes," and that it lends itself readily to the intolerant nationalism of the "American-Legion type of ideology," do the euphemisms begin to crack, revealing that what we are talking about sounds very much like nationalism.

the Caribbean, Central America, Korea, and the Philippines, America was a nation draped in flags, addicted to military ritual, and convinced that it was carrying out the will of a stern and highly partisan deity.

American's civil religion is limited, however, in ways that Nazism and State Shinto were not. Democracy guarantees, or at least has guaranteed so far, that Americans will not have some central, godlike figure—a Führer or an emperor—to focus and excite their nationalist zeal. Then there is the multiethnic and multiracial character of the American population. "America is no nation," the British ambassador observed dismissively at the outbreak of World War I, "just a collection of people who neutralize each other."[49] Lacking a Führer or a *Volk*, America's civil religion has the potential to focus on the American (and Enlightenment) ideals of democracy and freedom. This would be something truly unique among nationalisms: a loyalty to country tempered and strengthened by a vision of a just polity that extends to all of humankind.

Such inclusive visions—international socialism being another—have not, of course, fared well in the era of nationalism. Within the United States, a national loyalty based on Enlightenment ideals has had to compete, again and again, with the more fervent and *volkisch* forms of nationalism nourished by nativism and racism. The Christian right, for example, is as much a nationalist movement as a religious one and serves as an ardent lobby for the U.S. military. "The bearing of the sword by the government is correct and proper," Falwell wrote during the Cold War, segueing easily from bladed to nuclear weapons. "Nowhere in the Bible is there a rebuke for the bearing of armaments."[50]

But the Old Testament–style thunderings of the Christian right are only a particularly florid version of the civil religion shared by the great majority of Americans. Since the end of the Cold War, America's quasi-religious nationalism has continued to thrive without a "godless" enemy—without a consistent enemy at all—nourished by war itself. In other times and settings, outbursts of nationalist fervor have often served as a preparation for war, but in the United States, the causality increasingly works the other way, with war and warlike interventions serving, and sometimes apparently being employed, to whip up nationalist enthusiasm. Nations make war, and that often seems to be their most clear-cut function. But we should also recall Hegel's idea that, by arousing the passions of solidarity and transcendence, *war makes nations*, or at least revives and refreshes them.

The United States is hardly alone in its use of war to further domestic political aims. In 1982 Margaret Thatcher's brief war with Argentina over the Falkland Islands occasioned an outburst of British nationalism and an enormous boost for Thatcher in the polls. Serbian aggression in the former Yugoslavia temporarily salvaged the Miloševic government from the disastrous consequences of its economic policies. Or take the curious case of Ecuador, which is not normally thought of as a nationalistic society at all. After ordering his troops to resist Peruvian border incursions in early 1995, the deeply unpopular, seventy-three-year-old Ecuadorian president, Sixto Durán Ballen, found himself suddenly "bathed in the nationalist fountain of youth," as the *New York Times* put it. Flag-waving crowds welcomed him back from a diplomatic tour, and he could be seen daily on the balcony of the presidential palace, "energetically pumping the air with his right fist, and leading crowds in rhythmic chants of 'Not One Step Back!'"[51] No doubt, when the armed confrontations subsided, Ecuadorians went back to burning "Sixto dolls" in effigy.

In the post–Cold War United States, though, wars—or at least "interventions"—became the habitual cure for domestic malaise. Ronald Reagan used a Marxist coup in Grenada as the excuse to raid that island in 1983. George Bush discovered the energizing effects of military action early in his presidency, with his thrillingly swift invasion of Panama and capture of its de facto head of state. Two and a half years later, with the economy in recession and his approval ratings down, Bush decided to respond to the Iraqi invasion of Kuwait with a massive U.S.-led military intervention, "Operation Desert Storm." Public opinion was evenly divided on the necessity of war right up until the eve of hostilities, but once the killing began, it was popular enough to boost Bush's approval ratings to over 90 percent, which is very close to those of the deity.

The Gulf War evoked a burst of nationalist religiosity that, although clearly manipulated by television coverage of the war, seemed to be both spontaneous and deeply felt. Flags appeared everywhere, along with bumper stickers, T-shirts, and buttons urging Americans to SUPPORT OUR TROOPS. As if flags were not a sufficient proof of loyalty, they were joined by yellow ribbons, which had been originally displayed in solidarity with the U.S. hostages held by Iran from 1979 to 1981 and seemed to indicate that America was once again the wronged party or victim. In my town the Boy Scouts affixed yellow ribbons to every tree and bush lining the main street, and similar outbreaks of nationalistic fetishism occurred all over the country. Sports teams and public employees insisted on the right to wear American-flag patches on their uniforms; dissenters (and those deemed to look like Iraqis) were in some cases attacked or threatened with attack.[52]

In effect, the war had reduced a nation of millions to the kind of emotional consensus more appropriate to a primordial band of thirty or forty individuals. In their imaginations, Americans were being threatened by an outsize, barely human enemy, always represented by the lone figure of Iraqi leader Saddam Hussein. And like the primordial band confronted with a predator, we leaped into a frenzy of defensive action, brandishing the fetishes of our faith—our flags and yellow ribbons—against the intruding beast.

A number of scholars have proposed, in the words of social scientist Paul Stern, that nationalism "gets its force by drawing on a primordial sociality" rooted in our long prehistory as members of small-scale bands.[53] Mechanisms of entrainment—mass rallies in the case of Nazism, synchronized rituals in the case of State Shinto, televised war news in the contemporary United States—re-create for us the sense of being part of a unified and familiar group analogous to the primordial band. It may be, as Toynbee suggested, that capitalism, with its "war of each against all," leads individuals to crave this experience of unity all the more. To the alienated "economic actor," militant nationalism, with its parades and rituals, exhortations and flag-waving, holds out the tantalizing promise of a long-lost *Gemeinschaft* restored.

But socialism, in the twentieth century, has hardly been an effective antidote to the twin forces of capitalism and nationalism. It too promised community and self-loss in a collective undertaking, but the project of "socialist construction" turned out never to be quite so compelling as the project of war. People who would lay down their lives for their country will not necessarily give up a weekend to participate in a harvest or the construction of a dam. Love of our neighbors may stir us, but the threat posed by a common enemy stirs us even more.

The sociality of the primordial band is most likely rooted, after all, in the exigencies of defense against animal predators. We may *enjoy* the company of our fellows, but we *thrill* to the prospect of joining them in collective defense against the common enemy. Ultimately, twentieth-century socialism lost out to nationalism for the same reason the universalistic, post-axial religions did: It has no blood rite at its core, no thrilling spectacle of human sacrifice.

> War is like love; it always finds a way.[1]
>
> —Bertolt Brecht

14
The Further Evolution of War in the Twentieth Century

In the spring of 1990, two months before the beginning of "Operation Desert Storm," I gave a presentation on war and warrior elites to a small group of sociologists. They were interested and supportive, but a bit pitying about my choice of a topic: War, they were eager to remind me, had run its course. The Cold War had ended; communism was over; there were no longer any "sides" to take. Too bad I had elected to work on a subject of only historical interest.

The conviction that war is passé, or soon to become so, has a venerable history of its own. The introduction of the gun, and after that, artillery, seemed to promise levels of destruction so costly that no state would want to risk them. After the gruesome bloodletting of the Napoleonic Wars, philosophers Auguste Comte and John Stuart Mill prophesied that war would end as civilization turned, in relief, to the peaceful business of industrial production. World War I was, of course, the "war to end all wars"; a quarter-century later, the nuclear weapons developed and used in World War II seemed to doom war once and for all. Ghoulish wonks might play with scenarios for "limited nuclear war" and "flexible responses," but anyone with sense could see that "war has been vanquished," as Robert L. O'Connell has put it, defeated by its own weaponry.[2]

In the last few years, obituaries for war, or at least predictions of its imminent demise, have been coming thick and fast. In his 1989 book *Retreat from Doomsday*, John Mueller argued that "major war—war among developed countries—has gradually moved toward terminal disrepute because of its perceived repulsiveness and futility."[3] John Keegan, in his *History of Warfare*, expressed the hope that "at last, after five thousand years of recorded warmaking, cultural and material changes may be working to inhibit man's proclivity to take up arms."[4] And in his most recent book, *Ride of the Second Horseman*, O'Connell finds the grim horseman thrown from his mount: Thanks to the growth of international trade and the emergence of international economic institutions, war has ceased to be "functional."[5]

But no matter how futile, repulsive, or dysfunctional war may be, it persists. There have been 160 wars of various sizes since World War II,[6] and by 1994 these had taken the lives of an estimated 22 million people.[7] Many of these wars have been "conventional" in the sense of pitting one good-sized nation-state against another—Iran against Iraq, for example, or Iraq against the United States and its allies. Many others have been decidedly unconventional, featuring belligerents which are not nation-states but ethnic groups, factions, and religious movements. As Martin van Creveld argues, what we have been witnessing is not the death or atrophy of war but its "transformation":

> The nature of the entities by which war is made, the conventions by which it is surrounded, and the ends for which it is fought may change. However, now as ever war itself is alive and well.[8]

In a sense, war has found a way around the obstacles placed in its way by the scholars of militarism. Since armed conflict between the major nation-states is too costly and too likely to tip over into nuclear holocaust, war has taken other forms. Now it is likely to be "low-intensity" or, as German essayist Hans Magnus Enzensberger terms it, "molecular," with the diminutives referring to the size of the warring units rather than to the cost in human life. The new kind of war is less disciplined and more spontaneous than the old, often fought by ill-clad bands more resembling gangs than armies. But it is, from a civilian point of view, more lethal than ever. Recall that in World War I, 15 percent of the fatalities were civilians, with that proportion rising to 65 percent in World War II. In the "low-intensity" wars of the late twentieth century—the wars of Ivory Coast, Somalia, Sudan, Liberia, East Timor, and the former Yugoslavia—civilians constitute 90 percent of the dead.[9]

Whatever the psychology of this new type of war—and there has been much vaporizing about a recrudescence of "evil" in the world—one particular innovation has made it possible, and that is the emergence of an international market in small arms.[10] The modern nation-state came into being, as we have seen earlier, as a support system for the mass army. Today, however, anyone can purchase guns and almost anything else they might need—vehicles, canteens, boots, camouflage clothes—on the open market. Even military training and leadership is available, for a price, from mercenary groups and U.S. firms employing retired officers.[11] Somalia, for example, had no arms industry and very little infrastructure of any kind during the years it was being torn in shreds by warring factions; the guns were provided by the superpowers of the Northern Hemisphere. With a thriving black market in weapons recycled by the former guerrillas of Mozambique, Nicaragua, and Afghanistan, the nation-state is no longer necessary as the unit of militarism. A warlord with cash and a coterie of followers will do.

And it is not only the expertise and hardware of war that is available in the international marketplace. The very spirit of war—the glory and romance once associated with particular noble lineages and, later, nations—has become a commodity available in the global consumer culture. With Rambo and his ilk, Hollywood offers up a denationalized, generic warrior-hero, a man of few words and limited loyalties, suitable for universal emulation. An American journalist described Russian special-forces fighters in Chechnya this way:

> The soldiers were dressed in preposterous Rambo outfits: headbands, mirrored shades, sleeveless muscle shirts, bandoliers, belt packed with hunting knives. . . . [They] wanted nothing more than to look like their movie hero—they had seen all his movies on video—and how they melted at the sound of his name. "You know Sly?" [they asked]. . . . "You *really* know Sly?"[12]

It is in the postnational factions of today's "molecular wars" that these images are probably most effective, complementing and even substituting for makeshift notions of tribal and ethnic identity. Serbian soldiers also affect Rambo-style headbands and bandoliers;[13] a Liberian guerrilla fighter takes "General Rambo" as his nom de guerre.[14] Within the United States, the "Rambo culture" helps inspire a grass-roots "militia" movement dedicated to preserving and expanding the individual's right to bear arms, including assault weapons normally reserved for the police and the military.[15]

So the "democratization of glory," begun in the mass armies of the eighteenth and nineteenth centuries, may eventually outlive the mass army, with its oppressive discipline and its constitutionally ordained subordination to civilian government. "Every man a warrior-hero!" seems to be the great populist demand of the late twentieth century. And if every man is to have his experience of warrior-glory, every man must have his war: The right-wing rural American stockpiles weapons in preparation for eventual battle with immigrants, blacks, or government forces, while his suburban counterpart pays to spend weekends in mock wars fought with paint balls instead of bullets.

De-gendering War

One feature of the "transformed" war of the nuclear age is that it is less likely to be the exclusive province of males or even of adults. This "de-gendering" of war reflects, above all, the continuing revolution wrought by guns. There has never been a weapon that *some* women could not wield, but the gun—easy to carry and dependent for its lethal force on chemical rather than muscular energy—is potentially within reach of all. The "democratizing" trend it set in motion, which began in the sixteenth century with the elevation of the foot soldier's role, extends now increasingly to the human categories traditionally excluded from combat: women and even children.

Nationalism has been another force militating toward the greater inclusion of women. Unlike the elite-warrior ethos of another era, nationalism does not discriminate on the basis of gender or class. Women as well as men are expected to participate in the worship of their nations' flags and other sacred symbols, to cheer at parades and rallies, to "sacrifice" for the war effort. World War I, as we saw at the beginning of this book, inspired the same transports of enthusiasm among women as it did among men. In wartime England, for example, suffrage leaders abandoned their cause for war-related efforts, such as attempts to publicly shame men they judged to be "shirkers."

In the United States, the change has occurred more rapidly than anyone could have imagined just a couple of decades ago. At that time, the prospect of women dying in combat was sufficiently alarming that it helped mobilize votes against the Equal Rights Amendment to the Constitution.[16] But a few years later the deaths of eleven women, and the capture of two, in the U.S.-led Gulf War aroused no special indignation. The idea of a "weaker sex," requiring male protection, had lost its grip. Though still largely barred from direct combat, women now serve in a variety of new roles: directing artillery, piloting helicopters, operating supply depots. Meanwhile, a few bold and sturdy women have gained admission to the service academies where the officer elite is trained, have become fighter pilots, and have even found berths on combat vessels. We no longer hail "our boys" as they go forth to war, but "our men and women."[17]

And in some settings, children. The warring factions in Liberia routinely recruited young boys as "men"-at-arms. During the war between Iran and Iraq, both nations fielded troops consisting of boys in their teens or younger. There is nothing about the gun, after all, which says it cannot be wielded by a child. But when little boys, and occasionally also girls, can be enlisted, then clearly war can no longer serve its ancient function as a male ritual of initiation—if gender remains a meaningful category at all. In Liberia, fighters in one armed faction carried out some of their massacres while dressed, bizarrely, in blond wigs and tutus.

The de-gendering of war does not mean that "masculinity" will cease to be a desirable attribute; only that it will be an attribute that women as well as men can possess. Already, in popular usage, the dismissive term "wimp" is applied almost as readily to women as to men, implying that the appropriate stance for both sexes is tough and potentially battle-ready. The division of humanity into "masculine" and "feminine" may persist, but these categories may have less and less to do with the biological sexes. This is not an entirely negative development, from a woman's perspective: With the admission of women to warrior status, we may be ready for the long overdue recognition that it was not only human males who made the transition from prey to predator, but the entire human race.

How far the de-gendering of war will go is still very much an open question. Van Creveld, for one, sees the "transformation of war" inevitably stopping short of the continued incorporation of women, if only because of entrenched and irrational male resistance.[18] Indeed, at every step toward their incorporation into the military, women have been met with coarse, misogynist resistance—jeers, hazings, and, above all, sexual assaults and harassment aimed at reminding them that, in the most primitive calculus, women are still not predators, but prey.[19] There is no reason to think that men, as a sex, will give up their starring role in war any more easily than mounted knights once gave up theirs.

But the inclusion of women has gone far enough to cast serious doubts on any theory of war that derives exclusively from considerations of gender. War *has been* seen by many cultures as a male initiation rite and a defining male activity, but it need not remain so. When war ceases to serve one "function"—for example, the capture of prisoners for human sacrifice or the seizure of land for agricultural expansion—it generally finds another.

So war has come to depend less on the human social institutions that have sustained it for centuries, if not millennia. One of these is male supremacy, as embodied in the all-male warrior elite; another is that superb social instrument of war, the nation-state, in whose name all major wars have been fought for more than two hundred years. To anyone who had believed that war could be abolished by severing its links to male privilege, or by healing the artificial division of our species into nations, the end of the twentieth century can only bring gloom. War has little loyalty to even the most warlike of human institutions and may, ominously enough, have little use for humans themselves. Twentieth-century military technologists have already begun preparations for a version of war in which "autonomous weapons" will be "given the responsibility for killing human beings without human direction or supervision."[20]

The Beast in Modern Form

Looking back on the developments of the twentieth century—and on the four centuries of gun-based warfare that preceded it—one is tempted to reformulate the ancient puzzle of what it is that gives war its iron grip on human cultures. Traditionally, the puzzle has been posed as a question about "human nature": What is it in us that draws us, over and over, to an undertaking we know to be destructive and suspect, in most cases, to be thoroughly immoral? But when we reflect on war's remarkable resilience in the face of changing circumstances, we cannot help wanting to turn the question around for a moment to ask instead: What *is* this thing that humans have been so fatally drawn to? If war is not firmly rooted in some human subgroup (adult males, for example, or any other relative elite), if it is not the product of some particular form of human social organization (feudalism, the nation-state, or capitalism)—then what exactly is it?

This is not, I should remind the reader, the question I set out to answer in this book. The aim of the book was not to explain the existence of war but, more modestly, to understand the uniquely "religious" feelings humans bring to it. These feelings are not indissolubly wedded to the project of war: As William James wisely observed, the kind of courage and altruism people bring to war could, conceivably, be redirected to some more worthy enterprise, or "moral equivalent of war." Nor is war dependent, for its existence, on the special feelings we attach to it. War can be waged, and often has been, without any great and noble sentiments. It is routinely waged, in fact, by ants.

In trying to understand what war is, we have been misled, I would argue, by the apparent linkage between war and various other institutions—hierarchies of class, gender, and political leadership, for example. Analyze any war-making society and, sure enough, you will find the practice of war apparently embedded in and dependent upon that society's economy, culture, system of gender relations, and so forth. But change that economy and culture—as in going from a hunting-gathering to an agricultural way of life, or from agriculture to industry—and war will, most likely, be found to persist. So it is the *autonomy* of war as an institution that we have to confront and explain. Is war something which really does have "a life of its own"?

As we observed in chapter 9, war can be analogized, in a mathematical sense, to a process caused by living things—in particular, to a disease brought about by microorganisms. War is "contagious," as we have noted, spreading readily from one culture to the next. And once the famous "cycle of violence" has begun, there is, of course, no stopping it; each injury demands the counterinjury known as revenge. Thus war is, in some not yet entirely defined sense, a *self-replicating* pattern of behavior, possessed of a dynamism not unlike that of living things.

Social science provides us with no category for such an entity, but other fields are beginning to offer what look, at least for now, like promising frameworks. One of these is the biologist Richard Dawkins's concept of a "meme." Searching for a way to describe cultural evolution, he proposed the concept of self-replicating "units of culture" analogous to genes. Like genes, these "memes" seek to copy themselves as widely as possible and, also like genes, are subject to certain (so far unexamined) selective forces. The underlying idea—which gains a certain respectability from the new "dual inheritance model" of evolution[21]—is that culture, like biology, may be subject to evolutionary laws of its own, with the "fittest" memes winning out, in time, over the other cultural possibilities.

Unfortunately, it is not too easy to say what the evolutionarily significant "units of culture" may be. Sometimes Dawkins and his followers in what is optimistically called the "science of memetics" refer to the slenderest bits of cultural ephemera—tunes, phrases, images—as memes. But while tunes or phrases can be "infectious" in their own way, their reproduction—on compact discs or printed pages—seems largely a matter of human whim. At other times, Dawkins includes rather grander notions, such as the idea of a deity, as memes, though clearly the idea of a deity exists at a vastly higher level of complexity than, say, a particular image of a deity. The image—a particular painting of Jesus, for example—will be more or less the same for all who behold it and can be described, more or less adequately, by a simple code suitable for electronic transmission. Not so, however, with the idea of God: Not only does the idea vary from person to person (and within each person, depending on mood and the vicissitudes of faith), but it often contains within it a complex set of behavioral instructions—love thy neighbor, light candles on *shabbos*, avoid pork and alcohol, or whatever.

If war can be thought of as a meme, clearly it is a meme like religion rather than like, for example, a popular tune. It cannot be reduced, as a tune can, to any simple sequence of symbols. Rather, it would have to be conceived as a loose assemblage of algorithms or programs (in the computer sense) for action: When living in the vicinity of a tribe that possesses large numbers of spears, it is wise to make spears of one's own. When approached by a group of men brandishing spears, it is a good idea to muster up a spear-bearing group of one's own. When attacked, fight back, or run very fast. And so forth.

Considered as a self-reproducing cultural entity or meme, war appears to be far more robust than any particular religion, perhaps more robust than religion in general. Compare, for example, the "reproductive" efficacy of war to that of a superficially rather similar religious practice: human sacrifice. Both involve killing people, and both tend to invoke rather exalted explanations for why the killing must be done. But human sacrifice can spread only by imitation; war, on the other hand, requires far less by way of human acquiescence. You may admire the religious fervor that leads the neighboring tribe to immolate its children, but you are not required to follow suit. In the case of war, there is very little choice; if the neighboring band decides to capture and immolate *your* children (or steal your herds and grain stores), your group can fight back—or prepare to face extinction. Given its tenacity and near universality, war is surely one of the "fittest" of memes.

"Memetics" remains in its infancy, but for our purposes, the truly sobering aspect of Dawkins's idea is that "fitness," for a meme, may have little or nothing to do with the biological fitness or well-being of the people who act in conformity with it. If culture is governed by laws analogous to those of natural selection, these laws are not selecting for stronger or happier people, but for more successful memes. "What we have not previously considered," Dawkins writes, apparently referring to a century of social science, "is that a cultural trait may have evolved in the way that it has, simply because it is *advantageous to itself*."[22]

Thus, if war is understood as a self-replicating entity, we should probably abandon the many attempts to explain it as an evolutionary adaptation which has been, in some ecological sense, useful or helpful to humans. Biology instructs us to raise large numbers of healthy children—the clearest possible measure of biological fitness—but culture can countermand this instruction with the idea that it is glorious to die young in war. Culture, in other words, cannot be counted on to be "on our side." Insofar as it allows humans to escape the imperatives of biology, it may do so only to entrap us in what are often crueler imperatives of its own.

Another possible way of thinking about war as a self-replicating activity comes from computer science—though not from the part that seeks to provide models for the human mind. Perhaps surprisingly, this infant science has come up with a new notion of "life," and one that goes well beyond the water-and-carbon-based chemical engines that we usually recognize as animals, plants, and microorganisms. Computer scientists are generating new "life forms" that have no material substance at all; they are programs—computer "viruses" would be the most familiar example—that have been designed to reproduce themselves and, in some cases, even to undergo spontaneous "mutations." Such "creatures," which can be represented on a computer screen as dots or fish or lions or anything else one fancies, can be programmed to evolve in response to selective forces imposed by the experimenter. If two or more species of them are present, they may quite spontaneously enter into such lifelike relationships as those of symbiosis and parasitism.

These self-reproducing computer programs demand a definition of a living being as "a pattern in space/time . . . rather than a specific material object."[23] Such a being must be able not only to reproduce itself, but to undergo mutations, and hence to evolve over the course of generations. If technological changes in weaponry, transportation, and so on are understood as the relevant "mutations," then war, in some rough sense, may fit this kind of expanded definition. With the introduction of the horse as part of the technology of war some 4,000 years ago, war "mutated" into an occupation for mounted elites. With the introduction of the gun, it mutated again—this time into an activity potentially accessible to the common man and woman. And following each such mutation in the mechanism of war, human social institutions, with their ancient hierarchies of class and gender, can only scramble to keep up.

But whether we base our analogies on genes or computer programs, we are looking for a way to understand how human societies may, in a sense, fall prey to "living" entities that were, originally, of our own creation. This tragic possibility is implicit, it seems to me, in Marx's description of capitalism. In *Capital*, as in that other nineteenth-century classic, *Frankenstein*, human creativity brings forth something—market system or monster—which humans can no longer control. Humans invented market systems and bring strong feelings to them—greed, most notably, but also the desire for adventure and sometimes even altruistic concerns for the general welfare. But once under way, market systems (and perhaps especially those of the industrial-capitalist variety) have a dynamism of their own, which no socialist enclave has yet found a way to resist for any length of time. The market comes to act like a force of nature, dictating—or at least severely circumscribing—the choices of anyone who hopes to remain a "player." This outcome would seem fit Andrew Bard Schmookler's observation that "with the rise of civilization human creativity ceased to drive the mill of cultural evolution but rather became its grist."[24]

War is not the only self-replicating social institution. The familiar hierarchies of race, gender, and class are also endowed with a certain ability to reproduce themselves. Insofar as the members of a supposedly inferior group are denied adequate nutrition or education or access to important resources, they will indeed remain "inferior." Girls who are barred from education on the basis of their sex's presumed intellectual deficits may well end up as examples of why women *can't* be educated, and will often pass this implicit judgment on to their own daughters. Black children who are underfed and consigned to underfunded schools will, very often, be handicapped for life. This does not mean that social hierarchies cannot be overthrown; only that those who would overthrow them should be aware of their almost lifelike power to persist. As reformers have had to learn again and again, simply declaring a group equal does not end the dreary dynamic that has condemned it to inequality thus far.

Someday, perhaps, social theory will be in a position to understand human culture as a medium—a primeval soup, as it were—within which abstract entities like war, and possibly also capitalism, religion, and science, not only "live" and reproduce but also interact. For now, let us content ourselves with observing that they do indeed interact, and in complex, evolving ways. War, for example, has for millennia existed in a symbiotic relationship with male domination, both drawing strength from and giving nourishment to it. But this mutual dependence only goes so far. There have been cultures, like that of the Inuit, which are both peaceable and male dominated, just as there is now a culture—that of the United States—which is both militaristic and (at least officially) egalitarian with respect to gender. War has thrived through its symbiosis with male domination, but it can also do quite nicely on its own.

Market systems have an even more complex history of interaction with the self-replicating pattern that is war. During the feudal era, for example, the European warrior elite disdained the nascent market and the men who made it work. But, as William H. McNeill argues in *The Pursuit of Power*, it was the eventual synergy of markets and militarism that helped pave the way for the burst of European imperial expansionism from the sixteenth century on. Something like that synergy persists in the United States, where the market economy has become thoroughly addicted to the manufacture of weapons and the government expenditures that underwrite it. But on a global scale, the interaction between war and the market system (or, if you will, the memes for war and markets) has grown more complex and sometimes hostile: The now global marketplace tends to homogenize cultures and produce a single "community" of, say, Coca-Cola drinkers or Marlboro smokers; at the same time, the far older war system exerts a centripetal force, fractionating the human population into warring subgroups.[25]

I should emphasize that the notion of a cultural entity as a quasi-"living" being does not impute to that entity any intentions or objectives of its own. In fact, I was being overly colorful at the beginning of this discussion in saying that such entities "seek" to reproduce. They "seek" nothing; as with strands of viral DNA, it is just that those that *have* managed to reproduce successfully are still around. For anything like intentionality, or passion, or ambition or hope, these self-replicating cultural entities are dependent entirely on us.

And in this sense we have more than served their "purpose." This book has been about the passions of war, and they are, as we have seen, among the "highest" and finest passions humans can know: courage, altruism, and the mystical sense of belonging to "something larger than ourselves." But if we concede to war at least some measure of the autonomy enjoyed by living things, then we must acknowledge that we have invested these lofty passions in a peculiar kind of god indeed—an entity that is ultimately alien to us and supremely indifferent to our fate. We have sacrificed our loved ones for what is worse than nothing: we have sacrificed them for something that has no use for us.

To return to the question I posed at the beginning of this section: What is war that it exerts such cruel demands on us? It is first, in an economic sense, a *parasite* on human cultures—draining them of the funds and resources, talent and personnel, that could be used to advance the cause of human life and culture. But "parasitism" is too mild a term for a relationship predicated on the periodic killing of large numbers of human beings. If war is a "living" thing, it is a kind of creature that, by its very nature, devours us. To look at war, carefully and long enough, is to see the face of the predator over which we thought we had triumphed long ago.

Fighting War

War, at the end of the twentieth century, is a more formidable adversary than it has ever been. It can no longer be localized within a particular elite and hence overthrown in a brilliant act of revolution. Revolution, in fact, was redefined by Lenin and others as little more than a species of war, fought by disciplined "cadres" organized along the same hierarchical lines as the mass armies of the modern era.

Meanwhile, war has dug itself into economic systems, where it offers a livelihood to millions, rather than to just a handful of craftsmen and professional soldiers. It has lodged in our souls as a kind of religion, a quick tonic for political malaise and a bracing antidote to the moral torpor of consumerist, market-driven cultures.

In addition, our incestuous fixation on combat with our own kind has left us ill prepared to face many of the larger perils of the situation in which we find ourselves: the possibility of drastic climatic changes, the depletion of natural resources, the relentless predations of the microbial world. The wealth that flows ceaselessly to the project of war is wealth lost, for the most part, to the battle against these threats. In the United States, military spending no longer requires a credible enemy to justify it, while funding for sanitation, nutrition, medical care, and environmental reclamation declines even as the need mounts. In the third world and much of the postcommunist world, the preparedness for war far surpasses the readiness to combat disease—witness Zaire's fumbling efforts to contain the Ebola outbreak of 1995, or the swiftly declining life expectancy of the former Soviets.

But in at least one way, we have gotten tougher and better prepared to face the enemy that is war. If the twentieth century brought the steady advance of war and war-related enterprises, it also brought the beginnings of organized human resistance to war. Anti-war movements, arising in massive force in the latter half of the century, are themselves products of the logic of modern war, with its requirements of mass participation and assent. When the practice and passions of war were largely confined to a warrior elite, popular opposition to war usually took the form of opposition to that elite. But in the situation where everyone is expected to participate in one way or another, and where anyone can become a victim whether they participate or not, opposition could at last develop to the institution of war itself.

This represents an enormous human achievement. Any anti-war movement that targets only the human agents of war—a warrior elite or, in our own time, the chieftains of the "military-industrial complex"—risks mimicking those it seeks to overcome. Anti-war activists can become macho and belligerent warriors in their own right, just as revolutionaries all too often evolve into fatigue-clad replacements for the oppressors they overthrow. So it is a giant step from hating the warriors to hating the war, and an even greater step to deciding that the "enemy" is the abstract institution of war, which maintains its grip on us even in the interludes we know as peace.

The anti-war movements of the late twentieth century are admittedly feeble undertakings compared to that which they oppose. They are reactive and ad hoc, emerging, usually tardily, in response to particular wars, then ebbing to nothing in times of peace. They are fuzzy-minded, moralistic, and often committed to cartoonish theories of the sources of war—that it is a product of capitalism, for example, or testosterone or some similar flaw.

But for all their failings, anti-war movements should already have taught us one crucial lesson: that the passions we bring to war can be brought just as well to the struggle *against* war. There is a place for courage and solidarity and self-sacrifice other than in the service of this peculiarly bloody institution, this inhuman "meme"—a place for them in the struggle to shake ourselves free of it. I myself would be unable to imagine the passions of war if I had not, at various times in my life, linked arms with the men and women around me and marched up, singing or chanting, to the waiting line of armed and uniformed men.

And we will need all the courage we can muster. What we are called to is, in fact, a kind of war. We will need "armies," or at least networks of committed activists willing to act in concert when necessary, to oppose force with numbers, and passion with forbearance and reason. We will need leaders—not a handful of generals but huge numbers of individuals able to take the initiative to educate, inspire, and rally others. We will need strategies and cunning, ways of assessing the "enemy's" strength and sketching out the way ahead. And even with all that, the struggle will be enormously costly. Those who fight war on this war-ridden planet must prepare themselves to lose battle after battle and still fight on, to lose security, comfort, position, even life.

But what have all the millennia of warfare prepared us for, if not this Armageddon fought, once more, against a predator beast?

Notes

Citations given here only in part can be found in full in the bibliography.

Foreword

1. Tolstoy, *War and Peace*, p. 730.

Chapter 1

1. Van Creveld, *The Transformation of War*, p. 166.
2. See, for example, Stoessinger, *Why Nations Go to War*, pp. 14–20.
3. Stromberg, *Redemption by War*, p. 82.
4. O'Connell, *Of Arms and Men*, p. 119.
5. Kroeber and Fontana, *Massacre on the Gila*, p. 166.
6. Fox, "Fatal Attraction: War and Human Nature," p. 15.
7. McCauley, Clark, "Conference Overview," in Haas, *The Anthropology of War*, p. 2.
8. Quoted in Mitchell, *Colonizing Egypt*, p. 42.
9. Delbrück, *History of the Art of War*, p. 303.
10. See Grossman, *On Killing*.

11. In the mythologies of the Indo-European tradition, Dumézil relates, thanks "either to a gift of metamorphosis, or to a monstrous heredity, the eminent warrior possesses a veritable animal nature." Dumézil, *Destiny of the Warrior*, p. 140.
12. Davidson, *Myths and Symbols in Pagan Europe*, p. 84.
13. Keeley, *War Before Civilization*, p. 146.
14. Hanson, *The Western Way of War*, p. 126.
15. Griffith, Samuel B., in his introduction to Sun Tzu, *The Art of War*, p. 37.
16. Rolle, *The World of the Scythians*, pp. 94–95.
17. Keeley, p. 144.
18. Sagan, *Cannibalism*, p. 18
19. Métraux, "Warfare, Cannibalism, and Human Trophies," p. 397.
20. Stromberg, p. 182.
21. Ibid, p. 233.
22. LeShan, *The Psychology of War*, p. 67.
23. Quoted in Alberti, *Beyond Suffrage*, p. 50.
24. Mosse, *Confronting the Nation*, p. 64.
25. Quoted in Stromberg, p. 2.
26. Hirschman, *Shifting Involvements*, p. 5.
27. Partridge, *The Psychology of Nations*, p. 23.
28. Ibid., p. 22.
29. Stromberg, p. 190.
30. Ibid., p. 53.
31. Toynbee, *A Study of History*, p. 18.
32. Le Bon, *The Crowd*, p. 34.
33. Quoted in Fornari, Franco, *The Psychoanalysis of War*, p. 151.
34. Mosse, *Confronting the Nation*, p. 32.
35. Vagts, *A History of Militarism*, p. 21.
36. Quoted in Mosse, *Confronting the Nation*, p. 70.
37. Ibid., p. 25.
38. Ibid., pp. 74–75.
39. Turney-High, *Primitive War*, p. 214.
40. Ibid., p. 215.
41. Ibid., p. 213.
42. Van Creveld, p. 158.
43. I would include in this category LeShan, Mosse, Fornari, Partridge, and Young, as well as bits and pieces of many others.
44. Quoted in Sun Tzu, p. 22.

Chapter 2

1. Bakunin, *God and the State*, pp. 25–26.
2. Burkert, *Homo Necans*, p. 3.
3. Schele, Linda, "Human Sacrifice Among the Classic Maya," in Boone, *Ritual Human Sacrifice in Mesoamerica*, p. 44.
4. Ewers, *The Blackfeet*, p. 183 and following.
5. See Favazza, *Bodies Under Siege*.
6. Ibid., p. 95.
7. Burkert, *Homo Necans*, p. 5.
8. Keegan, *The Mask of Command*, p. 47.
9. Xenophon, *The March Up Country*, p. 73.
10. Burkert, *Homo Necans*, p. 9.
11. Girard, *Violence and the Sacred*, p. 23.
12. Ibid., p. 78.
13. Ibid., p. 251.
14. Ibid., p. 249.
15. Jameson, "Sacrifice and Ritual: Greece," p. 966.
16. Valeri, *Kingship and Sacrifice*, p. 56.
17. Hubert and Mauss, *Sacrifice*, p. 37.
18. Quoted in Bergmann, *In the Shadow of Moloch*, p. 35.
19. Bataille, *Theory of Religion*, pp. 49–50.
20. See, for example, Young, *Origins of the Sacred*, p. 349.
21. Lincoln, *Death, War, and Sacrifice*, pp. 170–71.
22. Quoted in Neumann, *The Great Mother*, p. 152.
23. Heesterman, *The Broken World of Sacrifice*, p. 7.
24. Ingold, *Hunters, Pastoralists and Ranchers*, p. 210.
25. Hubert and Mauss, p. 33.
26. Burkert, *Homo Necans*, p. 11.
27. Girard, p. 1.
28. Frazer, *The Golden Bough*, p. 101.
29. Hughes, *Human Sacrifice in Ancient Greece*, p. 85.
30. Burkert, "The Problem of Ritual Killing," in Hamerton-Kelly, *Violent Origins*, p. 163.
31. Hartog, "Self-cooking Beef and the Drinks of Ares," p. 174.

Chapter 3

1. From the *Protagoras*, quoted in Vernant and Vidal-Naquet, *Myth and Tragedy in Ancient Greece*, p. 143.
2. Quoted in Montagu, *Man and Aggression*, p. 5.
3. Luckert, *Egyptian Light, Hebrew Fire*, p. 21.
4. Burkert, *Homo Necans*, p. 16.
5. See, for example, Anderson, "Predation and Primate Evolution"; Gould and Yellen, "Man the Hunted"; Zihlman, "Sex, Sexes and Sexism in Human Origins."
6. Haraway, *Simians, Cyborgs and Nature*, p. 86.
7. Wenke, *Patterns in Prehistory*, pp. 120–21.
8. Ibid.
9. Blumenschine and Cavallo, "Scavenging and Human Evolution"; Binford, "Human Ancestors"; and Binford, "The Hunting Hypothesis."
10. Binford, "The Hunting Hypothesis."
11. Quoted in Clark, J. Desmond, "Comments" on Rose and Marshall, "Meat Eating," p. 323.
12. Ardrey, *African Genesis*, p. 190.
13. Brain, *The Hunters or the Hunted*?
14. Cited in Rose and Marshall, p. 313.
15. Tsukahara, "Lions Eat Chimpanzees."
16. Richard, *Primates in Nature*, p. 276.
17. Tsukahara.
18. Pfeiffer, *The Emergence of Man*, p. 117.
19. Kortlandt, "How Might Early Hominids Have Defended Themselves?"
20. Saberwal et al., "Lion-Human Conflict in the Gir Forest, India."
21. Boyles, *Man Eaters Motel*, pp. 130–40.
22. Russell, *The Hunting Animal*, pp. 40–41.
23. Ibid., p. 44.
24. Montgomery, *Spell of the Tiger*, p. 9.
25. Brain, pp. 97–98.
26. Ibid., p. 65.
27. Quoted in Hodges-Hill, *Man-Eater*, p. 18.
28. See, for example, the videotape *The Wolf: Real or Imagined*? by Bruce Weide and Lori Hudak, funded by the Montana Committee for the Humanities, the Idaho Humanities Council, and KSPS Spokane Public Television (no date).
29. Burns, John F., "In India Attacks by Wolves Spark Old Fears and Hatreds," *New York Times*, September 1, 1996, p. 1.

30. Quoted in Kortlandt, p. 79.
31. Pfeiffer, p. 165.
32. Fagan, *People of the Earth*, pp. 208–9.
33. Chang, *Art, Myth, and Ritual*, p. 61 and following.
34. Luckert, *The Navajo Hunter Tradition*, pp. 70–79.
35. Dumézil, *Destiny of the Warrior*, p. 145.
36. Lonsdale, *Creatures of Speech*, p. 20.
37. Pritchard, *The Ancient Near East*, p. 48.
38. Lonsdale.
39. Quoted in King, *Achilles*, p. 22.
40. *Iliad*, Book XXII, ll. 346–47.
41. Mumford, *The City in History*, pp. 22–23.
42. Bergmann, *In the Shadow of Moloch*, p. 75.
43. Lonsdale, pp. 103–4n.
44. Faraone, *Talismans and Trojan Horses*, pp. 36–53.
45. Maurer, A., "What Children Fear," *Journal of Genetic Pscyhology* 106 (1965); 265–77. See also Marks, *Fears, Phobias, and Rituals*, p. 149.
46. Mundkur, "Human Animality," pp. 161–62.
47. Stanley, *Children of the Ice Age*, p. 175.
48. Robin Fox, personal communication. March, 1995.
49. Janson, "Evolutionary Ecology of Primate Social Structure." For earlier examples of the emphasis on predation, see Alexander, Richard D., "The Evolution of Social Behavior," *Annual Review of Ecological Systems* 5 (1974): 324–82, and Rubenstein, "On Predation."
50. Gould and Yellen.
51. Some predators, bears for instance, tend not to attack human groups of six or more, at least in daylight. Stephen Herrero, personal communication, December 4, 1995.
52. Bowlby, *Attachment and Loss*, p. 85. See also Marks and Nesse, "Fear and Fitness."
53. Anderson, "Predation and Primate Evolution."
54. Young, *Origins of the Sacred*, p. 82.
55. Alcock, *Animal Behavior*, p. 472.
56. O'Connell, *Ride of the Second Horseman*; see ch. 3, "The Soul of a Hunter."
57. Keegan, *The History of Warfare*, pp. 81–84. He mentions, at one point, the skeleton of a young man from about 10,000 years ago found at Arene Candide in Italy: "Part of his lower jaw, his collar-bone and the shoulder-blade, together with the top of the thigh bone, had been carried away by the bites of a large, savage animal." But Keegan can imagine only that

this savage animal was itself the intended prey—"perhaps a bear which had been cornered in a pit or cave that the hunters dug or adapted as a trap" (p. 117).

58. Young, p. 165.

Chapter 4

1. Detienne and Svenbro, "The Feast of the Wolves," p. 162.
2. Burkert, *Structure and History in Greek Mythology and Ritual*, p. 51.
3. Ibid., p. 71.
4. Ibid., p. 72.
5. Quoted in Tierny, *The Highest Altar*, p. 10.
6. Law, "Human Sacrifice in Pre-Colonial West Africa."
7. Davies, Nigel, "Human Sacrifice in the Old World and the New: Some Similarities and Differences," in Boone, *Ritual Human Sacrifice in Mesoamerica*, pp. 211–26.
8. Saggs, *Civilization Before Greece and Rome*, p. 287.
9. Wilford, John Noble, "New Analysis of the Parthenon's Frieze Finds It Depicts a Horrifying Legend," *New York Times*, July 4, 1995, p. 19.
10. Bergmann, *In the Shadow of Moloch*, p. 103.
11. Stager and Wolff, "Child Sacrifice at Carthage," pp. 31–51.
12. Davies, p. 217.
13. Bergmann, p. 24.
14. Lewis, *A Goddess in the Stones*, pp. 226–27.
15. Davidson, *Myths and Symbols in Pagan Europe*, p. 64.
16. Tierny, pp. 14–15.
17. Clendinnen, *Aztecs*, p. 91.
18. Bernardino de Sahagún, quoted in Bataille, *Theory of Religion*, p. 50.
19. Miguel León Portilla, quoted in Demarest, Arthur, "Overview: Mesoamerican Human Sacrifice in Evolutionary Perspective," in Boone, pp. 227–47.
20. Canetti, *Crowds and Power*, p. 139.
21. Mumford, *The City in History*, p. 44
22. Ingham, "Human Sacrifice at Tenochtitlán." p. 395.
23. Demarest, p. 228.
24. Quoted in Jay, *Throughout Your Generations Forever*, p. 66.
25. Tierny, p. 23.
26. Graves, *The Greek Myths*, p. 105.
27. Mahapatra, "The Meria Sloka."

28. Quoted in ibid., p. 74.
29. Marean, "Sabertooth Cats."
30. Robert J. Blumenschine, personal communication. May, 1994.
31. Nelson, *Make Prayers to the Raven*, p. 159.
32. Ibid., p. 159.
33. Bolgiano, *Mountain Lion*, p. 26.
34. Luckert, *Egyptian Light, Hebrew Fire*, p. 21.
35. Eliade, *Rites and Symbols of Initiation*, p. 23.
36. "Prehistoric Art Treasure Is Found in French Cave," *New York Times*, January 19, 1995, p. 1.
37. Mundkur, *The Cult of the Serpent*, p. 118.
38. Ibid., p. 127.
39. Saunders, "Tezcatlipoca."
40. Montgomery, *Spell of the Tiger*, p. 147.
41. Quoted in ibid., p. 144.
42. Valeri, *Kingship and Sacrifice*, p. 23.
43. Quoted in Lewis, p. 158.
44. Ziegler, Rebecca Lea, "Odin and His Warriors: The Volsung-Tradition and Its Mythic Function" (Ph.D. diss., UCLA, 1985), abstract in *Dissertation Abstracts International*, Vol. 46/08-A, p. 2,331.
45. Edmonson, Munro S., "Human Sacrifice in the Books of Chilam Balam of Tizimin and Chumayel," in Boone, pp. 91–100.
46. Robicsek, Francis, and Donald Hales, "Maya Heart Sacrifice: Cultural Perspectives and Surgical Technique," in Boone, p. 73.
47. Saunders, p. 171.
48. Robicsek and Hales, p. 73.
49. Ibid., p. 51.
50. Ibid., p. 56.
51. Lorenz, *On Aggression*, pp. 260–61.
52. Quoted in Burkert, *Creation of the Sacred*, p. 31.
53. Canetti, p. 209.

Chapter 5

1. Lorenz, *On Aggression*, p. 261.
2. Blomberg, *The Heart of the Warrior*, p. 63.
3. Sjoo, Monica, and Barbara Mor, *The Great Cosmic Mother: Rediscovering the Religion of the Earth* (San Francisco: Harper & Row, 1987), p. 250.

4. Campbell, *The Hero with a Thousand Faces*, pp. 285–86.
5. Weil, "The Illiad or the Poem of Force," p. 165.
6. Quoted in Pritchard, *The Ancient Near East*, p. 113.
7. Cosmides and Tooby, "From Evolution to Behavior," p. 296.
8. Graves, *The Greek Myths*, p. 228.
9. Pfeiffer, *The Emergence of Man*, p. 129.
10. Rose and Marshall, "Meat Eating."
11. McNeill, *Keeping Together in Time*.
12. Pfeiffer, p. 308.
13. Stanford, "To Catch a Colobus."
14. Handoo, Jawaharlal, "Cult Attitudes to Birds and Animals in Folklore," in Willis, *Signifying Animals*, pp. 37–42.
15. Bloch, *Prey into Hunter*, p. 10. Unfortunately Bloch does not develop this point in a historical direction, and leaves open the possibility that "the predator" is a largely metaphorical concept. I thank Rosa Ehrenreich for bringing Bloch's work to my attention.
16. Eliade, *Rites and Symbols of Initiation*, p. 24.
17. Ibid., p. 131.
18. Bloch, pp. 9–10.
19. Eliade, p. 105.
20. Lopez, *Of Wolves and Men*, pp. 129–31.
21. Mundkur, *The Cult of the Serpent*, p. 58.
22. Eliade, p. 23.
23. Ibid., p. 79.
24. Dumézil, *Destiny of the Warrior*, pp. 139–47.
25. Eliade, p. 81.
26. Ibid., p. 72.
27. Buchanan, *Roman Sport and Entertainment*, p. 44.
28. Quoted in Tucker, *Life in the Roman World*, p. 287.
29. Ibid., p. 285.
30. Yoon, Carol Kaesuk, "Pronghorn's Speed May Be Legacy of Past Predators," *New York Times*, Dec. 12, 1996, p. B9. Yoon was reporting on the work of Dr. John A. Byers, to be published under the title *American Pronghorn: Social Adaptations and the Ghosts of Predators Past* (Chicago: University of Chicago Press, 1997).
31. Quoted in Marks, *Fears, Phobias, and Rituals*, p. 112.
32. Dawkins, *The Selfish Gene*, p. 331.
33. See, for example, Sokolov, "Phobias and Anxiety."
34. Nesse, "Evolutionary Explanations of Emotions."

35. Marks and Nesse, "Fear and Fitness."
36. As in the case of humans, the initial effect of Prozac is to heighten anxiety in mice, or at least to intensify their anti-predator vigilance. Then, after a few doses—and again parallel to the pattern of its action on humans—the drug begins to exert its anxiolytic, or anxiety-quelling, effects. Griebel et al., "Differential Modulation."
37. See Marks and Nesse for a review of the literature.
38. Saladin D'Anglure, Bernard, "Nanook, Super-male: The Polar Bear in the Imaginary Space and Social Time of the Inuit of the Canadian Arctic," in Willis, p. 184.
39. Marks's 1987 volume *Fears, Phobias and Rituals*, for example, offers nothing on the role of child-rearing practices in the etiology of anxiety and phobias.
40. Dawkins, p. 198.

Chapter 6

1. Neumann, *The Great Mother* (see ch. 2, n. 23), p. 279.
2. On the prominence of "the goddess" in archaic Middle Eastern and Mediterranean religions, see Graves, *The Greek Myths: I* (see ch. 4, n. 26); Gimbutas, *The Language of the Goddess*; Eisler, *The Chalice and the Blade*; Campbell and Muses, *In All Her Names*. Evidence for archaic goddess worship in other parts of the world is fragmentary but suggestive. According to some interpretations, the principal deity of the Harappan culture of pre-Aryan-invasion India was female; certainly Harappan art features bold and powerful-looking female figures. In Aztec mythology, the preeminent (male) deity Huitzilopochtli, the god of war, comes to power by defeating his sister, the moon goddess Coyolxuahqui, in battle. The prehistoric Japanese worshipped Amaterasu, goddess of the sun, who is still the principal Shinto deity. And until the coming of Islam, Mecca was the site of the worship of the three goddesses Allat, al-Uzza, and Manat. On this point, see Hodgson, *The Venture of Islam*, vol. 1, p. 156.
3. As one expert says disparagingly of the Mesopotamian goddess Inanna: "We see her . . . in all the roles a woman may fill except the two which call for maturity and a sense of responsibility. She is never depicted as a wife and helpmate or as a mother." Jacobsen, Thorkild, *The Treasures of Darkness: A History of Mesopotamian Religion* (New Haven: Yale University Press, 1976), p. 141.

4. Quoted in Baring and Cashford, *The Myth of the Goddess*, p. 170.
5. Tiwari, *Goddess Cults in Ancient India*, p. 70.
6. Baring and Cashford, p. 217.
7. Ibid., p. 460.
8. Quoted in ibid., p. 325.
9. Neumann, p. 183.
10. Ibid., p. 172.
11. Burkert, *Greek Religion*, p. 149.
12. Young, *Origins of the Sacred* (see ch. 2, n. 21), p. 180.
13. Burkert, p. 152.
14. Baring and Cashford, p. 170.
15. Quoted in Vernant and Vidal-Naquet, *Myth and Tragedy in Ancient Greece* (see ch. 3, n. 1), p. 157.
16. Baring and Cashford, p. 460.
17. Stager and Wolff, "Child Sacrifice at Carthage" (see ch. 4, n. 12).
18. Kosambi, *Myth and Reality*, p. 86.
19. Brown, C. Mackenzie, "Kali, the Mad Mother," in *The Book of the Goddess Past and Present*, ed. Carl Olson (New York: Crossroad, 1994), pp. 110–23.
20. Nilsson, *A History of Greek Religion*, p. 16.
21. Burkert, *Ancient Mystery Cults*, p. 120.
22. Brown, p. 115.
23. Baring and Cashford, p. 114.
24. Eisler, p. 43.
25. Ibid., p. 20.
26. Gimbutas, p. 141.
27. Lerner, *The Creation of Patriarchy*, p. 39.
28. On the chronic scarcity of game for surviving Amazonian Indian peoples, see Ferguson, R. Brian, "War and the Sexes in Amazonia," in *Dialectics and Gender*, eds. R. Randolph, M. Diaz, and D. Schneider (Boulder, Colo.: Westview Press, 1988), pp. 136–54.
29. Olsen, "Solutré."
30. Ewers, *The Blackfeet* (see ch. 2, n. 4), p. 13.
31. Harris, *Cultural Materialism*, p. 82.
32. As discussed, for example, by Turke, "Effects of Ovulatory Concealment and Synchrony on Protohominid Mating Systems and Parental Roles."
33. Quoted in Knight, Chris, "Menstrual Synchrony and the Australian Rainbow Snake," in Buckley and Gottliber, *Blood Magic*, pp. 232–56.
34. Marshack, *The Roots of Civilization*, pp. 37–44.

35. Knight, *Blood Relations*, pp. 246–48.
36. Quoted in Detienne and Svenbro, "The Feast of the Wolves, or the Impossible City" (see ch. 4, n. 1), p. 147.
37. King, Helen, "Bound to Bleed: Artemis and Greek Women," p. 117. See also Dean-Jones, *Women's Bodies in Classical Greek Science.* On page 225, Dean-Jones states that "menstrual blood is the linchpin of both the Hippocratic and the Aristotelian theories on how women differed from men. Whether a woman was healthy, diseased, pregnant, or nursing, in Classical Greece her body was defined scientifically in terms of blood hydraulics."
38. Power, "The Woman with the Zebra's Penis," pp. 8–10.
39. Valeri, *Kingship and Sacrifice* (see ch. 2, n. 17), p. 114.
40. Wilkerson, S. Jeffrey K., "In Search of the Mountain of Foam: Human Sacrifice in Eastern Mesoamerica," in Boone, *Ritual Human Sacrifice in Mesoamerica*, pp. 115–16.
41. De Heusch, *The Drunken King or The Origin of the State*, p. 171.
42. Lévi-Strauss, *The Origin of Table Manners*, p. 349.
43. Ibid., pp. 400–401.
44. Grahn, *Blood, Bread, and Roses*, p. 76.
45. Knight, Chris, "Lévi-Strauss and the Dragon: *Mythologiques* Reconsidered in the Light of an Australian Aboriginal Myth," *Man* 18 (1983): 21–50.
46. Quoted in ibid., p. 22.
47. Grahn, pp. 32–33.
48. Ibid., p. 54.
49. Ibid., pp. 5–6.
50. Knight, *Blood Relations*.
51. Sandars, *The Epic of Gilgamesh*, p. 85.
52. Ibid., p. 93.
53. Knight, "Lévi-Strauss and the Dragon," pp. 34–35.
54. Mithen, "The Mesolithic Age," pp. 106–7.
55. Mithen, "To Hunt or to Paint: Animals and Art in the Upper Paleolithic." He argues that the stalking strategy was employed in Upper Paleolithic Europe in years when game shortages would have obviated the "drive" strategy. Since the long-term trend in Europe and other places was toward diminishing game populations, the long-term trend in hunting strategies would have been toward stalking.
56. Ferrill, *The Origins of War*, p. 18; Fagan, *People of the Earth*, pp. 208–9. While Ferrill locates this invention in the Mesolithic, between 12,000

and 8,000 years ago, Fagan puts it slightly earlier, at about 15,000 years ago, or on the eve of the Mesolithic.

57. Leibowitz, "In the Beginning . . . : The Origins of the Sexual Division of Labour and the Development of the First Human Societies," pp. 43–75. Leibowitz, it should be noted, connects this change in hunting strategies not to the decline of game populations but to the invention of projectile weapons, which she locates in the Upper Paleolithic epoch but which was probably closer to the Mesolithic.
58. Cucchiari, "The Gender Revolution and the Transition from Bisexual Horde to Patrilocal Band: The Origins of Gender Hierarchy," pp. 30–79.
59. On the deleterious effects of women's blood on male weapons, see, for example, Meggitt, *Blood Is Their Argument*, p. 60.
60. Jay, *Throughout Your Generations Forever* (see ch. 4, n. 24), p. 29.
61. Euripides, *The Bacchae and Other Plays*, p. 203.
62. Ibid., p. 204.
63. Ibid., pp. 216–17.
64. Ibid., p. 220.
65. Ibid., p. 196.
66. Aeschylus, *The Furies*, in Lowell, *The Oresteia*, p. 107.
67. Virgil, *The Aeneid*, pp. 179–80.
68. Evans-Grubb, "Abduction Marriage in Antiquity: A Law of Constantine (CTH IX. 24. 1) and Its Social Context."
69. Bloch, *Prey into Hunter* (see ch. 5, n. 15), pp. 69–72.
70. Schuster, Angela M. H., "A Woman's Place," *Archaeology* (November/December 1995): 78–79.
71. King, Helen, "Sacrificial Blood: The Role of the *Amnion* in Ancient Gynecology," *Helios* 13, no. 2 (1986): 117–26.
72. King, "Bound to Bleed," p. 120.

Chapter 7

1. McCarthy, Cormac, *Blood Meridian, Or the Evening Redness in the West* (New York: Vintage, 1985), p. 248.
2. O'Connell, *Ride of the Second Horseman*, pp. 45–52.
3. Mithen, "The Mesolithic Age," p. 134.
4. Wenke, *Patterns in Prehistory*, pp. 179, 375.
5. O'Connell, *Of Arms and Men*, p. 37.
6. McRandle, *The Antique Drums of War*, p. 45.
7. Martin, "Prehistoric Overkill."

8. Schüle, "Human Evolution."
9. Bower, "Extinctions on Ice."
10. Ibid.
11. Paul Martin, personal communication. February, 1993.
12. Zimmer, Carl, "Carriers of Extinction," *Discover* (July 1995): 28–30.
13. Paul Martin, same personal communication.
14. Cohen, N. M., *The Food Crisis in Prehistory* (New Haven and London: Yale University Press, 1977), cited in Wenke, p. 263.
15. Ingold, *Hunters, Pastoralists and Ranchers*, p. 281.
16. Lopez, *Of Wolves and Men*.
17. Ingold, *Hunters*, p. 281.
18. Wenke, p. 325.
19. O'Connell, *Ride*, chapter 6.
20. Keeley, *War Before Civilization*, p. 37.
21. On human trophy-hunting by South American native peoples, see, for example, Métraux, "Warfare, Cannibalism, and Human Trophies."
22. Keeley, p. 100.
23. Mumford, *The City in History*, p. 22.
24. Vidal-Naquet, *Forms of Thought and Forms of Society in the Greek World*, p. 3.
25. Mumford, p. 22.
26. Dyer, *War*, p. 10.
27. Kroeber and Fontana, *Massacre on the Gila*, p. 168.
28. Haas, *The Anthropology of War*.
29. *Iliad*, Book VI, ll. 490–92.
30. Barber, Elizabeth Wayland, *Women's Work: The First 20,000 Years* (New York: W. W. Norton, 1994).
31. For more examples of "warrior queens," see Fraser, *The Warrior Queens*.
32. Wheelwright, *Amazons and Military Maids*, p. 75.
33. Davie, *The Evolution of War*, p. 29.
34. Quoted in Fornari, *The Psychoanalysis of War*, p. 46.
35. Garlan, *War in the Ancient World*, pp. 26–31.
36. Quoted in Barber, Richard, *The Knight and Chivalry*, p. 21.
37. Davie, p. 44.
38. Hogbin, Ian, quoted in Walsh and Scandalis, "Institutionalized Forms of Intergenerational Male Aggression," p. 146.
39. Turney-High, *Primitive War*, p. 145.
40. Apple, R. W., "War: Bush's Presidential Rite of Passage," *New York Times*, December 21, 1989, p. A1.

41. Elshtain, *Women and War*, p. 168.
42. Shoumatoff, Alex, "The 'Warlord' Speaks," *The Nation*, April 4, 1994, p. 442.
43. Quoted in Sagan, *Cannibalism*, p. 4.
44. Quoted in LeShan, *The Psychology of War*, p. 91.
45. Quoted in Sanday, *Female Power and Male Dominance*, p. 78.
46. Lerner, *The Creation of Patriarchy*, p. 81.
47. Euripides, *The Trojan Women*, in *Euripides: Four Tragedies*, pp. 152–53.
48. See, for example, Ferguson, "War and the Sexes in Amazonia." Ferguson suggests that, for the war-prone Amazonian Indians, "raiding for women itself may further lower female status in society," and he notes that men's attempts to bring a captive woman into the household may be "blocked by the resident females, who would descend on the new wife 'like white cells on a virus.'"

Chapter 8

1. Quoted in Theweleit, Klaus, "Homosexuelle Aspekte von Männerbünden unter besonderer Berücksichtigung des Faschismus," in Völger, Gisela and Karin v. Welck, *Männerbände, Männerbünde: Zur Rolle des Mannes im Kulturvergleich, Zweibändige Materialiensammlung zu einer Ausstellung des Rautenstrach-Joest-Museums für Völkerkunde in der Josef-Haubrich-Kunsthalle Köln* (Cologne: 1990).
2. Siverson and Starr, *The Diffusion of War*, p. 16.
3. Houweling, "The Epidemiology of War."
4. Keeley, *War Before Civilization*, p. 128.
5. Ibid., p. 148.
6. Schmookler, *The Parable of the Tribes*, p. 37.
7. Ibid., p. 23.
8. Fox, "Fatal Attraction."
9. Benedict, "The Natural History of War."
10. On the obsidian trade, see Wenke, *Patterns in Prehistory*, p. 327.
11. Hinde, R. A., "Patriotism: Is Kin Selection Both Necessary and Sufficient?" *Politics and the Life Sciences* 8 (1989): 58–61.
12. Keeley, p. 122.
13. Ibid.
14. Quoted in Schmookler, p. 54.
15. Van Creveld, *The Transformation of War*, p. 174.

16. "Blood Revenge and War Among the Jibaro Indians of Eastern Ecuador," in Bohannan, *Law and Warfare*, pp. 303–32.
17. Ruth Benedict, quoted in Sagan, *Cannibalism*, p. 37.
18. Quoted in Métraux, "Warfare, Cannibalism, and Human Trophies," p. 385.
19. Morren, "Warfare on the Highland Fringe of New Guinea," p. 201.
20. Kroeber and Fontana, *Massacre on the Gila*, p. 91.
21. Sagan, *Cannibalism*, p. 21.
22. Lopez, *Of Wolves and Men*, p. 119.
23. Lamb, *Genghis Khan*, p. 20.
24. Quoted in Bataille, *The Accursed Share*, p. 51.
25. Quoted in Barber, Richard, *The Knight and Chivalry*, p. 209.
26. Hubert and Mauss, *Sacrifice*, p. 82.
27. Oldenbourg, *The Crusades*, p. 39.
28. Quoted in Packer, George, "Communication by Gunpowder," *New York Times Book Review* (February 12, 1995): 13.
29. Divale, "An Explanation for Primitive Warfare."
30. Andrzejewski, *Military Organization and Society*, pp. 33–74.
31. For the phrase "means of destruction" I am indebted to Goody, *Technology, Tradition and the State in Africa*.

Chapter 9

1. Quoted in Seward, *The Hundred Years War*, p. 15.
2. Blomberg, *The Heart of the Warrior*, p. 125.
3. White, L., quoted in Goody, *Technology, Tradition and the State in Africa*, p. 34.
4. Ibid., pp. 36–37.
5. McNeill, *The Pursuit of Power*, pp. 8–11.
6. Andrzejewski, *Military Organization and Society*, pp. 28–33.
7. Blomberg, p. 47.
8. The African example is from Andrzejewksi, p. 32.
9. McNeill, *Pursuit*, p. vii.
10. Ibid., p. 2.
11. Quoted in Keegan, *The History of Warfare*, p. 242.
12. Quoted in Fields, *The Code of the Warrior*, pp. 187–88.
13. Quoted in Waite, *Vanguard of Nazism*, p. 42.
14. *From the War of Rebellion: Official Records of the Union and Confederate Armies*, ser. 1, vol. 12, part 3 (Washington: Government Printing Office, 1885), p. 844.

15. Atkinson, *The Long Gray Line*, p. 58.
16. Nye, *The Patton Mind*, p. 6.
17. Atkinson, p. 39.
18. Vagts, *A History of Militarism*, p. 18.
19. Barber, Richard, *The Knight and Chivalry*, p. 45.
20. Quoted in Anderson, *Imagined Communities*, p. 9, n. 2.
21. Goodrick-Clarke, *The Occult Roots of Nazism*, pp. 192–204.
22. Goody, p. 35.
23. Quoted in Schmookler, *The Parable of the Tribes*, p. 165.
24. Kolko, *Century of War*, p. 47.
25. Nash, June, "The Aztecs and the Ideology of Male Dominance," *Signs* 4 (1978–9): 349.
26. Quoted in Turnbull, *Samurai Warlords*, p. 105.
27. Byock, *The Saga of the Volsungs*, pp. 40–43.
28. Barber, Richard, pp. 38–39.
29. Blomberg, p. 97.
30. Froissart, *Chronicles*, p. 92.
31. Quoted in Theweleit, *Male Fantasies*, p. 33.
32. Jay, *Throughout Your Generations Forever*, p. 32.
33. Quoted in Eliade, *Rites and Symbols of Initiation*, p. 55.
34. Quoted in Fields, p. 76.
35. Davidson, *Myths and Symbols in Pagan Europe*, p. 98.
36. Hiltebeitel, *The Ritual of Battle*, p. 319. See also O'Flaherty, *The Origins of Evil in Hindu Mythology*, p. 261.
37. Ritter, *Shaka Zulu*, pp. 308–9.

Chapter 10

1. Quoted in Fields, *The Code of the Warrior*, p. 147.
2. Sandars, *The Epic of Gilgamesh*, p. 62.
3. Murray, *Early Greece*, p. 179.
4. Barber, Richard, *The Knight and Chivalry*, p. 61.
5. Contamine, *War in the Middle Ages*, pp. 275–76.
6. Sherratt, Andrew, "The Emergence of Elites: Early Bronze Age Europe, 2500–1300 B.C.," in Cunliffe, *The Oxford Illustrated Prehistory of Europe*, p. 253.
7. Murray, p. 47.
8. Barber, Richard, p. 186.
9. Quoted in ibid., p. 47.

10. Law, "Human Sacrifice in Pre-Colonial West Africa."
11. There is some disagreement about the number of young people owed to Crete by Athens. Bulfinch (*Bulfinch's Mythology*) puts the Athenian tribute at seven youths and seven maidens annually, while Hamilton (*Mythology*) has fourteen victims being sent to Crete only every nine years.
12. Davidson, *Myths and Symbols in Pagan Europe,* p. 62.
13. Demarest, Arthur, "Overview: Mesoamerican Human Sacrifice in Evolutionary Perspective," in Boone, *Ritual Human Sacrifice in Mesoamerica*, pp. 227–43.
14. Quoted in Bergmann, *In the Shadow of Moloch*, pp. 57–58.
15. Quoted in Bainton, *Christian Attitudes Toward War and Peace*, p. 48.
16. Hodgson, *The Venture of Islam*, p. 134.
17. Kosambi, *An Introduction to the Study of Indian History*, p. 166.
18. Luckert, *Egyptian Light, Hebrew Fire*, p. 24.
19. Hodgson, p. 133, and Armstrong, *A History of God*, p. 27.
20. Kosambi, *An Introduction*, p. 167.
21. Luckert, *Egyptian Light*, p. 24.
22. Griffin, "New Heaven, New Earth."
23. Byock, *The Saga of the Volsungs*, p. 7.
24. Burkert, *Creation of the Sacred*, p. 42.
25. See Seidel, *Mithras-Orion.*
26. Contamine, p. 302.
27. Quoted in Bainton, p. 110.
28. Bernstein, "Just War, Holy War."
29. Contamine, p. 277.
30. Oldenbourg, *The Crusades,* pp. 35–36.
31. Contamine, pp. 269–70.
32. Bainton, p. 104.
33. Frend, *The Rise of Christianity*, p. 804.
34. McNeill, *The Pursuit of Power*, p. 63: He observes that "very little is known about the manufacture and distribution of the arms and armor upon which the knights of Latin Christendom relied."
35. Contamine, pp. 67–68.
36. Seward, *The Hundred Years War*, p. 57.
37. Barber, Richard, pp. 47–48.
38. Oldenbourg, p. 47.
39. Contamine, pp. 298–99.
40. Ibid., pp. 300–301.

41. Quoted in Bainton, pp. 111–12.
42. Contamine, p. 294.
43. Bainton, p. 115.
44. Blomberg, *The Heart of the Warrior*, p. 49.
45. Quoted in Froissart, *Chronicles*, p. 212.
46. Ibid., p. 152.
47. Ibid., p. 249.
48. Hibbert, *Agincourt*, p. 119.
49. Quoted in O'Connell, *Ride of the Second Horseman*, p. 233.
50. Hibbert, p. 38.
51. Quoted in Froissart, p. 89.
52. Vagts, *A History of Militarism*, p. 42.
53. Quoted in ibid.

Chapter 11

1. Cervantes, Miguel de, *Don Quixote*, trans. John Ormsby (New York: W. W. Norton & Co., 1981), p. 303.
2. On the "early modern military revolution," see especially Delbrück, *History of the Art of War*; Parker, *The Military Revolution*; McNeill, *The Pursuit of Power*, chapter 4; O'Connell, *Of Arms and Men*, chapters 7 and 8.
3. Quoted in O'Connell, *Of Arms and Men*, p. 114.
4. Quoted in Barber, Richard, *The Knight and Chivalry*, p. 200.
5. Gies, *Joan of Arc*, p. 56.
6. Ibid., p. 86.
7. O'Connell, *Of Arms and Men*, p. 114.
8. Perrin, *Giving Up the Gun*, p. 25.
9. Phillippe de Comines, quoted in Vagts, *A History of Militarism*, p. 44.
10. Quoted in ibid., p. 48.
11. Delbrück, p. 258.
12. Frend, *The Rise of Christianity*, pp. 266–7, fn. 41.
13. Parker, pp. 20–21.
14. Quoted in O'Connell, *Of Arms and Men*, p. 155.
15. De Landa, *War in the Age of Intelligent Machines*.
16. Parker (p. 148) reports that the drill books of the Prussian army contained no command for "take aim."
17. O'Connell, *Of Arms and Men*, p. 154.
18. Parker, p. 53.

19. Rothenberg, *The Art of Warfare in the Age of Napoleon*, p. 12.
20. Delbrück, p. 224.
21. Howard, *The Lessons of History*, p. 52.
22. Parker, p. 3.
23. Mosse, *Confronting the Nation*, p. 15.
24. Parker, p. 57.
25. At least none are cited in the sources I have consulted, and it is hard to believe that scholars of the caliber, for example, of O'Connell or McNeill would overlook the journals or letters of ordinary soldiers if such records were available.
26. McNeill, *Pursuit*, p. 131; McNeill, *Keeping Together in Time*, chapter 2.
27. McNeill, *Keeping Together*, p. 8.
28. McNeill, *Pursuit*, p. 132.
29. Ibid., p. 124.
30. Quoted in Palmer, R. R., "Frederick the Great, Guibert, Bülow: From Dynastic to National War," in Paret, *The Makers of Modern Strategy*, p. 99.
31. Vagts, p. 95.
32. O'Connell, *Of Arms and Men*, pp. 171–72.
33. Quoted in Keeley, *War Before Civilization*, p. 74.
34. Vagts, p. 96.
35. Mosse, *Fallen Soldiers*, p. 18.
36. Herrold, *The Age of Napoleon*, p. 46.
37. Rothenberg, p. 82.
38. Ibid., p. 86.
39. Quoted in Delbrück, p. 413.
40. Quoted in ibid., p. 414.
41. Vagts, p. 100.
42. Palmer, p. 93.
43. Quoted in Delbrück, p. 187.
44. Vagts, p. 107.
45. McNeill, *Pursuit*, p. 213.
46. Anderson, *Imagined Communities*, p. 9.
47. Herrold, p. 29.
48. Hegel, *Elements of the Philosophy of Right*, p. 364.

Chapter 12

1. Keegan, *The Mask of Command*, p. 3.
2. Howard, *The Lessons of History*, p. 39.
3. Quoted in Vagts, *A History of Militarism*, p. 409.
4. Mosse, *Confronting the Nation*, p. 23.
5. Fichte, *The Science of Rights*, p. 228.
6. Anderson, *Imagined Communities*, p. 26.
7. Howard, *The Causes of Wars*, pp. 26–27.
8. Reischauer, *Japan*, p. 185.
9. Hegel, *Elements of the Philosophy of Right*, p. 290.
10. Quoted in Lake, "Mission Impossible," p. 309.
11. Friedrich, *The Philosophy of Hegel*, p. 322.
12. Gowans, *Selections from Treitschke's Lectures on Politics*, pp. 23–24.
13. Keen, *Faces of the Enemy*, pp. 60–64.
14. See Hope and Hope, *Symbols of the Nations*.

Chapter 13

1. Quoted in Vagts, *A History of Militarism*, p. 440.
2. Anderson, *Imagined Communities*, p. 10.
3. Bainton, *Christian Attitudes Toward War and Peace*, p. 209.
4. Quoted in ibid., p. 207.
5. O'Connell, *Of Arms and Men*, p. 270.
6. Strada, "The Horror of Land Mines."
7. Dower, *War Without Mercy*, p. 36.
8. O'Connell, *Of Arms and Men*, p. 286.
9. Quoted in Nation, *Black Earth, Red Star*, p. 137.
10. Ibid., p. 129.
11. Ibid., p. 138.
12. Mayer, *Why Did the Heavens Not Darken?*, p. 96.
13. Quoted in Waite, *The Psychopathic God*, p. 29.
14. Ibid., p. 31.
15. Ibid., p. 31.
16. Ibid., p. 30.
17. Ibid., p. 30.
18. Goodrick-Clarke, *The Occult Roots of Nazism*, p. 68.

19. Keegan, *The Mask of Command*, pp. 235–58.
20. Quoted in Toland, *Adolf Hitler*, p. 77.
21. Ibid., p. 80.
22. Ibid., p. 103.
23. Quoted in Waite, *The Psychopathic God*, p. 26.
24. Ibid., p. 224.
25. Ienaga, *Japan's Last War*, p. 23.
26. Quoted in ibid., p. 26.
27. "Because the Zen masters did not preach the easy way to salvation as did the masters of the Pure Land sects, Zen did not become a mass movement. Instead it tended to be a religion of the elite." Hane, *Premodern Japan*, p. 80.
28. Hardacre, *Shinto and the State*, pp. 23–25.
29. Ienaga, p. 22.
30. Ibid., p. 109.
31. Benedict, *The Chrysanthemum and the Sword*, pp. 88–89.
32. Hardacre, p. 32.
33. Ibid.
34. Fridell, Wilbur M., "A Fresh Look at State Shinto," *Journal of the American Academy of Religion* 44/3 (1976): 547–61.
35. Quoted in Blomberg, *The Heart of the Warrior*, p. 192.
36. Ibid., p. xii.
37. Quoted in Dower, p. 225.
38. Ibid., p. 216.
39. Quoted in ibid., p. 231.
40. Cousins, "*In God We Trust*," p. 95.
41. Quoted in Sherry, *In the Shadow of War*, p. 159.
42. Mosse, *Fallen Soldiers*, p. 33.
43. Quoted in Goldstein, *Saving "Old Glory,"* p. 13.
44. Quoted in ibid., p. 14.
45. Ibid., p. 93.
46. Bellah, Robert N., "Civil Religion in America," in Hudson, *Nationalism and Religion in America*, pp. 146–52.
47. Falwell, *Listen, America!*, p. 106.
48. Bennett, "*. . . So Gallantly Streaming*," pp. 72–73.
49. Quoted in Barnet, *The Rockets' Red Glare*, p. 145.
50. Falwell, p. 98.
51. Brooke, James, "Two Leaders Seek Laurels Along Peru-Ecuador Border," *New York Times*, February 9, 1995.

52. See, for example, "It's a Grand Old (Politically Correct) Flag," *Time*, February 25, 1991, p. 55.
53. Stern, Paul, "Why Do People Sacrifice for Their Nations?" in Comaroff and Stern, *Perspectives on Nationalism and War*, pp. 99–121.

Chapter 14

1. From Brecht's play *Mother Courage and Her Children*, in Bentley, *Seven Plays by Bertolt Brecht*, p. 303.
2. O'Connell, *Of Arms and Men*, p. 301.
3. Mueller, *Retreat from Doomsday*, p. 4.
4. Keegan, *The History of Warfare*, p. 56.
5. O'Connell, *Ride of the Second Horseman*, p. 241.
6. Kaplan, Robert D., "Into the Bloody New World: A Moral Pragmatism in an Age of Mini-Holocausts," *The Washington Post*, April 17, 1994, Outlook section.
7. Cranna, *The True Cost of Conflict*, p. xvii.
8. Van Creveld, *The Transformation of War*, p. 223.
9. Strada, "The Horror of Land Mines."
10. See Boutwell et al., *Lethal Commerce*.
11. Kim, Lucian, "The Private Security State," *In These Times* (April 15–28, 1996): 17–18.
12. Remnick, David, "Letter from Chechnya: In Stalin's Wake," *New Yorker* (July 24, 1995): 46–62.
13. "Serb Soldiers 'Still Holding Heights,'" *Daily Telegram*, August 13, 1993, p. 9.
14. Goldberg, Jeffrey, "A War Without a Purpose in a Country Without Identity," *New York Times Magazine* (January 22, 1995): 37.
15. See Gibson, *Warrior Dreams*.
16. Mansbridge, *Why We Lost the ERA*.
17. On women's gains in the U.S. military, see, for example, Stiehm, *It's Our Military Too!*
18. Van Creveld, p. 222.
19. For more on the harassment of women within the U.S. military, see Zimmerman, *Tailspin*.
20. Quoted in De Landa, *War in the Age of Intelligent Machines*, p. 128.
21. See, for example, Boyd and Richerson, *Culture and the Evolutionary Process*.

22. Dawkins, *The Selfish Gene*, p. 200.
23. Emmeche, *The Garden in the Machine*, p. 38.
24. Schmookler, *The Parable of the Tribes*, p. 32.
25. See, for example, Barber, Benjamin R., *Jihad vs. MacWorld*.

Bibliography

Aeschylus. *The Oresteia of Aeschylus.* Edited by Robert Lowell. New York: Farrar, Straus and Giroux, 1978.

Alberti, Johanna. *Beyond Suffrage: Feminists in War and Peace, 1914–1928.* New York: St. Martin's, 1989.

Alcock, John. *Animal Behavior: An Evolutionary Approach.* Sunderland, Mass.: Sinauer Associates, 1975.

Anderson, Benedict. *Imagined Communities: Reflections on the Origin and Spread of Nationalism.* London: Verso, 1983.

Anderson, Connie. "Predation and Primate Evolution." *Primates* 27, no. 1 (1986): 15–39.

Andrzejewski, Stanislaw. *Military Organization and Society.* London: Routledge and Kegan Paul, 1908.

Ardrey, Robert. *African Genesis.* New York: Dell, 1961.

———. *The Territorial Imperative.* New York: Delta, 1966.

Armstrong, Karen. *A History of God: The 4,000 Year Quest of Judaism, Christianity and Islam.* New York: Knopf, 1994.

Atkinson, Rick. *The Long Gray Line.* New York: Pocket Books, 1989.

Bainton, Roland H. *Christian Attitudes Toward War and Peace: A Historical Survey and Critical Re-evaluation.* Nashville: Abingdon, 1960.

Bakunin, Mikhail. *God and the State.* New York: Dover, 1970.

Barber, Benjamin R. *Jihad vs. MacWorld.* New York: Times/Random House, 1995.

Barber, Richard. *The Knight and Chivalry.* New York: Harper and Row, 1974.

Baring, Anne, and Jules Cashford. *The Myth of the Goddess: Evolution of an Image.* London: Arkana/Penguin, 1991.

Bibliography

Barnet, Richard J. *The Rockets' Red Glare: When America Goes to War.* New York: Simon and Schuster, 1990.

———. *Roots of War: The Men and Institutions Behind U.S. Foreign Policy.* New York: Penguin, 1972.

Bartov, Omer. *Hitler's Army: Soldiers, Nazis, and War in the Third Reich.* New York: Oxford University Press, 1992.

Bataille, Georges. *The Accursed Share.* New York: Zone Books, 1991.

———. *Theory of Religion.* New York: Zone Books, 1992.

Benedict, Ruth. *The Chrysanthemum and the Sword: Patterns of Japanese Culture.* Cleveland: Meridian Books, 1967.

———. "The Natural History of War." In *An Anthropologist at Work: The Writing of Ruth Benedict*, edited by Margaret Mead. Boston: Houghton Mifflin, 1959.

Bennett, M. R., "*. . . So Gallantly Streaming": The Story of Old Glory; the History and Proper Use of Our Flag from 1776 to the Present.* New York: Drake Publishers, 1974.

Bentley, Eric, ed. *Seven Plays by Bertolt Brecht.* New York: Grove Press, 1961.

Bergmann, Martin S. *In the Shadow of Moloch: The Sacrifice of Children and Its Impact on Western Religions.* New York: Columbia University Press, 1992.

Bernstein, Alan E. "Just War, Holy War." *University Publishing* (Spring 1979): 21–26.

Binford, Lewis R. "Human Ancestors: Changing Views of Their Behavior." *Journal of Anthropological Archaeology* 4 (1985): 292–327.

———. "The Hunting Hypothesis: Archaeological Methods and the Past." *The Yearbook of Physical Anthropology*, supp. 8 to *American Journal of Physical Anthropology* (1987): 1–9.

Bloch, Maurice. *Prey into Hunter: The Politics of Religious Experience.* New York: Cambridge University Press, 1992.

Blomberg, Catharina. *The Heart of the Warrior: Origins and Religious Background of the Samurai System in Feudal Japan.* Sandgate, Folkestone, Kent: Japan Library, 1994.

Blumenschine, Robert J., and John A. Cavallo. "Scavenging and Human Evolution." *Scientific American* (October 1992): 90–96.

Bohannan, Paul. *Law and Warfare: Studies in the Anthropology of Conflict.* Garden City, N.Y.: The Natural History Press, 1967.

Bolgiano, Chris. *Mountain Lion: An Unnatural History of Pumas and People.* Mechanicsburg, Pa.: Stackpole Books, 1995.

Boone, Elizabeth H., ed. *Ritual Human Sacrifice in Mesoamerica.* Washington, D.C.: Dumbarton Oaks Research Library and Collection, 1984.

Boutwell, Jeffrey, Michael T. Klare, and Laura W. Reed. *Lethal Commerce: The Global Trade in Small Arms and Light Weapons.* Cambridge, Mass.: Committee on International Security Studies, American Academy of Arts and Sciences, 1995.

Bower, Bruce. "Extinctions on Ice." *Science News* 32 (October 31, 1987): 284–85.

Bowlby, John. *Attachment and Loss*, vol. 2, *Separation: Anxiety and Anger.* New York: Basic Books, 1973.

Boyd, Robert, and Peter J. Richerson. *Culture and the Evolutionary Process.* Chicago: University of Chicago Press, 1985.

Boyles, Denis. *Man Eaters Motel.* New York: Ticknor and Fields, 1991.

Brain, C. K. *The Hunters or the Hunted? An Introduction to African Cave Taphonomy.* Chicago: University of Chicago Press, 1981.

Brown, C. Mackenzie. "Kali, the Mad Mother." In *The Book of the Goddess, Past and Present*, edited by Carl Olson. New York: Crossroad, 1994.

Buchanan, David. *Roman Sport and Entertainment.* London: Longman, 1976.

Buckley, Thomas, and Alma Gottlieb, eds. *Blood Magic: The Anthropology of Menstruation*. Berkeley: University of California Press, 1988.

Bulfinch, Thomas. *Bulfinch's Mythology*, abridged by Edward Fuller. New York: Dell, 1963.

Burenhalt, Göran, ed. *The First Humans: Human Origins and History to 10,000 B.C.* San Francisco: Harper San Francisco, 1993.

Burkert, Walter. *Ancient Mystery Cults.* Cambridge, Mass.: Harvard University Press, 1987.

———. *Creation of the Sacred: Tracks of Biology in Early Religions.* Cambridge: Harvard University Press, 1996.

———. *Greek Religion.* Cambridge: Harvard University Press, 1985.

———. *Homo Necans: The Anthropology of Ancient Greek Sacrificial Ritual and Myth.* Berkeley: University of California Press, 1983.

———. *Structure and History in Greek Mythology and Ritual.* Berkeley: University of California Press, 1979.

Byock, Jesse L., trans. *The Saga of the Volsungs: The Norse Epic of Sigurd the Dragon Slayer.* Berkeley: University of California Press, 1990.

Campbell, Joseph. *The Hero with a Thousand Faces.* Princeton, N.J.: Princeton University Press, 1968.

Campbell, Joseph, and Charles Muses, eds. *In All Her Names: Explorations of the Feminine in Divinity.* San Francisco: Harper San Francisco, n.d.

Canetti, Elias. *Crowds and Power.* New York: Continuum, 1962.

Carrasco, David. *Religions of Mesoamerica: Cosmovision and Ceremonial Centers.* New York: Harper & Row, 1990.

Carsten, Francis L. "Interpretations of Fascism." In *Fascism: A Reader's Guide*, edited by Walter Laqueur. Berkeley: University of California Press, 1976.

Chang, K. C. *Art, Myth, and Ritual: The Path to Political Authority in Ancient China.* Cambridge: Harvard University Press, 1983.

Clendinnen, Inga. *Aztecs: An Interpretation.* Cambridge: Cambridge University Press, 1995.

Comaroff, John. L. and Paul Stern. *Perspectives on Nationalism and War.* New York: Gordon and Breach, 1995.

Contamine, Philippe. *War in the Middle Ages*, translated by Michael Jones. Oxford: Basil Blackwell, 1993.

Coon, Carleton. *The Hunting Peoples.* Boston: Little, Brown, 1971.

Coontz, Stephanie, and Peta Henderson, eds. *Women's Work, Men's Property: The Origins of Gender and Class.* London: Verso, 1986.

Cosmides, Leda, and John Tooby. "From Evolution to Behavior: Evolutionary Psychology as the Missing Link." In *The Latest and the Best: Essays on Evolution and Optimality*, edited by J. Dupré. Cambridge: MIT Press, 1987.

Cousins, Norman. *"In God We Trust": The Religious Beliefs and Ideas of the American Founding Fathers.* New York: Harper and Bros., 1958.

Cranna, Michael, ed. *The True Cost of Conflict: Seven Recent Wars and Their Effects on Society.* New York: New Press, 1994.

Crile, G. W. *A Mechanistic View of War and Peace* (1915), quoted in Quincy Wright, *A Study of War*, vol. 2. Chicago: University of Chicago Press, 1942.

Cucchiari, Salvatore. "The Gender Revolution and the Transition from Bisexual Horde to Patrilocal Band: The Origins of Gender Hierarchy." In Ortner and Whitehead, *Sexual Meanings*.

Cunliffe, Barry, ed. *The Oxford Illustrated Prehistory of Europe.* Oxford: Oxford University Press, 1994.

Davidson, Hilda Ellis. *Myths and Symbols in Pagan Europe: Early Scandinavian and Celtic Religions.* Syracuse, N.Y.: Syracuse University Press, 1988.

Davie, Maurice R. *The Evolution of War: A Study of Its Role in Early Societies.* New Haven: Yale University Press, 1929.

Dawkins, Richard. *The Selfish Gene.* Oxford: Oxford University Press, 1989.

Dean-Jones, Lesley. *Women's Bodies in Classical Greek Science.* Oxford: Clarendon Press, 1994.

De Heusch, Luc. *The Drunken King or The Origin of the State*, translated by Roy Willis. Bloomington: Indiana University Press, 1982.

De Landa, Manuel. *War in the Age of Intelligent Machines.* New York: Zone Books, 1991.

Delbrück, Hans. *History of the Art of War*, vol. 4, *The Dawn of Modern Warfare.* Lincoln: University of Nebraska Press, 1985.

Detienne, Marcel, and Jesper Svenbro. "The Feast of the Wolves, or the Impossible City." In *The Cuisine of Sacrifice Among the Greeks*, edited by Marcel Detienne and Jean-Pierre Vernant, translated by Paula Wissing. Chicago: University of Chicago Press, 1989.

Divale, William T. "An Explanation for Primitive Warfare: Population Control and the Significance of Primitive Sex Ratios." *The New Scholar* (Fall 1970): 173–91.

Dower, John W. *War Without Mercy: Race and Power in the Pacific War.* New York: Pantheon, 1986.

Dumézil, Georges. *Destiny of the Warrior.* Chicago: University of Chicago Press, 1969.

Dyer, Gwynne. *War.* New York: Crown, 1985.

Eisler, Riane. *The Chalice and the Blade.* San Francisco: Harper and Row, 1987.

Eksteins, Modris. *Rites of Spring: The Great War and the Birth of the Modern Age.* New York: Anchor/Doubleday, 1989.

Eliade, Mircea. *Rites and Symbols of Initiation: The Mysteries of Birth and Rebirth.* New York: Harper and Row, 1958.

Elshtain, Jean Bethke. *Women and War.* New York: Basic Books, 1987.

Emmeche, Claus. *The Garden in the Machine.* Princeton, N.J.: Princeton University Press, 1994.

Euripides. *The Bacchae and Other Plays*, translated by Philip Vellacott. Baltimore, Md.: Penguin Books, 1965.

Euripides. *The Trojan Woman*, translated by Richmond Lattimore. In *Euripides III: Four Tragedies*, edited by David Grene and Richmond Lattimore. Chicago: University of Chicago Press, 1958.

Evans-Grubb, Judith. "Abduction Marriage in Antiquity: A Law of Constantine

(CTH IX. 24. 1) and Its Social Context." *Journal of Roman Studies* 79 (1989): 59–83.

Ewers, John C. *The Blackfeet: Raiders on the Northwestern Plains.* Norman and London: University of Oklahoma Press, 1958.

Fagan, Brian M. *People of the Earth.* New York: HarperCollins, 1992.

Falwell, Jerry. *Listen, America!* Garden City, N.Y.: Doubleday, 1980.

Faraone, Christopher A. *Talismans and Trojan Horses: Guardian Statues in Ancient Greek Myth and Ritual.* New York: Oxford University Press, 1992.

Favazza, Armando R. *Bodies Under Seige: Self-mutilation in Culture and Psychiatry.* Baltimore, Md.: Johns Hopkins University Press, 1987.

Ferguson, R. Brian. "Game Wars? Ecology and Conflict in Amazonia." *Journal of Anthropological Research* 45 (1989): 179–206.

———. "War and the Sexes in Amazonia." In *Dialectics and Gender*, edited by R. Randolph, M. Diaz, and D. Schneider. Boulder, Colo.: Westview Press, 1988.

Ferrill, Arthur. *The Origins of War: From the Stone Age to Alexander the Great.* London: Thames and Hudson, 1985.

Fichte, J. G. *The Science of Rights*, translated by A. E. Kroeger. London: Trubnor and Co., 1889.

Fields, Rick. *The Code of the Warrior.* New York: HarperPerennial, 1991.

Fornari, Franco. *The Psychoanalysis of War*, translated by Alenka Pfeifer. Bloomington: Indiana University Press, 1975.

Fox, Robin. "Fatal Attraction: War and Human Nature." *The National Interest* (Winter 1992/93): 11–20.

———. *The Search for Society: Quest for a Biosocial Science and Mortality.* New Brunswick, N.J.: Rutgers University Press, 1989.

Fraser, Antonia. *The Warrior Queens.* New York: Vintage Books, 1988.

Frazer, James G. *The Golden Bough: The Roots of Religion and Folklore.* New York: Avenel Books, 1981; originally published 1890.

Frend, W. H. C. *The Rise of Christianity.* Philadelphia: Fortress Press, 1984.

Friedrich, Carl J. *The Philosophy of Hegel.* New York: Modern Library, 1953.

Froissart, Jean. *Chronicles*, translated by Geoffrey Brereton. London: Penguin, 1978.

Fromm, Erich. *The Anatomy of Human Destructiveness.* New York: Holt, Rinehart and Winston, 1973.

Fussell, Paul. *The Great War in Modern Memory.* London: Oxford University Press, 1975.

Garlan, Yvon. *War in the Ancient World: A Social History.* London: Chatto and Windus, 1975.

Garrett, Laurie. *The Coming Plague: Newly Emerging Diseases in a World Out of Balance.* New York: Farrar, Straus and Giroux, 1994.

Gibson, James William. *Warrior Dreams: Paramilitary Culture in Post-Vietnam America.* New York: Hill and Wang, 1994.

Gies, Frances. *Joan of Arc: The Legend and the Reality.* New York: Harper and Row, 1981.

Gimbutas, Marija. *The Language of the Goddess.* San Francisco: Harper, 1989.

Girard, René. *Violence and the Sacred.* Baltimore, Md.: Johns Hopkins University Press, 1979.

Gochman, Charles S., and Alan Ned Sabrosky, eds. *Prisoners of War? Nation-States in the Modern Era.* Lexington, Mass.: D. C. Heath & Co., 1990.

Goldstein, Robert Justin. *Saving "Old Glory": The History of the American Flag Desecration Controversy.* Boulder, Colo.: Westview Press, 1995.

Goodrick-Clarke, Nicholas. *The Occult Roots of Nazism: Secret Aryan Cults and Their Influence on Nazi Ideology.* New York: New York University Press, 1992.

Goody, Jack. *Technology, Tradition and the State in Africa.* London: Oxford University Press, 1971.

Gould, Richard A., and John E. Yellen. "Man the Hunted: Determinants of Household Spacing in Desert and Tropical Foraging Societies." *Journal of Anthropological Archaeology* 6 (1987): 77–102.

Government Printing Office. *From the War of Rebellion: Official Records of the Union and Confederate Armies.* Series 1, vol. 12, part 3. Washington, D.C., 1885.

Gowans, Adam L., trans. and ed. *Selections from Treitschke's Lectures on Politics.* New York: Frederick A. Stokes Co., 1914.

Grahn, Judy. *Blood, Bread, and Roses: How Menstruation Created the World.* Boston: Beacon Press, 1993.

Graves, Robert. *The Greek Myths: I.* New York: Penguin, 1977; originally published 1955.

Griebel, G., D. C. Blanchard, R. S. Agnes, and R. J. Blanchard. "Differential Modulation of Antipredator Defensive Behavior in Swiss-Webster Mice Following Acute or Chronic Administration of Imipramine and Fluoxetine." *Psychopharmacology* 120, no. 1 (1995): 57–66.

Griffin, Jasper. "New Heaven, New Earth." *New York Review of Books*, December 22, 1994, pp. 23–28.

Gross, Rita M. "Menstruation and Childbirth as Ritual and Religious Experience." In *Unspoken Worlds: Women's Religious Lives*, edited by Rita M. Gross and Nancy Auer Falk. Belmont, Calif.: Wadsworth, 1989.

Grossman, Lt. Col. Dave. *On Killing: The Psychological Cost of Learning to Kill in War and Society.* Boston: Little, Brown, 1995.

Haas, Jonathan, ed. *The Anthropology of War.* Cambridge: Cambridge University Press, 1990.

Hamerton-Kelly, Robert G., ed. *Violent Origins: Walter Burkert, René Girard, and Jonathan Z. Smith on Ritual Killing and Cultural Formation.* Stanford: Stanford University Press, 1987.

Hamilton, Edith. *Mythology.* New York: New American Library, 1969.

Hane, Mikiso. *Premodern Japan: A Historical Survey.* Boulder, Colo.: Westview Press, 1991.

Hanson, Victor Davis. *The Western Way of War: Infantry Battle in Classical Greece.* New York: Alfred A. Knopf, 1989.

Haraway, Donna J. *Simians, Cyborgs and Nature: The Reinvention of Nature.* New York: Routledge, 1991.

Hardacre, Helen. *Shinto and the State: 1868–1988.* Princeton, N.J.: Princeton University Press, 1989.

Harris, Marvin. *Cannibals and Kings: The Origins of Cultures.* New York: Vintage Books, 1977.

———. *Cultural Materialism: The Struggle for a Science of Culture.* New York: Random House, 1979.

Harrison, Jane Ellen. *Prolegomena to the Study of Greek Religion.* Cambridge: Cambridge University Press, 1922.

Hartog, François. "Self-cooking Beef and the Drinks of Ares." In *The Cuisine of Sacrifice Among the Greeks*, edited by Marcel Detienne and Jean-Pierre Vernant. Chicago: University of Chicago Press, 1989.

Heesterman, J. C. *The Broken World of Sacrifice: An Essay in Ancient Indian Ritual.* Chicago: University of Chicago Press, 1993.

Hegel, G. W. F. *Elements of the Philosophy of Right*, edited by Allan W. Wood and translated by H. B. Nisbet. Cambridge: Cambridge University Press, 1991.

Herrold, J. Christopher. *The Age of Napoleon.* Boston: Houghton Mifflin, 1987; originally published 1963.

Hibbert, Christopher. *Agincourt.* Philadelphia: Dufour Editions, 1964.

Hiltebeitel, Alf. *The Ritual of Battle: Krishna in the Mahabharata.* Ithaca, N.Y.: Cornell University Press, 1976.

Hirschman, Albert O. *Shifting Involvements: Private Interest and Public Action.* Princeton, N.J.: Princeton University Press, 1982.

Hobbs, Richard. *The Myth of Victory: What Is Victory in War?* Boulder, Colo.: Westview Press, 1979.

Hobsbawm, E. J. *Nations and Nationalism Since 1780: Programme, Myth, Reality.* Cambridge: Cambridge University Press, 1990.

Hodges-Hill, Edward, ed. *Man-Eater: Tales of Lion and Tiger Encounters.* Heathfield U.K.: Cockbird Press, 1992.

Hodgson, Marshall G. S. *The Venture of Islam*, vol. 1, *The Classical Age of Islam.* Chicago: University of Chicago Press, 1974.

Hope, A. Guy, and Janet Barker Hope. *Symbols of the Nations.* Washington, D.C.: Public Affairs Press, 1973.

Houweling, Henk W. "The Epidemiology of War, 1816–1980." *Journal of Conflict Resolution* 29, no. 4 (1985): 641–63.

Howard, Michael. *The Causes of Wars.* Cambridge: Harvard University Press, 1983.

———. *The Lessons of History.* New Haven: Yale University Press, 1991.

Hubert, Henri, and Marcel Mauss. *Sacrifice: Its Nature and Function.* Chicago: University of Chicago Press, 1964; originally published in French in 1898.

Hudson, Winthrop S., ed. *Nationalism and Religion in America: Concepts of American Identity and Mission.* New York: Harper Forum Books, 1970.

Hughes, Dennis D. *Human Sacrifice in Ancient Greece.* London: Routledge, 1991.

Ienaga, Saburo. *Japan's Last War: World War II and the Japanese, 1931 to 1945.* Oxford: Basil Blackwell, 1979.

The Iliad of Homer. Translated by Richmond Lattimore. Chicago: University of Chicago Press, 1951.

Ingham, John M. "Human Sacrifice at Tenochtitlán." *Comparative Studies in Society and History* 26 (1984): 379–400.

Ingold, Tim. *Hunters, Pastoralists and Ranchers: Reindeer Economics and Their Transformations.* Cambridge: Cambridge University Press, 1980.

———, ed. *What Is an Animal?* London: Unwin Hyman, 1988.

Jacobsen, Thorkild. *The Treasures of Darkness: A History of Mesopotamian Religion.* New Haven: Yale University Press, 1976.

Jameson, Michael H. "Sacrifice and Ritual: Greece." In *Civilization of the Ancient Mediterranean*, vol. 2, *Greece and Rome*, edited by Michael Grant and Rachel Kitziner. New York: Charles Scribner's Sons, 1988.

Janson, Charles H. "Evolutionary Ecology of Primate Social Structure. In *Evolutionary Ecology and Human Behavior*, edited by E. A. Smith and B. Winterhalder. New York: Aldine, 1992.

Jay, Nancy. *Throughout Your Generations Forever: Sacrifice, Religion, and Paternity.* Chicago: University of Chicago Press, 1992.

Johanson, Donald C., and Maitland A. Edey. *Lucy: The Beginnings of Humankind.* New York: Simon and Schuster, 1981.

Keegan, John. *The History of Warfare.* New York: Knopf, 1995.

———. *The Mask of Command.* New York: Viking, 1987.

Keeley, Lawrence H. *War Before Civilization: The Myth of the Peaceful Savage.* New York: Oxford University Press, 1996.

Keen, Sam. *Faces of the Enemy: Reflections of the Hostile Imagination.* San Francisco: Harper San Francisco, 1991.

King, Helen. "Bound to Bleed: Artemis and Greek Women." In *Images of Women in Antiquity*, edited by Averil Cameron and Amelie Kuhrt. Detroit: Wayne State University Press, 1983.

———. "Sacrificial Blood: The Role of the *Amnion* in Ancient Gynecology." *Helios* 13, no. 2 (1986): 117–26.

King, Katherine Callen. *Achilles: Paradigms of the War Hero from Homer to the Middle Ages.* Berkeley: University of California Press, 1987.

Knight, Chris. *Blood Relations: Menstruation and the Origins of Culture.* New Haven: Yale University Press, 1991.

Kolko, Gabriel. *Century of War: Politics, Conflicts, and Society Since 1914.* New York: New Press, 1994.

Kortlandt, Adriaan. "How Might Early Hominids Have Defended Themselves Against Large Predators and Food Competitors?" *Journal of Human Evolution* 9 (1980): 79–112.

Kosambi, Damodar Dharmanand. *An Introduction to the Study of Indian History.* Bombay: Popular Prakashan, 1991.

———. *Myth and Reality: Studies in the Formation of Indian Culture.* Bombay: Popular Prakashan, 1992.

Kroeber, Clifton, B., and Bernard L. Fontana. *Massacre on the Gila: An Account of the Last Major Battle Between American Indians, with Reflections on the Origin of War.* Tucson: University of Arizona Press, 1986.

Lake, Marilyn. "Mission Impossible: How Men Gave Birth to the Australian Nation—Nationalism, Gender and Other Seminal Acts." *Gender and History* 4, no. 3 (1992): 305–22.

Lamb, Harold. *Genghis Khan: The Emperor of All Men.* Garden City, N.Y.: Doubleday, 1927.

Law, Robin. "Human Sacrifice in Pre-Colonial West Africa." *African Affairs* 84 (1985): 53–87.

Le Bon, Gustave. *The Crowd: A Study of the Popular Mind.* Atlanta: Cherokee Publishing Co., 1982.

Leibowitz, Lila. "In the Beginning . . . : The Origins of the Sexual Division of Labour and the Development of the First Human Societies." In Coontz and Henderson, *Women's Work, Men's Property.*

Lerner, Gerda. *The Creation of Patriarchy.* New York: Oxford University Press, 1986.

LeShan, Lawrence. *The Psychology of War: Comprehending Its Mystique and Its Madness.* Chicago: Noble Press, 1992.

Lévi-Strauss, Claude. *The Origin of Table Manners*, translated by John and Doreen Weightman. Chicago: University of Chicago Press, 1990.

Lewis, Norman. *A Goddess in the Stones: Travels in India.* New York: Henry Holt and Co., 1991.

Lewthwaite, James. "The Transition to Food Production: A Mediterranean Perspective." In *Hunters in Transition: Mesolithic Societies of Temperate Eurasia and Their Transition to Farming*, edited by Marek Zvelebil. Cambridge: Cambridge University Press, 1986.

Liljegren, Ronnie. "Animals of Ice Age Europe." In *The First Humans: Human Origins and History to 10,000 B.C.*, edited by Gören Burenhalt. San Francisco: Harper San Francisco, 1993.

Lincoln, Bruce. *Death, War, and Sacrifice: Studies in Ideology and Practice.* Chicago: University of Chicago Press, 1991.

Lonsdale, Steven H. *Creatures of Speech: Lion, Herding, and Hunting Similes in the Iliad.* Stuttgart: B. G. Teubner, 1990.

Lopez, Barry Holstun. *Of Wolves and Men.* New York: Charles Scribner's Sons, 1978.

Lorenz, Konrad. *On Aggression.* New York: Bantam, 1966.

Luckert, Karl W. *Egyptian Light, Hebrew Fire.* Albany: State University of New York Press, 1992.

———. *The Navajo Hunter Tradition.* Tucson: University of Arizona Press, 1975.

McNeill, William H. *Keeping Together in Time: Dance and Drill in Human History.* Cambridge: Harvard University Press, 1995.

———. *The Pursuit of Power: Technology, Armed Force and Society Since A.D. 1000.* Chicago: University of Chicago Press, 1982.

———. *The Rise of the West: A History of the Human Community.* Chicago: University of Chicago Press, 1963.

McRandle, James H. *The Antique Drums of War.* College Station: Texas A & M Press, 1994.

Mahapatra, Sitakant. "The Meria Sloka: Songs of the Kondh Accompanying the Rite of Ritual Sacrifice." *Man in India* 54 (1974): 73–82.

Mansbridge, Jane J. *Why We Lost the ERA.* Chicago: University of Chicago Press, 1986.

Marean, Curtis W. "Sabertooth Cats and Their Relevance for Early Hominid Diet and Evolution." *Journal of Human Evolution* 18 (1989): 559–82.

Marks, Isaac M. *Fears, Phobias, and Rituals: Panic, Anxiety, and Their Disorders.* New York: Oxford University Press, 1987.

Marks, Isaac M., and Randolph M. Nesse. "Fear and Fitness: An Evolutionary Analysis of Anxiety Disorders." *Ethology and Sociobiology* 15 (1994): 247–61.

Marshack, Alexander. *The Roots of Civilization.* Mount Kisco, N.Y.: Moyer Bell, 1991.

Martin, Paul S. "Prehistoric Overkill: The Global Model." In *Quaternary Extinctions: A Prehistoric Revolution*, edited by Paul S. Martin and Richard G. Klein. Tucson: University of Arizona Press, 1984.

Mayer, Arno J. *Why Did the Heavens Not Darken? The "Final Solution" in History.* New York: Pantheon, 1988.

Meggitt, Mervyn. *Blood Is Their Argument: Warfare Among the Mae Enga Tribesmen of the New Guinea Highlands.* Mountain View, Calif.: Mayfield, 1977.

Métraux, Alfred. "Warfare, Cannibalism, and Human Trophies." In *Handbook of South American Indians*, vol. 5, edited by Julian H. Steward. New York: Cooper Square Publishers, 1963.

Mitchell, Timothy. *Colonizing Egypt.* Berkeley: University of California Press, 1991.

Mithen, Steven J. "The Mesolithic Age." In Cunliffe, *The Oxford Illustrated Prehistory of Europe.*

———. "To Hunt or to Paint: Animals and Art in the Upper Paleolithic." *Man* 23 (1988): 671–95.

Montagu, Ashley, ed. *Man and Aggression.* New York: Oxford University Press, 1973.

Montgomery, Sy. *Spell of the Tiger: The Man-Eaters of Sundarbans.* Boston: Houghton Mifflin, 1995.

Moorhouse, Geoffrey. *Hell's Foundations: A Social History of the Town of Bury in the Aftermath of the Gallipoli Campaign.* New York: Henry Holt, 1992.

Morren, George E. B., Jr. "Warfare on the Highland Fringe of New Guinea: The Case of the Mountain Ok." In *Warfare, Culture and Environment*, edited by R. Brian Ferguson. New York: Academic Press, 1984.

Mosse, George L. *Confronting the Nation: Jewish and Western Nationalism.* Hanover and London: Brandeis University Press, 1993.

———. *Fallen Soldiers.* New York: Oxford University Press, 1990.

Mueller, John. *Retreat from Doomsday.* New York: Basic Books, 1989.

Mumford, Lewis. *The City in History: Its Origins, Its Transformations, Its Prospects.* New York: Harcourt, Brace and World, 1961.

Mundkur, Balaji. *The Cult of the Serpent: An Interdisciplinary Survey of Its Manifestations and Origins.* Albany: State University of New York Press, 1983.

———. "Human Animality, the Mental Imagery of Fear, and Religiosity." In Ingold, *What Is an Animal?*

Murray, Oswyn. *Early Greece.* 2d ed. Cambridge: Harvard University Press, 1993.

Nation, R. Craig. *Black Earth, Red Star: A History of Soviet Security Policy, 1917–1991.* Ithaca, N.Y.: Cornell University Press, 1992.

Nelson, Richard K. *Make Prayers to the Raven: A Koyukon View of the Northern Forest.* Chicago: University of Chicago Press, 1983.

Nesse, Randolph M. "Evolutionary Explanations of Emotions." *Human Nature* 1, no. 3 (1989): 261–89.

Neumann, Erich. *The Great Mother: An Analysis of the Archetype.* Princeton, N.J.: Princeton University Press, 1963.

Nilsson, Martin P. *A History of Greek Religion.* Westport, Conn.: Greenwood Press, 1949.

Nye, Roger H. *The Patton Mind: The Professional Development of an Extraordinary Leader.* Garden City Park, N.Y.: Avery, 1993.

O'Connell, Robert L. *Of Arms and Men: A History of War, Weapons, and Aggression.* New York: Oxford University Press, 1989.

———. *Ride of the Second Horseman: The Birth and Death of War.* New York: Oxford University Press, 1995.

O'Flaherty, Wendy Doniger. *The Origins of Evil in Hindu Mythology.* Berkeley: University of California Press, 1976.

Oldenbourg, Zoé. *The Crusades.* New York: Pantheon, 1966.

Olsen, Sandra L. "Solutré: A Theoretical Approach to the Reconstruction of Upper Paleolithic Hunting Strategies." *Journal of Human Evolution* 18 (1989): 295–327.

Ortner, Sherry B., and Harriet Whitehead. *Sexual Meanings: The Cultural Construction of Gender and Sexuality.* Cambridge: Cambridge University Press, 1981.

Paret, Peter, ed. *The Makers of Modern Strategy: From Machiavelli to the Nuclear Age.* Princeton, N.J.: Princeton University Press, 1986.

Parker, Geoffrey. *The Military Revolution: Military Innovation and the Rise of the West, 1500–1800.* Cambridge: Cambridge University Press, 1989.

Partridge, G. E. *The Psychology of Nations: A Contribution to the Philosophy of History.* New York: Macmillan, 1919.

Perrin, Noel. *Giving Up the Gun: Japan's Reversion to the Sword, 1543–1879.* Boston: David R. Godine, 1979.

Pfeiffer, John E. *The Emergence of Man.* New York: Harper and Row, 1972.

Pick, Daniel. *War Machine: The Rationalisation of Slaughter in the Modern Age.* New Haven: Yale University Press, 1993.

Power, Camilla. "The Woman with the Zebra's Penis: Evidence for the Mutability of Gender Among African Hunter-Gatherers" (monograph). Department of Anthropology, University College, London, 1994.

Pritchard, James B., ed. *The Ancient Near East*, vol. 1, *An Anthology of Texts and Pictures.* Princeton, N.J.: Princeton University Press, 1958.

Profet, Margie. "Menstruation as a Defense Against Pathogens Transported by Sperm." *Quarterly Review of Biology* 68, no. 3 (1993): 335–86.

Radin, Paul. *Primitive Religion: Its Nature and Origin.* New York: Dover, 1957; originally published in 1937.

Reischauer, Edwin O. *Japan: The Story of a Nation.* New York: Knopf, 1970.

Richard, Alison F. *Primates in Nature.* New York: W. H. Freeman and Co., 1985.

Ritter, E. A. *Shaka Zulu.* London: Penguin Books, 1988.

Robarchek, Clayton A., and Carole J. Robarchek. "Cultures of War and Peace: A Comparative Study of the Waorani and Semai." In *Aggression and Peacefulness in Humans and Other Primates*, edited by James Silverberg and J. Patrick Gray. New York: Oxford University Press, 1992.

Rolle, Renate. *The World of the Scythians.* Berkeley: University of California Press, 1989.

Rose, Lisa, and Fiona Marshall. "Meat Eating, Hominid Sociality, and Home Bases Revisited." *Current Anthropology* 37, no. 2 (1996): 307–19.

Rothenberg, Gunther E. *The Art of Warfare in the Age of Napoleon.* Bloomington: Indiana University Press, 1980.

Rubenstein, Daniel I. "On Predation, Competition, and the Advantages of Group Living." In *Perspectives in Ethology*, vol. 3, edited by P. P. G. Bateson and P. H. Klopfer. New York: Plenum Press, 1978.

Russell, Franklin. *The Hunting Animal.* New York: Harper and Row, 1983.

Saberwal, Vasant K., James P. Gibbs, Ravi Chellam, and A. J. T. Johnsingh. "Lion-Human Conflict in the Gir Forest, India." *Conservation Biology* 8, no. 2 (1994): 501–7.

Sagan, Eli. *Cannibalism: Human Aggression and Cultural Form.* New York: Harper and Row, 1974.

Saggs, H. W. F. *Civilization Before Greece and Rome.* New Haven: Yale University Press, 1989.

Sandars, N. K. , ed. *The Epic of Gilgamesh.* New York and London: Penguin Books, 1972.

Sanday, Peggy Reeves. *Female Power and Male Dominance: On the Origins of Sexual Inequality.* Cambridge: Cambridge University Press, 1981.

Saunders, Nicholas J. "Tezcatlipoca: Jaguar Metaphors and the Aztec Mirror of Nature." In Willis, *Signifying Animals*.

Schaller, George B., and Gordon R. Lowther. "The Relevance of Carnivore Behavior to the Study of Early Hominids." *Southwestern Journal of Anthropology* 25, no. 4 (1969): 307–41.

Schmookler, Andrew Bard. *The Parable of the Tribes: The Problem of Power in Social Evolution.* Boston: Houghton Mifflin, 1984.

Schüle, W. "Human Evolution, Animal Behaviour, and Quaternary Extinctions: A Paleo-ecology of Hunting." *Homo* 41/3 (1991): 228–50.

Seidel, Michael P. *Mithras-Orion: Greek Hero and Roman Army God.* Leiden: E. J. Brill, 1980.

Seward, Desmond. *The Hundred Years War: The English in France, 1337–1453.* New York: Atheneum, 1978.

Sherry, Michael S. *In the Shadow of War: The United States Since the 1930s.* New Haven and London: Yale University Press, 1995.

Shuttle, Penelope, and Peter Redgrove. *The Wise Wound: Eve's Curse and Everywoman.* New York: Richard Marek, 1978.

Siverson, Randolph M., and Harvey Starr. *The Diffusion of War: A Study of Opportunity and Willingness.* Ann Arbor: University of Michigan Press, 1991.

Sokolov, E. N. "Phobias and Anxiety in the Framework of the Defense Reflex." *Behavioral and Brain Sciences* 18, no. 2 (1995): 313.

Stager, Lawrence E., and Samuel R. Wolff. "Child Sacrifice at Carthage: Religious Rite or Population Control?" *Biblical Archaeological Review* 10 (January/February 1984).

Stanford, Craig B. "To Catch a Colobus." *Natural History* (January 1995): 48–54.

Stanley, Steven M. *Children of the Ice Age: How a Global Catastrophe Allowed Humans to Evolve.* New York: Harmony Books, 1996.

Stiehm, Judith Hicks, ed. *It's Our Military Too! Women and the U.S. Military.* Philadelphia: Temple University Press, 1996.

Stoessinger, John G. *Why Nations Go to War.* 6th ed. New York: St. Martin's Press, 1993.

Strada, Gino. "The Horror of Land Mines." *Scientific American* (May 1996): 40–45.

Stromberg, Roland. *Redemption by War: The Intellectuals and 1914.* Lawrence: University of Kansas Press, 1982.

Sun Tzu. *The Art of War.* Translated and with an introduction by Samuel B. Griffith. London: Oxford University Press, 1971.

Theweleit, Klaus. *Male Fantasies*, vol. 1, *Women, Floods, Bodies, History*. Minneapolis: University of Minnesota Press, 1987.

Tierny, Patrick. *The Highest Altar: Unveiling the Mystery of Human Sacrifice.* New York: Penguin, 1989.

Tiwari, J. N. *Goddess Cults in Ancient India.* Bombay: Sundeep Prakashan, 1985.

Toland, John. *Adolf Hitler.* New York: Ballantine Books, 1976.

Tolstoy, Leo. *War and Peace*, translated by Ann Dunnigan. New York: Signet Classic, 1968.

Toynbee, Arnold J. *A Study of History*, abridged and edited by D. C. Somevell. London: Oxford University Press, 1957.

Tsukahara, Takahiro. "Lions Eat Chimpanzees: The First Evidence of Predation by Lions on Wild Chimpanzees." *American Journal of Primatology* 29 (1993): 1–11.

Tucker, T. G. *Life in the Roman World.* New York: Macmillan, 1922.

Turke, Paul W. "Effects of Ovulatory Concealment and Synchrony on Protohominid Mating Systems and Parental Roles." *Ethology and Sociobiology* 5 (1984): 33–44.

Turnbull, Stephen. *Samurai Warlords: The Book of the Daimyo.* London: Blandford, 1989.

Turney-High, Harry Holbert. *Primitive War: Its Practice and Concepts.* Columbia: University of South Carolina Press, 1949.

Vagts, Alfred. *A History of Militarism: Civilian and Military.* New York: Free Press, 1959.

Valeri, Valerio. *Kingship and Sacrifice: Ritual and Society in Ancient Hawaii.* Chicago: University of Chicago Press, 1985.

Van Creveld, Martin. *The Transformation of War.* New York: Free Press, 1991.

Vernant, Jean-Pierre, and Pierre Vidal-Naquet. *Myth and Tragedy in Ancient Greece.* New York: Zone Books, 1988.

Vidal-Naquet, Pierre. *Forms of Thought and Forms of Society in the Greek World*, translated by Andrew Szegedy-Maszak. Baltimore, Md.: Johns Hopkins University Press, 1986.

Virgil. *The Aeneid*, translated by Allen Mandelbaum. New York: Bantam, 1971.

Waite, Robert G. L. *The Psychopathic God: Adolf Hitler.* New York: Da Capo Press, 1993.

———. *Vanguard of Nazism: The Free Corps Movement in Postwar Germany, 1918–1923.* New York: W. W. Norton, 1952.

Walsh, Maurice N., and Barbara G. Scandalis. "Institutionalized Forms of Intergenerational Male Aggression." In *War: Its Causes and Correlates*, edited by Martin Nettleship, R. D. Givens, and A. Nettleship. The Hague: Mouton, 1975.

Washburn, S. L., and C. S. Lancaster. "The Evolution of Hunting." In *Man the Hunter*, edited by R. Lee and I. DeVore. Chicago: Aldine, 1968.

Weil, Simone. "The Iliad or the Poem of Force." In *Simone Weil: An Anthology*, edited by Siân Miles. New York: Weidenfeld and Nicolson, 1986.

Wenke, Robert J. *Patterns in Prehistory: Humankind's First Three Million Years.* 3d ed. New York: Oxford University Press, 1990.

Wheelwright, Julie. *Amazons and Military Maids: Women Who Dressed as Men in Pursuit of Life, Liberty and Happiness.* London: Pandora, 1989.

Willis, Roy, ed. *Signifying Animals: Human Meaning in the Natural World.* London: Routledge, 1994.

Xenophon. *The March Up Country*, translated by W. H. D. Rouse. New York: New American Library, 1959.

Young, Dudley. *Origins of the Sacred: The Ecstasies of Love and War.* New York: HarperPerennial, 1992.

Zihlman, Adrienne L. "Sex, Sexes and Sexism in Human Origins." *The Yearbook of Physical Anthropology*, supp. 8 to the *American Journal of Physical Anthropology* (1987): 11–19.

Zimmerman, Jean. *Tailspin: Women at War in the Wake of Tailhook.* New York: Doubleday, 1995.

Index

Index